EXPLORATIONS IN LOCAL AND
REGIONAL HISTORY

Centre for English Local History, University of Leicester
and
Centre for Regional and Local History, University of Hertfordshire

SERIES EDITORS: HAROLD FOX AND NIGEL GOOSE

Also in this series

Volume 2: *The Self-Contained Village? The social history of rural communities, 1250–1900*
edited by CHRISTOPHER DYER
(ISBN 1-902806-59-X)

LANDSCAPES DECODED

The origins and development of Cambridgeshire's medieval fields

BY SUSAN OOSTHUIZEN

UNIVERSITY OF HERTFORDSHIRE PRESS

Explorations in Local and Regional History

Volume 1

CAMBRIDGESHIRE LIBRARIES	
0317	
Bertrams	23.02.07
C.15.6	£9.99

First published in Great Britain in 2006 by
University of Hertfordshire Press
Learning and Information Services
University of Hertfordshire
College Lane
Hatfield
Hertfordshire AL10 9AB

The right of Susan Oosthuizen to be identified as the author of this work has been asserted by her in accordance with the Copyright, Designs and Patents Act 1988.

© Copyright 2006 Susan Oosthuizen

All rights reserved. No part of this book may be reproduced or utilised in any form or by any means, electronic or mechanical, including photocopying, recording or by any information storage and retrieval system, without permission in writing from the publishers.

British Library Cataloguing in Publication Data
A catalogue record for this book is available from the British Library

ISBN 1-902806-58-1

Design by Geoff Green Book Design, CB4 5RA
Cover design by John Robertshaw, AL5 2JB
Printed in Great Britain by Alden Group Ltd, OX29 0YG

Publication grant
Publication has been made possible by a generous grant from the Aurelius Charitable Trust.

Contents

List of figures	vii
List of tables	ix
Abbreviations	x
Acknowledgements	xi
Series editors' preface	xiii
1 Common fields in their wider context	1
2 The Bourn Valley described	21
3 The medieval landscape in about 1300	46
4 Ancient fields into medieval furlongs	68
5 A proto-common field	91
6 Landscape and society in the eleventh century	114
7 Conclusions	140
Appendix A: Key to Figure 4.1	154
Appendix B: Key to Figure 5.1	156
Selected primary sources	159
Secondary sources	162
Index of place names	170
Index of subjects and people	172
List of Occasional Papers, Department of English Local History, University of Leicester	175

Figures

	Common fields at Barton, 1819	Cover
1.1	The Bourn Valley in the early nineteenth century	2
1.2	View south-west across the valley from Toft towards Great Eversden	5
1.3	Provinces of lowland Britain	13
1.4	A rare survival of a sixteenth-century plough	15
2.1	The Bourn Valley: relief and drainage	22
2.2	The Bourn Brook at its junction with the Roman road (A 603) in summer	22
2.3	The same view of the Bourn Brook, in winter	23
2.4	Densett, Bourn	23
2.5	The Bourn Valley: geology	24
2.6	Marsh Close, Little Eversden	26
2.7	The Bourn Valley: administrative boundaries	27
2.8	The Bourn Valley: modern roads and footpaths	28
2.9	Displacement of the alignment of the Roman road (A603) as the result of medieval ploughing	29
2.10	Romano-British occupation of the valley	31
2.11	Land-use in the valley in the later Anglo-Saxon period	32
2.12	Medieval boar from a bench-end at Swavesey parish church	36
2.13	Kingston Wood in its wider landscape in 1720	37
3.1	Common fields in the Bourn Valley in c. 1300	47
3.2	Common fields at Barton, 1819	49
3.3	Waterlogged ridge and furrow on the valley floor at Harlton	50
3.4	The Bourn Valley: greens and commons	52
3.5	Modern green at Haslingfield	53
3.6	Great Green, Haslingfield	54
3.7	Relic of Great Green, Haslingfield	54
3.8	View across Haslingfield Offal	55

3.9	Harlton Green	55
3.10	View towards the core of the extinct green at Great Eversden	57
3.11	Plan of settlement at Toft in 1815	61
3.12	Plan of the medieval settlement at Hardwick	62
3.13	View across the green, Hardwick	63
3.14	Distribution of moats in the Bourn Valley	65
4.1	The Bourn Valley: ancient alignments	70
4.2	Strympole Way, Caldecote	72
4.3	Looking south-west along Broadway, Bourn	73
4.4	Retrogressive and deconstructive analysis in the discovery of early field boundaries: case study of pre-enclosure fields in the north-western part of Toft in 1815	80
4.5	The relationship between a prehistoric alignment, reused in the northern section of the parish boundary between Comberton and Barton, and selions in Harborough Field, Comberton, in 1839	82
4.6	Curved furrows between medieval ridges revealed in plough-soil at Hardwick	83
4.7	Relationships between Roman roads and medieval furlong boundaries at Caxton and Harlton	84
4.8	Field boundaries and the Roman road at Caxton	85
4.9	A medieval headland survives as a low bank in modern fields	86
5.1	Framework of the proto-common field lying across the northern slopes of the Bourn Valley	92
5.2	Stallan Way at Comberton, looking east	94
5.3	The south-western common fields of Comberton in 1839	97
5.4	Intersection between Stallan Way and the Roman road (A603) in Barton in 1839	102
5.5	Relationship between the proto-common field and the Roman villa at Comberton	103
5.6	Whitland Furlong in Comberton in 1839	104
5.7	Reconstruction of an Anglo-Saxon drinking horn	112
6.1	Distribution of manors in the Bourn Valley in 1086	119
6.2	The landscape around Bourn Hall in the early nineteenth century, before parliamentary enclosure	126
6.3	Ancient bank along the boundary of the manorial complex at Bourn	127
6.4	Medieval field-divisions conserved in the hedges of the post-enclosure landscape of Great Eversden in 1886	135

Tables

2.1	Ploughlands and parish acreages in the Bourn Valley in 1086	44
3.1	Characteristics of moated sites in the Bourn Valley	66
6.1	The estates of Aelmer of Bourn in 1066 and 1086	125
6.2	Royal 'inland' and other bookland demesne in the Bourn Valley in 1066	128
6.3	Percentages of royal demesne, bookland, leaseland and warland in the Bourn Valley in 1066	130

Abbreviations

CC	Clare College, Cambridge
CCC HER	Cambridgeshire County Council Historic Environment Record
CCRO	Cambridge County Record Office
ChC	Christ's College, Cambridge
CUULM	Cambridge University Unit for Landscape Modelling
CUL	Cambridge University Library
DB	*Domesday Book*
EDR	Ely Diocesan Records
EHD	*English Historical Documents*
G&CC	Gonville and Caius College, Cambridge
ICC	*Inquisitio Comitatus Cantabrigiensis*
IE	*Inquisitio Eliensis*
LE	*Liber Eliensis*
MRO	Metropolitan Record Office
OED	*Shorter Oxford English Dictionary*
OS	Ordnance Survey
PC	Pembroke College, Cambridge
QC	Queens' College, Cambridge
Rot. Hund.	Rotuli Hundredorum (Hundred Rolls)
VCH	*Victoria County History of Cambridgeshire and the Isle of Ely*

Acknowledgements

I am very grateful to Professor Harold Fox for his kindness, many comments and help with earlier drafts of this book, which is based on and develops research undertaken for my Ph.D. thesis. Dr Robin Glasscock supervised that thesis and without him the groundwork for this book would never have been completed. Professor Brian Roberts, Professor Peter Fowler, Dr Debby Banham and Dr Tom Williamson not only discussed my work with me but also showed great generosity in allowing me access to pre-publication copies of all or part of manuscripts of forthcoming work. Dr Tim Bayliss-Smith and Dr Phil Howells of the University of Cambridge Department of Geography made helpful comments on the outline methodology and arguments. Phillip Judge kindly drew the maps. The research on which this book is based was undertaken during a sabbatical granted by my department, the University of Cambridge Institute of Continuing Education. I am very grateful for their support, and for that of my then College, Trinity Hall, which offered me a home and a bursary over the same period.

Mr Paul Tebbit (Great Eversden and Toft), Mr David Ellis (Great and Little Eversden), Mr Philip Clemmow (Great Eversden), Mrs Lynne Reynolds (Hardwick), Mr Andrew Smith (Hardwick), Mrs Caroline Chivers (Hardwick), Mr John Wilkinson (Kingston), Mr Peter Reynolds (Kingston), Mr Michael Coles and other members of the Cambridge Archaeological Field Group, Mr David Baxter (Bourn) and Mrs Catriona Campbell (Bourn) kindly shared local information with me and allowed me access to fields and buildings. Dr Colin Bibby shared his knowledge of buzzards and kites, and walked me across his fields in Caldecote.

Ms Ellie Clewlow (Gonville and Caius College, Cambridge), Professor Michael Lapidge (Clare College, Cambridge), Professor Geoffrey Martin (Christ's College, Cambridge) and Miss Jayne Ringrose (Pembroke College, Cambridge) were generous in allowing me access to relevant college archives. Mr Stephen Munday (Principal, Comberton Village College) kindly allowed me to photograph the copy of the pre-enclosure map of Comberton held by the College. Miss Ann Taylor of the University of Cambridge Library Map Department was helpful and patient in finding the appropriate maps on the basis of my obscure descriptions of what I was looking for. The staff of the Cambridgeshire County Record Office, the Cambridgeshire County Council Historic Environment Record, and the University of Cambridge Unit for Landscape Modelling were just as helpful and generous with their time.

I am grateful to Dr Stephen Bassett, Mr Stephen Baxter, Dr Paul Bowman, Mr A. E. Brown, Mr Stephen Coleman, Professor R. A. Dodgshon, Professor Christopher Dyer, Ms Judie English, Mr Christopher Evans, Dr Rosamund Faith, Mr Glenn Foard, Mr David Hall, Dr C. R. Hart, Professor Mary Hesse, Dr Catherine Hills, Dr Della Hooke, Mr John Hunter, Dr Nicholas James, Dr Graham Jones, Dr Richard Jones, Professor Tony Legge, Mr Tim Malim, Mr David McOmish, Dr Mark Page, Dr Max Satchell, Mrs Gillian Sheail, Mr Christopher Taylor, Dr Graham Winton and Dr Stuart Wrathmell for discussing aspects of my work with me and for the comments that they have made on it. Professor Alan Everitt and Dr Margaret Gelling kindly answered questions relating to this work. Students and colleagues at the University of Cambridge Institute of Continuing Education have also contributed to my understanding of this study.

I have gained a great deal from these discussions, but the mistakes and infelicities in this work reveal how much more I have to learn.

Series Editors' preface

This new series of *Explorations in Local and Regional History* is a continuation and development of the 'Occasional Papers' of the University of Leicester's Department of English Local History, a series started by Herbert Finberg in 1952.[1] Appropriately, the new series is published by the University of Hertfordshire Press, which has a strong and growing profile in English local and regional history. The Occasional Papers were described by Maurice Beresford, in a review, as 'the glory of Leicester University Press' and in Finberg's *Times* obituary as his 'brilliant series'. One can see why, for many of them introduced themes and methods which were new when they appeared, and which have been followed up and imitated in much subsequent work. Such was Alan Everitt's monograph on Kent in the Civil War, Finberg's own on continuity between Roman and Saxon settlement in the Cotswolds, David Hey's on rural by-employment, Charles Phythian-Adams' on early estates and their fission, Christopher Dyer's on the parish of Hanbury and Keith Snell's on the 1851 religious census. Many of the Occasional Papers did not sell well, for they were short in length – around 15–20,000 words or even fewer – and booksellers despaired of the fact that they had no spine, which meant they did not display well. A new, more substantial, series was started in 2001, but the publisher ceased operations almost immediately after the publication of the first volume and the series lapsed until its adoption by the University of Hertfordshire Press.

Explorations in Local and Regional History will have three distinctive characteristics. First, the series will be prepared to publish work on novel themes, to tackle fresh subjects – perhaps even unusual ones. We hope that it will serve to open up new approaches, prompt the analysis of new sources or types of source, and foster new methodologies. This is not to suggest that more traditional scholarship in local and regional history will be unrepresented, for it may well be distinctive in terms of its quality, and we also seek to offer an outlet for work of distinction that might be difficult to place elsewhere.

1. The Occasional Papers and related publications are listed at the end of this book.

This brings us to the second feature of the new series, which is the intention to publish mid-length studies, generally within the range of 40,000 to 60,000 words. Such studies are hard to place with existing publishers, for while there are current series that cater for mid-length overviews of particular historiographical topics or themes, there is none of which we are aware that offers similar outlets for original research. *Explorations*, therefore, intends to fill the publishing vacuum between research articles and full-length books (the latter, incidentally, might well be eligible for inclusion in the existing University of Hertfordshire Press series, *Studies in Regional and Local History*).

Third, while we expect this series to become required reading for both academics and students, it is also our intention to ensure that it is of interest and relevance to local historians operating outside an institutional framework. To this end we shall ensure that each volume is set at a price that individuals, and not only university libraries, can generally afford. Local and regional history is a subject taught at many levels, from schools to universities. As well as undergraduate modules, there are now numerous M.A. courses in local history, and a high percentage of Ph.D. theses on English social and economic history tackle themes at a local level. Bookshops without a 'local interest' section where history looms large are now rare and history features ever more prominently in other media such as television and radio, testifying to the vitality of research and writing outside the universities, as well as to the sustained growth of popular interest. It is hoped that *Explorations in Local and Regional History* will make a contribution to the continuing efflorescence of our subject.

This preface, finally, serves as a call for proposals. We ask authors to come forward, whether they are studying local themes in relation to particular places (rural or urban), regions, counties or provinces, whether their subject matter comprises social groups (or other groups), landscapes, interactions and movements between places, micro-history or total history. The editors can be consulted informally at the addresses given below, while a formal proposal form is available from the University of Hertfordshire Press at uhpress@herts.ac.uk.

Harold Fox	Nigel Goose
Centre for English Local History	Centre for Regional and Local History
Marc Fitch Historical Institute	Department of Humanities
5 Salisbury Road	University of Hertfordshire
Leicester LE1 7QR	College Lane
Fox@leicester.ac.uk	Hatfield AL10 9AB
	N.Goose@herts.ac.uk

1

Common fields in their wider context

The problem that lies at the heart of this book is how the field boundaries created and cultivated by the farmers of prehistoric and Roman Britain were transformed into the common fields of medieval England.[1] This is a puzzle that has exercised geographers, historians and archaeologists for many years. Christopher Taylor, for example, has commented that

> of all the problems concerning Roman fields, one of the most insoluble has been what happened to them at the end of the formal Roman period. Most historians and many archaeologists have seen a complete break, at least in physical terms, between the field systems of Roman Britain and the common or common fields of medieval England.[2]

The question has been neglected by landscape historians and archaeologists perhaps because it is so puzzling, and much work on field arrangements has instead confined itself to a particular period, like studies of common fields in particular counties, or to landscapes which, because they are agriculturally marginal, tend to preserve the field boundaries of just one or two periods as, for example, the prehistoric field systems of Dartmoor.

The case study within which the question is explored here focuses on the agricultural history of an area that has been intensively cultivated for at least the past 3,000 years: the Bourn Valley, a tributary of the River Cam just west of Cambridge (Figure 1.1). If it is possible to unravel the relationships between prehistoric and common-field boundaries in an area like this, then a significant step forward might be taken in our understanding of the origins of medieval common-field systems in general. We might begin to understand the processes

---

1. The period between about AD 400 and AD 1100 has been divided here into four general periods: the early Anglo-Saxon period, running from about 400 to about 650; the middle Anglo-Saxon period, roughly between about 650 and 900; the later Anglo-Saxon period, extending from between 900 and 1066; and the medieval period, calculated here from the date of the Norman Conquest.
2. Taylor and Fowler, 'Roman Fields', p. 159.

Figure 1.1 An early nineteenth-century map clearly depicts the flat floor of the Bourn Valley,

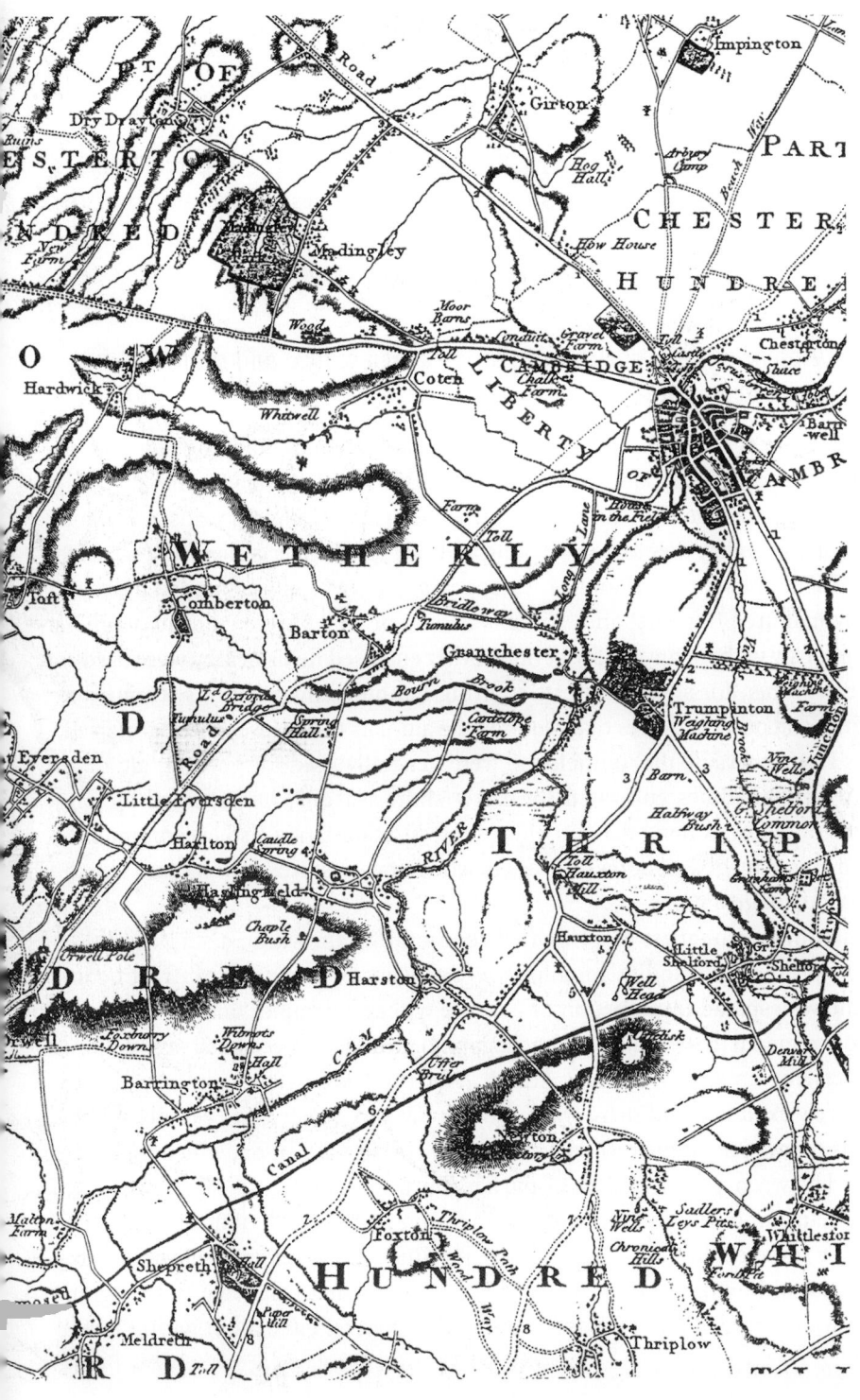

widening out to the south-east, and the plateaux which bound it to south and north

through which the fields, woods and pastures that had developed over the prehistoric millennia and the Roman centuries were organised into a completely new landscape between about 800 and 1100: that of the medieval common fields (Figure 1.2). The first step is to summarise what is presently judged to be the character of the agricultural landscape in central and southern England and the influences on its development between about 43 and 1150.

The development of the agricultural landscape in central and southern England: an overview

By the time of the arrival of the Romans in Britain in 43, lowland England was 'an almost totally exploited land'.[3] Dispersed hamlets and farmsteads were probably the typical form of settlement, often only between a few hundred yards and a mile apart. Just as today, they lay on all soils and facing all aspects, leaving few areas bare of settlement or cultivation. Each appears to have been surrounded by small, heavily manured 'infields' and 'gardens', some of which were cultivated almost continuously without any fallow period. Other enclosed fields nearby were used as home pastures, for sheep and cattle during lambing and calving, shearing and milking, and other activities that required the animals to be close to the farm itself. Lands further away – the 'outfields' – were generally used for grazing, although they were sometimes cultivated for a few short seasons, interspersed by long periods of fallow. Among the outfields of the different farms also lay communally owned and managed resources – areas of woodland, pasture, meadow and marsh, depending on geography.

The Roman conquest of 43 unified southern Britain within a single political authority. Political stability, the rapid development of a transport infrastructure and the widespread introduction of coinage within a complex and sophisticated economy meant that many farms began to produce specialised agricultural products for emerging urban markets. The rural landscape was increasingly intensively exploited and there was probably not very much more woodland than there is today. One of the results was a steady rise in population, which may have reached between 3 and 4 million by the late fourth century.[4]

Roman administration was withdrawn from Britain in 410. 'Within the span of what for some could have been a single life-time'[5] the economy appears to have collapsed, although the intensity of this process varied from region to region. Coins were hoarded and probably went out of general circulation within ten or

---

3. Taylor, *Village and Farmstead*, p. 83.
4. Millett, *Romanization of Britain*, p. 185.
5. Hinton, *Archaeology, Economy and Society*, p. 1.

Figure 1.2 View south-west across the valley from Toft towards Great Eversden. The medieval ridge and furrow in the foreground slopes gently down to the meadows across the Bourn Brook which lies in the middle distance, its winding course marked by trees and bushes

fifteen years. In those places where local authority survived, some towns seem to have retained a role as markets for their surrounding areas, perhaps until the middle years of the fifth century, but most – including Cambridge – were eventually abandoned during the sixth century. These processes went hand in hand with a period of political anarchy which seems to have intensified during the middle to later fifth century, as local and regional leaders competed to gain control over territories whose shifting boundaries reflected warlords' changing fortunes. In rural areas, the effects of these changes varied significantly from region to region. In some, but not all, places there appears to have been a decline in the number of rural settlements between the fifth and seventh centuries. For example, at Maxey in Cambridgeshire, field-walking has revealed the sites of six Romano-British farmsteads, but only three early Anglo-Saxon settlements.[6] In other regions, however, the number of settlements seems to have remained broadly stable, as for example, at Brixworth and Great Doddington in Northamptonshire, where the number of early Anglo-Saxon settlements discovered is equal to or even greater than the number of known Romano-British sites.[7]

6. Taylor, *Village and Farmstead*, p. 112 and Fig. 29.
7. RCHM(E), *North-West Northamptonshire*, p. 27; RCHM(E), *Central Northamptonshire*, p. xlix.

It is possible that in eastern England difficulties in the recognition of the fragile archaeological remains of early Anglo-Saxon settlement mean that the decline in settlement, and (extrapolated from this) of population, has been exaggerated. For example, intensive field-walking on the boulder clays of both north-west Essex and Northamptonshire has shown that there was considerable continuity of occupation of farms and hamlets in these areas from the Romano-British into the Anglo-Saxon periods (see 'Prehistoric and Romano-British fields' below).[8] On the boulder clays of the Bourn Valley in Cambridgeshire, too, there were thick spreads of sixth- to eighth-century Anglo-Saxon pottery overlying Romano-British ditches at Cambourne.[9] This evidence may just indicate that, in our region at least, population decline may not have been as intense as had previously been thought. On the other hand, there does seem to have been some change in agricultural practice. This is likely to have been driven partly by the loss of urban markets for specialised agricultural products and partly by climatic deterioration – the increased rainfall that created the wet and cold sixth and seventh centuries. While some arable land undoubtedly reverted to woodland in the post-Roman period (the Weald in Kent and Rockingham Forest in Northamptonshire being the best-known examples), it seems more often to have been converted to open pasture, often intensively grazed, indicating a considerable degree of continuity in the general exploitation of the agricultural landscape, despite changes in the form of that exploitation from the cultivation of grain to stock-rearing.[10] Evidence for such changes in agricultural practice has been found at Hockham Mere in Norfolk as well as at Cowdery's Down and Barton Court, both in Oxfordshire.[11]

At the same time, between about 400 and 600, groups of Anglo-Saxons moved into eastern and southern Britain from north-western Europe. Estimates of the numbers of these immigrants vary from about 10,000 over the 200-year period to very considerably more, and it is difficult to strike a balance between these very different points of view. Nevertheless, there is reason to think that the numbers are unlikely to have replaced the Romano-British population lost through malnutrition, civil war and the plagues of the fifth century. For example, if the population of Britain had already reached between 3 and 4 million by the late

8. Williamson, 'Early Co-Axial Fields', p. 127; Bellamy, 'Anglo-Saxon Dispersed Sites', p. 35.
9. Cambourne is a modern settlement, constructed within the past five years, on the northern watershed of the valley, straddling the parishes of Caxton and Bourn. Its construction has led to considerable archaeological work, both survey and excavation.
10. Everitt, Landscape and Community; Bellamy, 'Anglo-Saxon Dispersed Sites'. See other examples in Schumer, Wychwood, p. 13 and Dyer, Hanbury, pp. 15–19.
11. Carver, 'Kinship and Material Culture', p. 142; Bell, 'Environmental Archaeology', pp. 275 and 278.

fourth century[12] (declining to between 1.5 and 3 million people in 1086[13]), the number of Anglo-Saxon migrants who came to Britain between 400 and 600 must have been relatively small by comparison. It therefore seems unlikely that they will have had very much impact on changes in the population of Britain in that period, particularly since they themselves will have been as susceptible to malnourishment and illness as the indigenous population, and since the migrations occurred over an extended period, 'stretching over several generations, varying in intensity and character with time and place'.[14] The archaeological evidence, too, suggests that the transformation from Romano-British to Anglo-Saxon England was carried out by 'very small numbers of Germanic immigrants, most of whom were male'.[15]

Relatively low numbers, gender bias and the long period within which the migrations took place explain why it is now increasingly accepted that substantial proportions of the Romano-British population survived and continued to occupy lowland Britain after 400. While Anglo-Saxon migrants may sometimes have dispossessed Romano-British farmers or taken over abandoned land, most often they seem to have occupied the interstices of land between existing Romano-British farmsteads. Analysis of male burials in Anglo-Saxon cemeteries of the fifth and sixth centuries indicates that up to half the men buried there may actually have been of Romano-British stock.[16] DNA evidence, too, suggests that 'the genetic evidence does not support the hypothesis of the widespread destruction or displacement of the native population by invaders from what is now northern Germany'.[17] This means that it is often difficult to distinguish between Romano-British and Anglo-Saxon people in the archaeological evidence – both groups were using the same kinds of artefact, living in the same kinds of settlement, and seem to have been buried with the same kinds of grave goods. However, the material culture was different from that of the Roman period and more similar to that of the north-west European regions from which the migrants came. That is, both Romano-British and Anglo-Saxon peoples were using 'Anglo-Saxon' things in an 'Anglo-Saxon' way. At the same time, the British Romano-Celtic language was being supplanted by Germanic languages, since we now speak English rather than something more like Welsh. The dominance of Anglo-Saxon culture cannot be explained by the suggestion that the Anglo-Saxons killed or displaced the Romano-British population of Britain, since so much evidence suggests that the

12. Millett, Romanization of Britain, p. 185.
13. Higham, Frontier Landscape, p. 70.
14. Scull, 'Approaches to Material Culture', p. 73.
15. Hamerow, 'Migration Theory', p. 165.
16. Härke, 'Early Anglo-Saxon Social Structure', p. 150.
17. Evison, 'Lo', p. 8.

migrants were assimilated by the existing population. We are, therefore, thrown back on the possibility that these changes in language, burial practice and material culture resulted from a complex interplay of social, economic and political influences in which ethnicity played just a part. In Evison's epigram, 'The British survived by becoming English'.[18]

Nevertheless, despite the apparent dominance of Anglo-Saxon language and artefacts, it is clear that the Romano-British, too, made a substantial contribution to emerging Anglo-Saxon culture. Indeed, analysis of a recently excavated sixth-century cemetery at Sutton Hoo has concluded that 'early Anglo-Saxon kings seem to have been dressing up as Romans – claiming a right to rule as the spiritual descendants of the Roman emperors'.[19] The implications for the countryside are that post-Roman farmers, whether Romano-British or Anglo-Saxon in ancestry, continued to occupy and cultivate their holdings, even though the collapse of the coin-based economy and the disappearance of local and regional markets meant that there was an increased focus on economic self-sufficiency. It is important to say that there was no reversion to nomadism. On the contrary, the rural economy seems to have been based on settled farmers growing sufficient grain for subsistence, but perhaps concentrating on stock-raising in a landscape where little was truly 'waste'. Rough pastures, woods and intensively grazed pasture each had an important role to play in a stock-raising economy. Although little is known of the detail of the period, an analogy with the later Middle Ages may be appropriate: then, too, worsening climatic conditions and regional population decline were followed by a greater emphasis on sheep farming in the course of which the arable of whole parishes might be converted to pasture.

It is possible that the most obvious changes apparent to local men between about 400 and 600 were not changes in the layout of the physical landscape but the transformation of political and administrative landscapes. A national authority disappeared. Local leaders, initially based in towns, for a while retained control of their hinterlands. Sometimes these survived, but in many cases they were challenged by men building up a rural power base, local warlords constructing regional groupings which lasted as long as they had the strength and support to withstand confrontation with their neighbours or from aspiring challengers. This means that for much of that 200-year period up to 600, local political organisation was often uncertain and relatively transient, based on networks of closely or more distantly related kin, that frequently expanded to incorporate adjacent territories and as often shrank back again or even disappeared.

By the late seventh century England was almost completely dominated by the

---

18. Ibid., p. 9.
19. *Current Archaeology*, 'Sutton Hoo Before Redwald', p. 505.

major Anglo-Saxon kingdoms. The Bourn Valley lay on the frontier between Mercia to the west and East Anglia to the east.[20] Most of the local, political or ethnic groupings that had controlled regions of varying sizes during the fifth and sixth centuries had been absorbed into the new kingdoms, in a process that Bassett has memorably compared to a knock-out competition: 'most of the little teams have long gone, there are a few potential giant-killers left ... But the next round will see them off'.[21] A significant number of those that survived long enough to be recorded in the late seventh century – the Gifle, Hyrstingas, Willa and Gyrwe – appear to have controlled territories lying just west of the River Cam, suggesting that political organisation in this area remained volatile late into the seventh century, perhaps a buffer zone between the rival kingdoms. When they disappeared, their territories were absorbed into the ancestral estates of the emergent kings. These huge estates covered extensive areas, and portions were sometimes granted to monastic houses by land grant or charter (also called *boc*, from which the term 'bookland' is derived). From the eighth century the aristocracy of each kingdom also began to acquire estates by royal grant. Some of these estates had an ancient history, being based on Romano-British or even Iron Age territorial units; others developed from the 'clan territories' that had emerged during the anarchy of the fifth and sixth centuries; yet others may have been freshly created in the development of the new political order.[22] These estates, very often the size of ten to fifteen modern parishes, can sometimes be reconstructed from documents and place names.[23]

The development of extensive estates seems to have been one of the spurs to the increasing importance of arable agriculture from the eighth century onwards. The components of an estate were required to supply the estate centre (*caput*) with a range of agricultural products among which bread, grain and ale were as important as animals and animal products. The combination of centralised political control with the imposition of food renders seems to have resulted in the contribution of a specialist commodity from each community within the estate – some rendered barley, others sheep, and so on. Arable cultivation gradually became the predominant form of agriculture in the central area of southern England, stimulated by a period (lasting until about 1300) of warmer summers that extended the growing season and arable productivity. The movement towards

---

20. Bassett, *Anglo-Saxon Kingdoms*.
21. Ibid., p. 26.
22. For example, Bassett, 'Great Chesterford'; Blair, *Anglo-Saxon Oxfordshire*, pp. 79–80; Bassett, 'Continuity and Fission'.
23. For example, Bassett, *Anglo-Saxon Kingdoms* and 'Continuity and Fission'; Phythian-Adams, *Continuity, Fields and Fission*.

arable cultivation, which was more labour-intensive than pastoral farming, was supported by rising population levels from about 800 onwards.[24]

Between about 850 and 1150 the rural landscape of central and southern England changed dramatically. The infields and outfields of each hamlet and farmstead were replaced by an arrangement of two or more huge arable fields which were cultivated in common by the inhabitants of each vill.[25] The dispersed hamlets and farmsteads of earlier periods were abandoned, many lying under the new common fields. Settlement in each vill sometimes shifted to cluster on or around the edges of greens and commons, or was replaced by a single, nucleated settlement. It is this 'revolution' in agricultural practice and layout that is often taken to have initiated the division of lowland England between the 'ancient' landscapes in the north-west, west, south and east, where common fields were not introduced (although smaller fields were created within the older field boundaries and cultivated in common during the Middle Ages[26]), and the 'champion' landscapes of central and southern England where prehistoric and Romano-British fields were apparently swept away by the new common-field arrangements. This transformation of the landscape is quite unrelated to the early Anglo-Saxon settlement, which it post-dated by at least 250 years. Instead, it appears to have had some link, not properly understood, with rising population, centralised authority and economic demands of middle to late Anglo-Saxon extensive estates.

The development of the rural landscape between about 600 and 1100 is explored in more detail below, through the wider context of what is known about the forms of prehistoric and Romano-British fields, which continued to be cultivated into the middle Anglo-Saxon period; through what is known about the forms of new field layouts created between c. 850 and 1150; and through what is known about the physical links between the two.

Prehistoric and Romano-British fields

It is almost certain that the fields that the common fields replaced were created (and sometimes later amended) during the prehistoric or Roman periods. These fields took several forms. There are areas, for example in Cornwall or west Wales, where field arrangements appear to have grown 'organically' as successive intakes from wood, pasture or waste were added to the fields around a settlement over a period of many years – or even centuries or millennia – from the Bronze Age

---

24. Williamson, 'Preservation and Destruction', p. 6; Lamb, 'Climate and Landscape'.
25. Taylor, *Village and Farmstead*, pp. 130–1; Hall, *Medieval Fields*, Ch. 5.
26. For example, Williamson, 'Early Co-Axial Fields' and 'Scole-Dickleburgh'; although see also Hinton, 'Scole-Dickleburgh' for another view.

onwards. These landscapes are quite irregular, made up of fields of many different shapes and sizes on no particular alignment. Other early field arrangements are more regular, showing evidence of planning, and many are characterised as 'co-axial' (that is, where one axis is dominant over a considerable area), or are based on linear boundaries. Evidence of these regular field arrangements has been discovered across Britain, but it is only in areas of ancient countryside, away from central and southern England, that they survive as earthworks, walls or hedges, as, for example, on Dartmoor or on the Yorkshire Wolds.[27] In areas of common-field cultivation they were generally ploughed out by medieval farmers and are usually found today only in archaeological excavations or as soil- or cropmarks in aerial photographs. Co-axiality was a long-lived concept that was, until very recently, believed to have underpinned the creation of almost all large-scale planned land divisions across Britain from the Bronze Age until the Roman period. The essential character of these divisions of the landscape is that they were made up of long parallel boundaries along 'one prevailing axis of orientation', and that they ran, as far as possible, up valley slopes at right angles to the valley bottom, coming to a halt against a

> terminal reave, which ran along the contours some way below the crest of the hills. These long, regular layouts were usually sub-divided into small fields, often with a roughly square or rectangular shape. In Dorset, for example, fields are 'generally from ¼ acres to 1½ acres in size … [and their] sides are seldom over 70 yards long.[28]

Most appear to have been walled or hedged: at Heathrow in Middlesex fields dating to between 1500 and 1300 BC were limited by hedges that were already up to 500 years old by that date; at Farmoor in Oxfordshire, sloe and hawthorn hedges were planted.[29] Co-axial field patterns can often be demonstrated to have a relationship with the dispersed and shifting farmsteads and hamlets of the prehistoric and Roman periods, and provide a physical context for the relatively intensive patterns of manuring found close to Iron Age and Romano-British settlements.

Recent work on Salisbury Plain has, however, changed our understanding about the form and history of prehistoric field layouts.[30] Careful plotting of field boundaries on the plain suggests that most co-axial layouts probably date to the middle Bronze Age, that is, between about 1500 and 1000 BC. More significantly

---

27. Fleming, 'Dartmoor: Part 1'; 'Dartmoor: Part 2'; 'Dartmoor: Wider Implications'; 'Co-Axial Field Systems', p. 188; and *Dartmoor Reaves*, pp. 61–2; Fowler, *Landscape Plotted*; Darvill, *Prehistoric Britain*, Ch. 4.
28. RCHM(E), *Central Dorset*, p. 320.
29. Lewis, 'Heathrow Fields'; Robinson, 'Problem of Hedges', p. 156.
30. McOmish et al., *Salisbury Plain*.

for the Bourn Valley, they appear to have been replaced by arrangements of features called 'linear boundaries', often initially laid out between about 1020 and 1000 BC, but continuously reworked during the first millennium BC – during the Iron Age. Linear boundaries have several identifying characteristics. They are usually no shorter than about 500 yards and can extend up to 10 miles in length. They tend to fall into two categories: those called 'spinal linears' which, unlike terminal reaves, run along watersheds or false crests, and form the 'main backbone' or framework for subdividing land units; and those called 'subsidiary linears' which subdivide the areas between the spinal linears to 'define small parcels of land centred on valleys'.[31] It is possible that the extensive arrangements of grid-like fields in 'ancient' landscapes, which have previously been interpreted as Bronze Age 'co-axial landscapes', may in fact be the relics of later, Iron Age, linear boundaries. Rackham's portrait of South Elmham, Suffolk, appears to describe a typical East Anglian example: 'About 25 square miles divided into little fields by cross-hedges between bundles of parallel, not quite straight, main axes. There is no history of woodland or common field; the medieval greens and meadows intrude into the semi-regularity'.[32] A close examination of these field arrangements shows that they very often run up to a feature that is more like a spinal linear than a terminal reave in its relationship to the local topography – many run along watersheds or false crests, rather than lower down the slope. The rather 'wany' or irregular character of the field boundaries which run from valley floor to hilltop is also more like those of the subsidiary linears than like the much straighter Dartmoor reaves.

Whether they originated in the Bronze Age or in the Iron Age, and however they were reworked and altered over the intervening years, most fields cultivated by Romano-Britons continued to be used for arable or pasture into the early and middle Anglo-Saxon periods. It seems probable that the descendants of Romano-British farmers continued to tend their holdings alongside Anglo-Saxon migrants who, in many cases, were simply absorbed into the existing social and physical landscape. 'The development of Saxon fields, if such can be said to have existed, must be seen in the context of initial political and tenurial control over a basic and much older agricultural way of life'.[33]

Medieval common fields

Across central and southern England 'open' or common fields are generally considered to have completely replaced earlier field arrangements between about

---

31. Ibid., pp. 53–61.
32. Rackham, *History of the Countryside*, p. 156.
33. Taylor, *Fields*, p. 65.

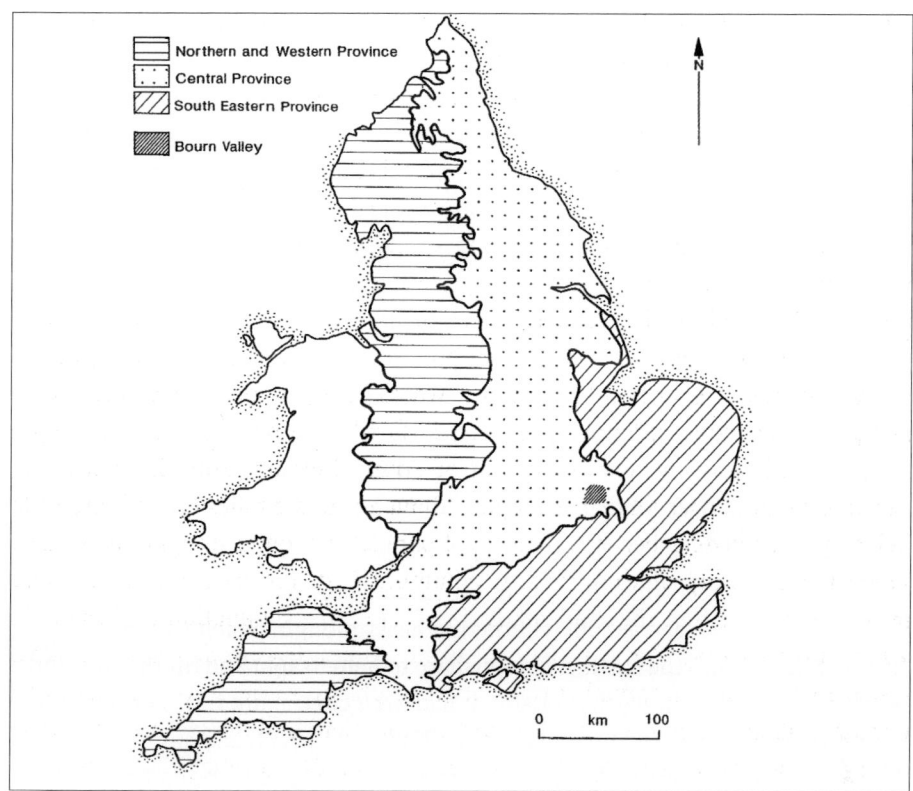

Figure 1.3 The Provinces of lowland Britain (after Roberts and Wrathmell, *Region and Place*, p. 10), showing the location of the Bourn Valley on the eastern side of the Central Province

850 and 1150 (Figure 1.3). The area within which the classic two- or three-field form of this kind of cultivation is found is sometimes called 'champion': a landscape of wide fields and few woods or enclosures, in which medieval arable lay in two or three very large fields. Classic common-field systems have distinctive characteristics: the division of between 70 per cent and 90 per cent of the available land of each community into two or three (though occasionally more) very large fields (which is why they are so often described as 'open'); the setting aside each year of one of the fields, or approximately one third of their total area, as fallow for common grazing; the subdivision of each field into smaller units, commonly known as 'furlongs';[34] the further subdivision of furlongs into individual units of cultivation, strips of land (also called selions) which ran from one end of the

34. 'Furlong' has two meanings: one as a unit of length and the other as a unit of area. As a unit of length, a furlong is 220 yards long or an eighth of a mile. As a unit of area, it is less well defined, simply referring to a subdivision of a common field, which might or might not be 220 yards long and which could contain any number of strips or selions within it (OED)

furlong to the other;[35] the distribution of selions among the freehold and tenant farmers of the vill, the lord and the church, sometimes in a regular sequence so that each field was held in common (hence the name 'common field'); and the practice of raising a single crop within each field. The classic cropping pattern was to grow wheat in one field, barley in the next, while the third lay fallow. The following year, barley would be grown where wheat had grown the year before, the fallow field would be ploughed up for wheat, while the previous year's wheat field would be turned to barley; and so on, year after year. Classic common fields therefore demonstrate distinctive patterns of physical form, cropping and tenure. On claylands like the Bourn Valley, selions were often ridged through ploughing to facilitate drainage, and they survive in the modern landscape as areas of ridge and furrow whose curved alignments reveal their medieval origins (Figure 1.2).

The heavy plough

It is generally agreed that the transition to medieval common-field agriculture could not have been carried out without the heavy plough, which used a coulter to cut more deeply into the earth, a ploughshare to help to split and lift the sod, and a mouldboard to turn the earth over after it had been cut (Figure 1.4). This plough, it has been argued, replaced the ard or 'scratch plough' which had simply scratched the surface of the land and required cultivation in two directions (from top to bottom and from side to side across a field) in order to raise a sufficient tilth. By cutting and turning the earth over, the heavy plough made possible a greater productivity, particularly on heavy clay soils on which Iron Age farmers must have used the ard with great difficulty.

The date at which the heavy plough came into common use in the Anglo-Saxon period is therefore of some importance in dating the origin of the common fields, and is also controversial. It appears originally to have been introduced into Britain during the Roman period, when it was used alongside the ard: the development of rectangular Romano-British fields, which were apparently ploughed in one direction only, has been explained as a product of the heavy plough.[36] There is a consensus that the heavy plough survived into the Anglo-Saxon period only in the

---

35. It is possible to recognise these strips of land, which were units of both cultivation and of tenure, by two characteristics that are distinctive of medieval ploughing. The first is that they are generally curved, either into a reversed S- (aratral), a C- or reversed C-shape; and the second is that, on claylands, they were ploughed into ridges usually between about 7 and 9 yards wide with furrows delineating the boundary between each strip. The landscape thus corrugated is very often called 'ridge and furrow' or 'high-backed'. On slopes, the strips were terraced and are called 'lynchets'.
36. Fowler, *Landscape Plotted*, p. 184.

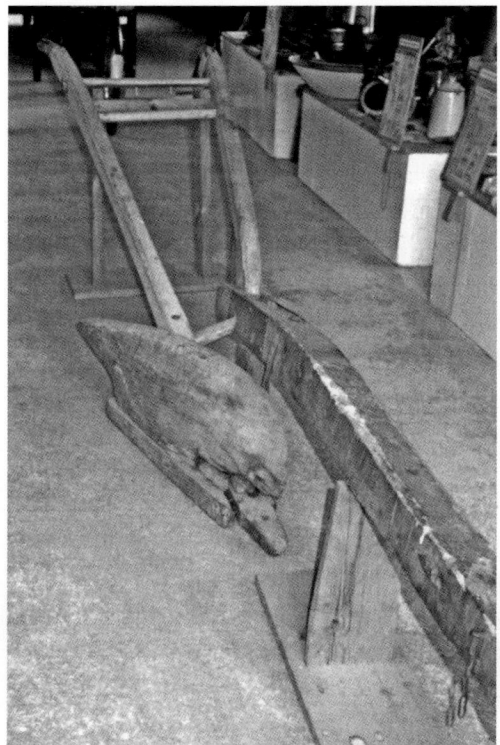

Figure 1.4 A rare survival of a sixteenth-century plough (Ramsey Rural Museum, Cambridgeshire). The heavy timbers which made up these ploughs are dramatically illustrated here and vividly evoke the skill and strength of medieval ploughmen

west of England, and was not reintroduced into central and eastern England before the tenth century.[37] Ploughmarks of the sixth to ninth centuries found at Gwithian, Cornwall, in the early 1960s were interpreted at the time as sod that had been turned by an 'implement … [that] employed a share, a coulter and, probably, a mouldboard', but the lack of definitive corroboratory evidence from elsewhere in Britain has led the excavators to revise their views, believing now that these marks were more probably the result of intensive cultivation by spade.[38] The most recent review of the evidence has concluded that 'a wooden ard without iron fittings was … most commonly in use in England at least until the tenth century' and that the use of the heavy plough – in widespread use by c. 1000 – seems to have been a late Anglo-Saxon reintroduction.[39]

The arguments about the reintroduction of the heavy plough – and therefore for the earliest date at which common fields might have been introduced into central and southern England – are complicated by the discovery across eastern

---

37. Ibid.; Hill, 'Sulh'.
38. Fowler and Thomas, 'Gwithian', p. 68; Fowler, 'Agriculture and Rural Settlement', p. 30; Fowler, *Farming*, Ch. 9.
39. Ibid.; Hill, 'Sulh', p. 7.

England of middle Anglo-Saxon iron implements that might have been fixed to an ard or to a plough. They have turned up at St Neots in Huntingdonshire and Westley Waterless in Cambridgeshire, Thetford in Norfolk, Nazeing in Suffolk and Flixborough in Lincolnshire.[40] The uncertainty about whether they were fixed to a heavy plough or an ard means that it is quite possible that the heavy plough did continue to be used in eastern England throughout the Anglo-Saxon period after all. An analogy might be the widespread consensus that the early Anglo-Saxon period was aceramic, when there are areas – of which Cambridgeshire is one – in which there is good evidence for pottery at this time. Perhaps the heavy plough did not disappear from eastern England altogether. The raw materials needed to make heavy ploughs were certainly available in eastern England – iron ore and wood were both available in the Bourn Valley, for example – and would not have been needed in very large quantities. Heavy timbers would have been needed as the sixteenth-century mouldboard plough at Ramsey Rural Museum in Cambridgeshire so graphically illustrates, but relatively small areas of managed woodland would have produced enough to fulfil these requirements, and there is some evidence for limited woodland regeneration before about 800. Blacksmiths would also have had the necessary expertise, since ironworking was an integral part of the Anglo-Saxon economy – as the weapons found in early burials demonstrate.

Poverty may offer a better explanation for a return to the ard for some early and middle Anglo-Saxon farmers.[41] Although the wealth of weapons and jewellery in burials in Anglo-Saxon cemeteries in the fifth and sixth centuries indicates that part of the population was probably able to afford a heavy plough and the oxen required to pull it, it is possible that the 53 per cent of adult males in eastern England who were buried without weapons in this period, and who have been interpreted as being members of subordinate groups who were probably largely British by descent, might be among those who had to be content with an ard.[42] These arguments have been recognised in the growing consensus that the heavy plough was almost certainly present in England from the middle Anglo-Saxon period (that is, from about 700) onwards. If this interpretation is correct, it suggests that ards and heavy ploughs were both in use throughout the Anglo-Saxon period, and their relative distributions were indicators of differences in material wealth between farmers in each region rather than of regional culture or agricultural practice, much as different makes of car are used as indicators of economic status today.

40. Langdon, 'Agricultural Equipment', pp. 88–9; Loveluck, 'Flixborough', p. 156; Hill, 'Sulh', p. 11.
41. D. Banham, personal communication.
42. Härke, 'Early Anglo-Saxon Social Structure', pp. 150–1.

Preservation of pre-medieval field boundaries into the Middle Ages

Most surviving examples of prehistoric landscapes are found in those areas of western and eastern England characterised as 'ancient' landscapes, where classic two- or three-field husbandry was never introduced. In Buckinghamshire, for example, just outside the Central Province,

> the majority of the roads and many of the footpaths are on the alignment of the bi-axial network, as are in most cases the alignment of field furlongs, and their associated balks and headlands ... The overall impression is that the topography of the common field village is adapted from an earlier [prehistoric] system and retains much of its former shape and form.[43]

In central and southern England the evidence for continuity of use of prehistoric and Roman field boundaries into medieval common-field boundaries is so contradictory and inconclusive that it is hardly considered a viable question for debate. David Hall, whose place among researchers of common-field arrangements is justifiably pre-eminent, has concluded that 'It is perhaps specious to look for continuity between "Celtic" [i.e. co-axial] fields and medieval fields on a large scale. In vain one looks for many extensive systems of Roman or prehistoric fields that could convincingly be converted to a recognisable furlong pattern'.[44] His extensive work in mapping the medieval common fields of the whole of Northamptonshire – work not replicated anywhere else in Britain – has led to the conclusion that 'there just is no continuity, and generally furlong boundaries have not the slightest relation to earlier landscape features'.[45] This view is widely accepted – implicitly or explicitly – among landscape historians, and is supported by evidence drawn from the overriding number of places throughout southern and central England where prehistoric or Roman fields survive only as crop- or soilmarks that are overlain and apparently ignored by medieval ridge and furrow.[46] The pessimistic view of continuity appears to have been confirmed by excavation. At Maxey and Faxton both in Northamptonshire, for example, medieval common fields and the furrows that subdivided them were laid out

---

43. Bull, 'Prehistoric Buckinghamshire', p. 16.
44. Hall, 'Origins of Open-Field Agriculture', p. 35.
45. Hall, *Medieval Fields*, p. 55; personal communication.
46. This point is vividly made by Roberts and Wrathmell, who have mapped all common-field cultivation in England, classic and irregular, against evidence for co-axial field systems surviving within common fields. Their illustration does not cite all the examples listed here and makes the point of lack of coincidence between the two more starkly. It shows evidence for co-axial fields in Norfolk and Cornwall, well outside the Central Province, and only one occurrence inside the Central Province, in the northern midlands, almost on the province's western boundary: *Region and Place*, p. 144, Fig. 5.10.

across the landscape as if it was a blank page, cutting across earlier settlements and fields as if they had never existed.[47] Similar conclusions may be drawn from studies of parish and other boundaries: in Nottinghamshire and Derbyshire 'township boundaries haphazardly cross the [earlier] fields as if they did not exist';[48] in north Nottinghamshire and south Yorkshire 'the Roman system of agriculture failed to survive through into the late Anglo-Saxon period';[49] in north Berkshire early fields, which survive only as cropmarks, are cut by parish boundaries at Letcombe Bassett and Lambourn.[50] Even in the ancient landscapes of East Anglia 'parish and manorial boundaries are unequivocally imposed in an arbitrary fashion on this early landscape'.[51]

Nevertheless, some evidence does sporadically suggest continuity or reuse of pre-medieval field boundaries in classic common-field layouts. At Teversham and Duxford, both Cambridgeshire, excavation has shown that Roman or earlier ditches consistently underlie medieval furlong boundaries. The Royal Commission on Historic Monuments (England) has noted that 'an early date can be inferred' for a co-axial field arrangement at Tadlow in Cambridgeshire, lying parallel to the Cam Valley and respected by both county and parish boundaries.[52] It has, though, as Christopher Taylor and others have noted, yet to be proved that these survivals represent continuity rather than reuse of abandoned features or even simply coincidence.[53]

Where other prehistoric landscapes have survived within or on the edges of the Central Province at Lichfield in Staffordshire, at Goltho in Lincolnshire (where 'every field boundary ... lies more or less parallel or at right-angles to all the others in its vicinity'), and at Wylye in Wiltshire, they tend to lie in areas which suffered early enclosure in the late Middle Ages.[54] Until now, each of these examples has been taken as an isolated case, the exception that proves the rule that prehistoric land divisions did not generally survive to become common-field furlongs. These examples do now seem to have appeared in sufficient numbers across a sufficiently wide area to suggest that they may represent another process of common-field creation. That is, while some common fields – like those in Northamptonshire – were laid out with no reference to the field and other

---

47. Addyman, 'Dark-Age Settlement', p. 24; Brown and Foard, 'Saxon Landscape', p. 74.
48. Unwin, 'Vills and Early Fields', p. 344. See also Upex 'Landscape Continuity' for a fresh and alternative view of continuity in Northamptonshire.
49. Unwin, 'Anglo-Scandinavian Rural Settlement', pp. 84–5.
50. Hooke, 'Regional Variation', p. 130.
51. Williamson, 'Early Co-Axial Fields', p. 427.
52. RCHM(E), *West Cambridgeshire*, p. xxx.
53. Taylor and Fowler, 'Roman Fields', p. 159; Taylor, 'Origins', p. 20.
54. Bassett, 'Lichfield', p. 97; 'Goltho', p. 32; Hooke, 'Regional Variation', p. 131.

boundaries that preceded them, there are other places where the process of medieval field creation incorporated elements of former field boundaries when they could be useful in the arrangement of common-field furlongs. One way of incorporating this evidence into the conventional model of common-field origins might be to suggest that these landscapes were not characteristic of classic common-field husbandry even though they lie in the Central Province. They are, after all, areas of late medieval or early post-medieval enclosure for pasture and this might mean that common-field agriculture was likely to be less securely entrenched here than in other places. This argument cannot, however, hold for south Cambridgeshire where the fields and furlongs of classic common fields continued to be used until the early to middle nineteenth century when they were overtaken by parliamentary enclosure.

'Ancient' and 'champion' landscapes

The survival of the remnants of prehistoric field systems into the modern landscape and the distribution of classic common fields are both closely related to Oliver Rackham's division of the lowland landscape of England into 'ancient' and 'champion'. Ancient countryside is 'the England of hamlets, medieval farms in the hollows of the hills, lonely moats and great barns in the clay-lands, pollards and ancient trees, cavernous holloways and many footpaths, fords, irregularly shaped groves with thick hedges colourful with maple, dogwood and spindle'.[55] Champion landscapes are characterised by 'the England of big villages, few, busy roads, thin hawthorn hedges, windswept brick farms, and ivied clumps of trees in the corners of fields; a predictable land of wide views, sweeping sameness and straight lines'.[56] This distinction has been the subject of a study by Brian Roberts and Stuart Wrathmell, whose analysis of nineteenth-century rural settlement, using a scale from dispersed to nucleated settlement (respectively characteristic of ancient and champion) has led them to propose the division of lowland Britain into three 'provinces', broadly agreeing with Rackham's divisions (Figure 1.3). Their Central Province is more or less coincident with the area of 'planned' or champion landscapes, while the Northern, Western and South-Eastern Provinces generally correspond with areas of ancient landscape.[57] To this general picture they have added a new and more subtle perception: that each province is made up of sub-regions with 'definitive' characteristics (including field arrangements) and more loosely defined 'associated' characteristics. In effect they have defined what

55. Rackham, *History of the Countryside*, pp. 4–5.
56. Ibid.
57. Roberts and Wrathmell, *Atlas*, pp. 2–4.

Everitt described years ago as 'the general framework or pattern of *pays* in the country as a whole'.[58] The Bourn Valley lies in the east midlands sub-province of the Central Province, an area dominated by nucleated villages. The valley offers the opportunity to examine the distinction between ancient and champion in greater detail since, as explained below in Chapters 3 to 5, it provides an imperfect fit with the characteristics of the Central Province, exhibiting some characteristics more typical of ancient landscapes.

So far, this analysis has concentrated attention on the suggestion that, while the introduction of common fields in champion England erased all traces of earlier landscapes in the Central Province, much of the landscape of ancient countryside is of late prehistoric or Romano-British origin. For example, it is generally concluded, on the basis of archaeological evidence, that dispersed settlement may represent the oldest pattern of settlement in the country. 'It is therefore possible to see at least part of the medieval dispersed settlement pattern [of ancient countryside] as an archaic survival, and it has been suggested that some farmsteads stand on or very near to their Roman predecessors'.[59] If this is the case, then it follows that landscapes across southern England before the introduction of common fields were all generally similar in layout and settlement pattern. The idea of a common origin for landscapes across all three provinces, predating the introduction of common fields across the Central Province, may however be an illusion, since the origins of divergence between ancient and champion landscapes do not seem to lie in population, soils, ethnicity, social differences or in strong or weak lordship, similar examples of which can be found in all three provinces. If this is so, then the idea of 'transitional' zones between ancient and champion should perhaps be supplanted by the identification of regional *pays* which were produced by regional cultures and created, as Dyer has remarked, 'from a complex combination of environmental and social factors. Soils, social structures, and lordship may not on their own have determined the distinction between champion and woodland, but acting in combination they may have had a cumulative effect'.[60]

---

58. Everitt, *Landscape and Community*, p. 15.
59. Dyer, 'Pendock', p. 99.
60. Ibid., p. 118.

2

The Bourn Valley described

Geography

The Bourn Brook runs just a few miles south-west of Cambridge (Figure 1.1). Its shallow valley opens out from its origin in Caxton in the north-west to its confluence with the River Cam at Grantchester in the south-east. The valley floor widens and flattens towards the south-east and is bounded to north and south by high ground, providing watersheds to the brook, whose southern slopes rise more steeply than those to the north (Figure 2.1). The brook itself is locally known as a 'flashy' stream.[1] Its waters are generally low, and in the late 1940s were shallow enough in summer to be dammed by children, but after heavy rain it rises rapidly to inundate the meadows of the flat valley bottom on either side (Figures 2.2 and 2.3).[2] The floods subside equally quickly. As long ago as 1600, Layer remarked that at Toft 'upon the fall of rains [the brook] overflowed the meadows adjoining and oft times denied passage, though it hath a wooden bridge over it erected to a good height'.[3] The waters of the brook are augmented by tributary streams, locally called 'deans' (Figure 2.4). The course of some, like Litlingdean and Granditch (both Great Eversden), or Puttockdean and Kingston Brook (both Kingston), are so smooth that their courses must have been straightened, perhaps in the Middle Ages, as they often follow the 'backward C' of medieval ploughing.

The geology of the valley is based on impervious Jurassic Gault clay, covered by more permeable layers of chalk laid down during the Cretaceous period (Figure 2.5). The upper chalks have since disappeared, and the surviving middle and lower chalks are capped by a layer of heavy boulder clay laid down during the Anglian

---

1. D. Ellis, personal communication.
2. Page, *Decline of an English Village*, p. 113.
3. Palmer, *John Layer*, p. 110. It is considered, for example, that the water table in Hampshire has dropped by between 36 and 60 metres in the last millennium: McOmish et al., *Salisbury Plain*, p. 10.

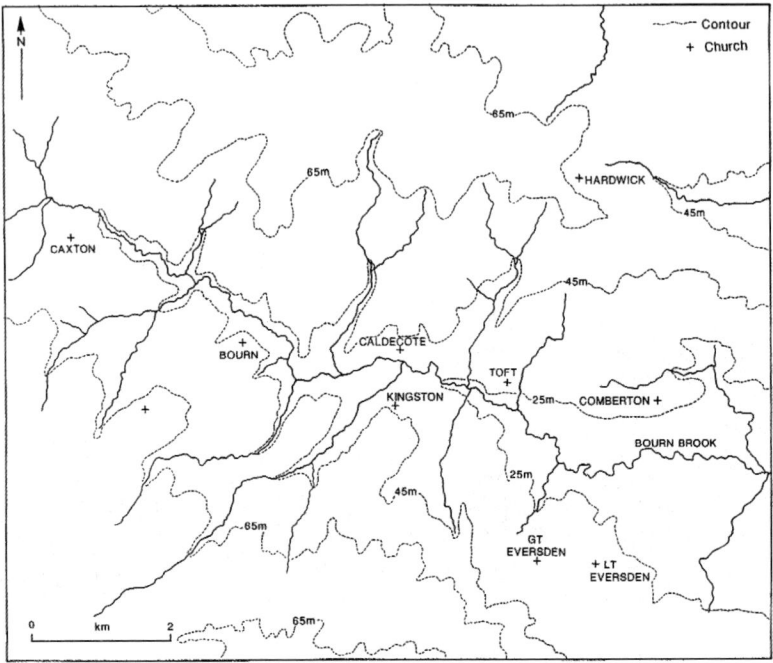

Figure 2.1 The Bourn Valley: relief and drainage. Relatively gentle slopes of the valley sides rise from the flat valley floor to the high, relatively level plateaux on top of the ridges. The narrow valleys of subsidiary streams divide the valley into relatively regular units

Figure 2.2 The Bourn Brook at its junction with the Roman road (A603) in summer. The level of water in the Brook is usually so low that it can barely be seen for summer undergrowth

Figure 2.3 The same view of the Bourn Brook, in winter. The water rises to flood within a matter of hours and subsides as quickly – a characteristic recorded by a local antiquarian in 1600 and familiar to medieval farmers

Figure 2.4 Densett – the settlement along the dean – at Crow End, Bourn

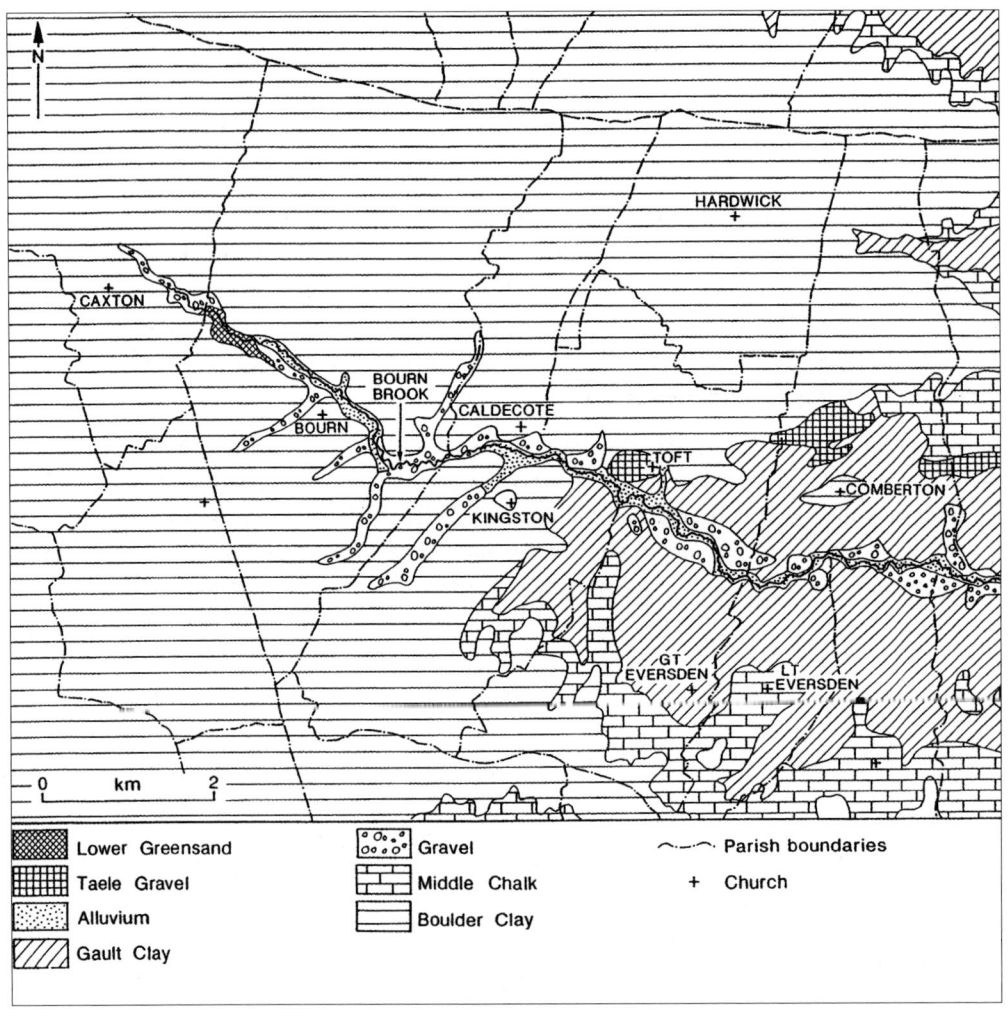

Figure 2.5 The Bourn Valley: geology. Gault clay is exposed on the valley floor which widens out towards the south-east, and boulder clay caps the ridges. More tractable Middle Chalk lies along the valley slopes

glaciation, sloping gently towards the south-east.[4] A thick sheet of heavy, waterlogged Gault clay is exposed in the flat valley bottom, where it is sometimes overlain by narrow bands of silt and alluvium along the beds of the Bourn Brook and its tributary streams, and by outcrops of Taele gravels, washed down from the higher slopes. The Gault clays are so difficult to work that a modern farmer finds it impossible to believe that his medieval predecessors could have cultivated the

4. British Geological Survey, Sheets 187 and 204; Jones, *Human Geography*, p. 56.

valley bottom, despite the physical evidence of curving ridge and furrow and documentary evidence from terriers. Some middle chalk is exposed along the south-eastern slopes of the valley, but the area is predominantly covered by boulder clay which severely inhibits the drainage of the flatter higher ground along the ridges, and explains why, by the sixteenth century, fields and furlongs along the northern watershed in Hardwick and Caldecote were called 'dams'.[5]

The tendency to waterlogging has directly affected land use along the relatively flat valley bottom and on the clay-topped ridges, where field names indicated extensive pastures in the late medieval and early modern periods (Figures 2.6 and 2.11). A description of Eversden in 1801 as 'wet and cold'[6] is typical of the valley as a whole: Guy Beresford has vividly described how

> many of the clayland soils retain to some extent the qualities of pure clay: they must not be worked in wet condition, since they become puddle and impervious to water, and they must not be overstocked in winter months when under grass, since treading 'poaches' the surface of the pastures and excludes the passage of air and moisture from the ground, which leads to eventual deterioration of foliage. Flocculation of the clay brings about aggregation of the particles, giving soil the texture of a coarse mass, with larger spaces between for the passage and percolation of water. This could have been assisted in medieval times by the spreading of manure, by early ploughing and by never attempting to work the ground until it had attained the correct degree of dryness ... Arable farming on claylands depends on reasonable weather. The land can be ploughed in the autumn when the ground is relatively dry; the winter frosts will break down the furrows ... If the land is very wet in autumn and the fields lie unploughed until the spring, the furrows will bake in the wind and sun, and a fine tilth will be impossible. Similar baking may occur if the furrows have been lying in water for long periods during the winter.[7]

Although the geology and topography of the valley offer local communities a fairly typical range of environmental and agricultural opportunities – meadow and marsh in the valley bottom, arable on the middle slopes, and pasture and woodland on the clay-topped ridges, the dominant Gault and boulder clays demanded a high degree of agricultural expertise and specialisation, as the following chapters demonstrate.

The defining outer parish and hundred boundaries of the Bourn Valley follow the River Cam in the east, and the watershed ridges to north and south (Figure

5. CUL EDR/H1; ChC Mun Caldecote L.
6. CUL QC 15/26/1.
7. Beresford, *Goltho and Barton Blount*, pp. 51–2.

Figure 2.6 Marsh Close, Little Eversden. Although modern drainage has made the cultivation of this land more feasible than it was during the Middle Ages, its situation on the flat valley floor on the Gault clay is revealed in the water which collects on this land each winter

2.7).[8] The antiquity of these is suggested by their continuous use as boundaries, by their sinuous character and by the way they follow natural features. The western boundary of the valley is more difficult to discern and may originally have been undefined because it lay in an area of intercommonable wood and wood pasture, along the watershed between the Ouse and the Cam Valleys. Within this unit, Bourn Brook is an almost continuous parish boundary dividing the valley in half. Other parish boundaries run between the outer ridgeways and the brook, subdividing the valley into fairly rectangular units. This impression of early cohesion in the valley is supported by the interlocking character of the early tenth-century hundred boundary between Longstow and Wetherley Hundreds, which indicates the later subdivision of an earlier integrated area.

The villages in the valley appear to have been nucleated from at least the late tenth or eleventh centuries. They tend to be sited on narrow promontories between the tributary streams of the brook, and the plans of most appear to be based on

8. The hundreds were late Anglo-Saxon administrative units created principally for the collection of tax and the organisation of defence. It is not unusual for hundreds to be based on earlier units, for example, fifth- or sixth-century clan territories or large estates created between about 700 and 900, but this is not always the case.

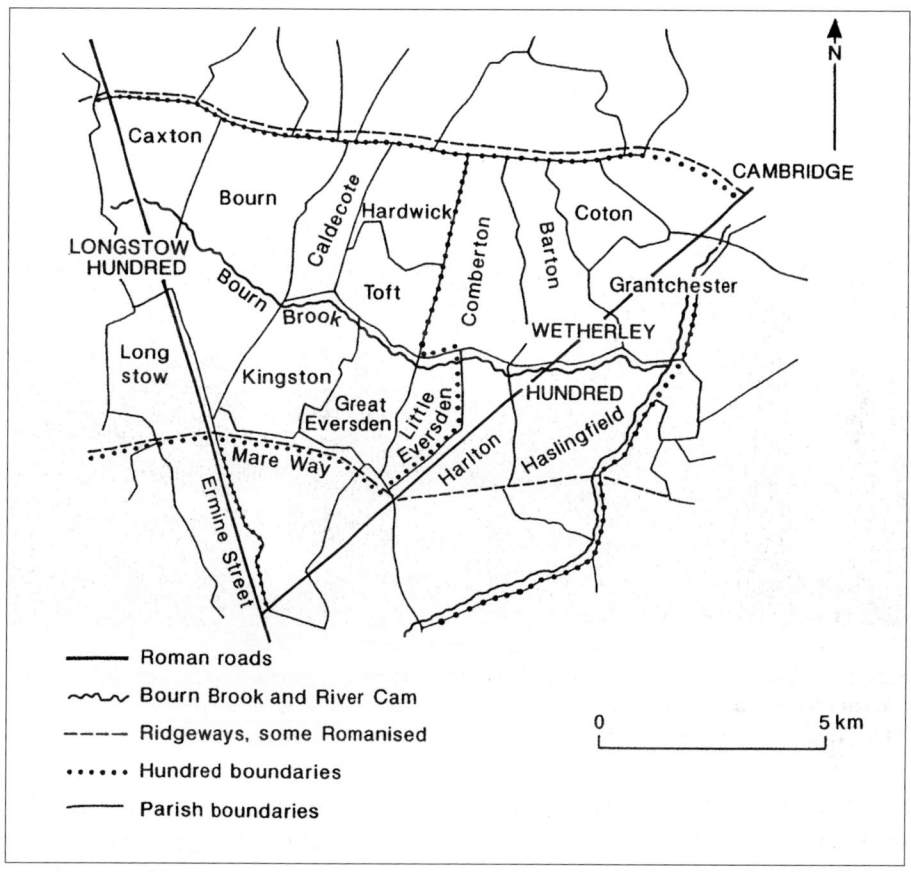

Figure 2.7 The Bourn Valley: administrative boundaries. The regular division of the valley allows most parishes access to meadows, valley slope and pasture on the ridges. The clumsy division of the valley between Longstow and Wetherley Hundreds is clearly later than the parish boundaries

grids of some form. Secondary settlement is found in the few isolated medieval moats situated in woods or on outlying pastures. Outlying secondary settlements without moats may have existed in some parishes during the Middle Ages, but none is known except for that at Highfields, Caldecote, where archaeological excavation has uncovered the remains of a few peasant houses, dating to between about 1200 and 1400, on either side of the northern section of the main north–south street.[9]

Routes in the Bourn Valley tend to run in two principal directions: either along the contours and generally parallel to the Bourn Brook and the ridges, or across the contours of the valley on a generally south-westerly/north-easterly alignment

9. Leith, *Highfields, Caldecote*, pp. 20–1.

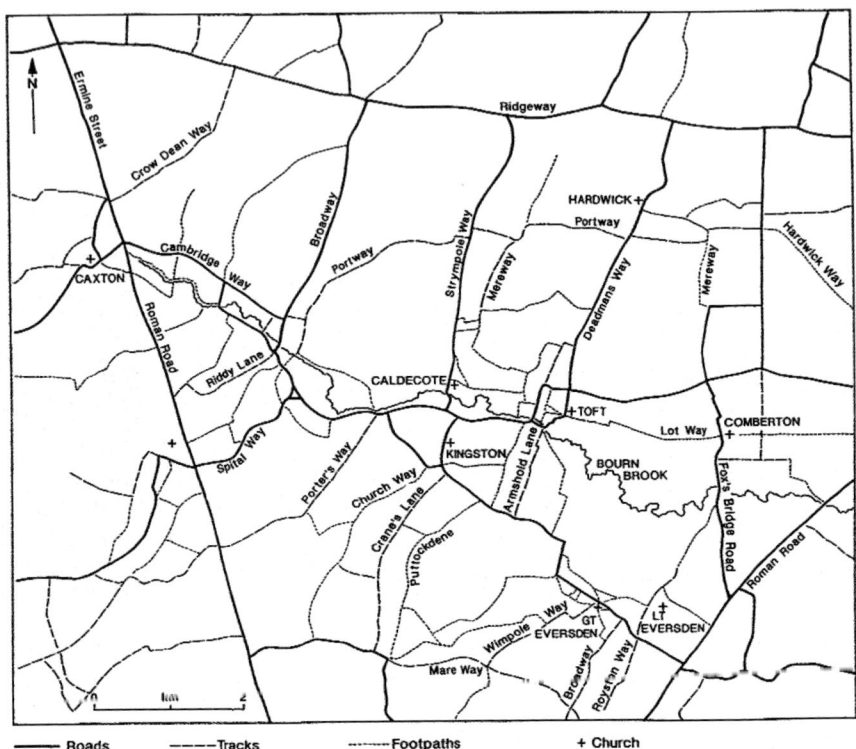

Figure 2.8 The Bourn Valley: modern roads and footpaths. Most rights of way in the valley still run from south-west to north-east, even though the modern dominant roads are those which follow the lower northern and southern slopes along the edge of the valley floor

(Figure 2.8). The sharp changes in direction of the present roads along the lower contours of the valley, both north and south of the Bourn Brook, make it likely that they amalgamate fragments of a number of other routes. Where stretches of these older ways became irrelevant to medieval or post-medieval communities, they went out of use, leaving only those fragments that make up the modern roads. This regular pattern of footpaths and boundaries is transected by two Roman roads: Ermine Street in the west and the present A603 from Wimpole to Cambridge in the east. Both appear to have been in continuous use since they were built. Although Ermine Street was first mentioned in 1012, it was the main route between London and York throughout the Anglo-Saxon and medieval periods. The A603 was called *fferdmanweye* in the sixteenth century – that is, it was a major route for the *fyrd*, the army of middle and later Anglo-Saxon England.[10] Although a section of this Roman road appears to have been lost between Barton and Cambridge, the southern part of its course, between Barton and Wimpole, appears

10. CUL QC13/3; Reaney, *Cambridgeshire*, pp. 22 and 18.

Figure 2.9 Displacement of the alignment of the Roman road (A603) as the result of medieval ploughing. This is one of three or four consecutive aratral curves, each about 200 yards long, to which the original straight alignment of the Roman road in Little Eversden was adapted during the Middle Ages by ploughmen who cultivated the fields on either side

relatively intact, although its alignment has been affected by medieval ploughing in the fields to either side (Figure 2.9).

The early history of the Bourn Valley

Archaeological evidence demonstrates that Cambridgeshire has been densely occupied since the prehistoric period. Iron Age hill forts at Wandlebury, Sawston and Arbury imply the existence of sophisticated political and administrative structures from an early date, but the place of the Bourn Valley in this organisation eludes us. By the Roman period, the valley was divided into a number of estates with Romano-British villas at Comberton, Grantchester, Harlton, Haslingfield and Kingston (Figure 2.10). While place names like Comberton and Grantchester may imply survival of Romano-British estate centres in the valley into the two or three centuries after 410, this continuity must be seen within the wider context of the unregulated and competing local warlords who controlled all or part of the valley at different times from different centres, as the areas over which they ruled expanded or contracted, were subdivided into new groupings or were absorbed into those of their neighbours. Warrior households, which derived their land and status from groupings based on kinship or clans, seem to have flourished in the valley between the fifth and early seventh centuries at the same time that the agricultural economy was predominantly focused on herding cattle and sheep. The names of three of these groupings survive in place names – at Haslingfield (Hæslingas 1086),[11] Armingford, Armshold Lane, Arrington and Ermine Street (Earningas 1012)[12] and Grantchester (Grantasæte 1086)[13] – but it is likely that there were once more. As has already been noted, there is no evidence that these local changes in political control were in any way related to cultural differences between competing groups, either locally or regionally. That is, this history does not seem to be one of competition between Britons and Anglo-Saxons. The archaeology suggests that the people of the Bourn Valley shared a common culture with people across East Anglia and the east midlands, and differences in political allegiance are most unlikely to reflect differences in ethnic or cultural traditions.[14] The names they chose for their groupings by the sixth or seventh centuries suggest that they saw themselves as local rather than ethnic groups – the Grantasæte took their name from the Granta, the Romano-British name for the River Cam, and the Hæslingas may also have named themselves after a local feature.[15] It seems possible that by the end of the seventh century the Hæslingas were one of the most powerful of these local groups. This is because the core estates of the Hæslingas seem to have been included in the ancestral demesnes of the Mercian kings who absorbed Cambridgeshire into Mercia between about 655 and 700, perhaps to legitimise their regional appropriations. An extensive estate, covering the whole Bourn Valley and at least initially dominated by pasture, seems to have emerged by the eighth century, although there is no sure way of knowing whether its extent was derived from an earlier small kingdom (regio), or whether it was created ab novo by a new Mercian overlord. This process is very likely to have coincided with an increase in demand for tributes paid in grain.

The lack of manorial structure in the late eleventh century and the high percentage of free landholders in the Bourn Valley in that period (both explored in more detail in Chapter 6) suggest that between the eighth and eleventh centuries the valley was an administrative backwater in which at least some elements of middle Anglo-Saxon social status and landholding survived simply because – for reasons we cannot elucidate – there was little impetus for change. It conforms to Dyer's characterisation of older land units 'with demesnes of such small size that the bulk of their revenues must have come from peasant rents. They are better

---

11. Ibid., pp. 77–8; Gelling, Place-Names, p. 244; Rackham, 'Trees and Woodland', p. 8; names derived from DB are shown as (1086) and are not referenced with footnotes.
12. Reaney, Cambridgeshire, pp. 51, 163, 70 and 23; Meaney, 'Gazetteer', p. 70.
13. Reaney, Cambridgeshire, pp. 75–6; Gelling, West Midlands, p. 82.
14. Stafford, East Midlands, p. 91.
15. Reaney, Cambridgeshire, pp. 75–6 and 77–8.

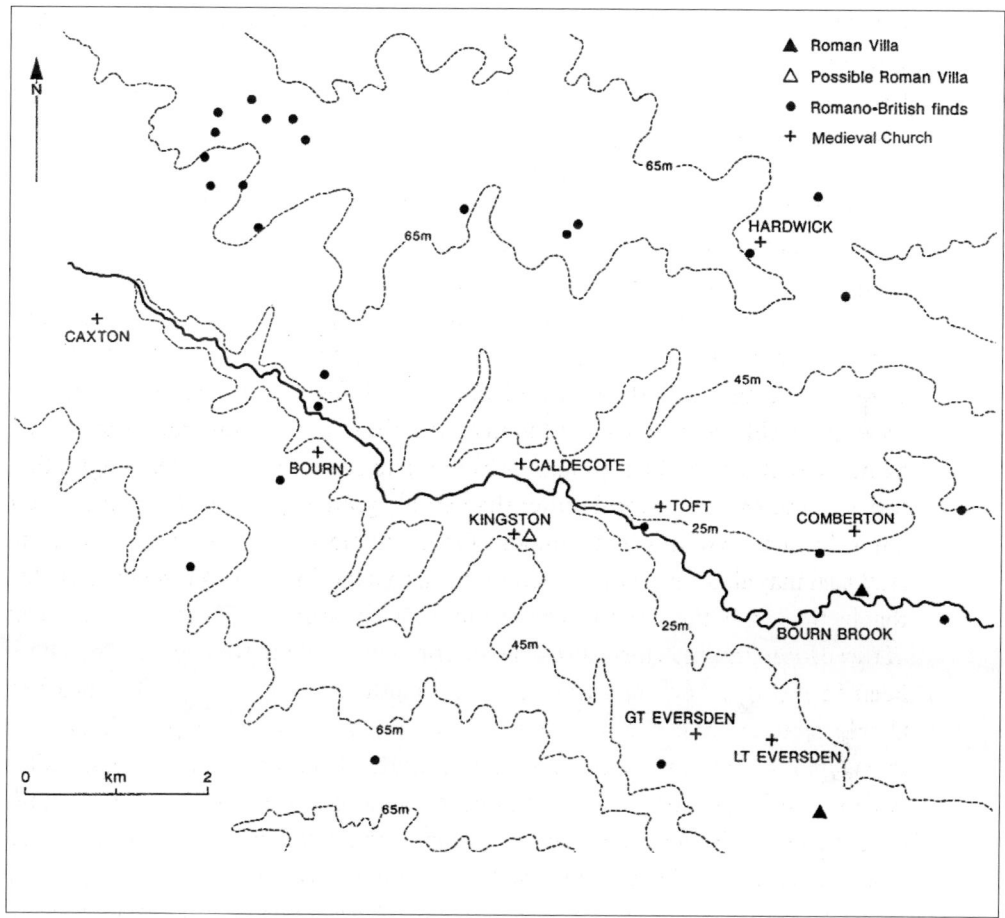

Figure 2.10 Romano-British occupation of the valley. The valley was evidently completely occupied during the Romano-British period, with farmsteads liberally placed along the upper and middle slopes, and villas and other farmsteads towards the valley floor. The information on this map is derived from stray finds and some archaeological excavation; systematic fieldwork across every field of the valley would, no doubt, record very much more

described as centres for the collection of tribute, preserving pre-manorial forms'.[16] Those processes of fission and disintegration of large estates in the ninth and tenth centuries that have been well documented elsewhere do not seem to have occurred widely in the Bourn Valley until the late tenth or eleventh centuries, and those that can be discerned suggest a much slower pace and a conservatism about that change compared with other places.

16. Dyer, 'Lords, Peasants', p. 303.

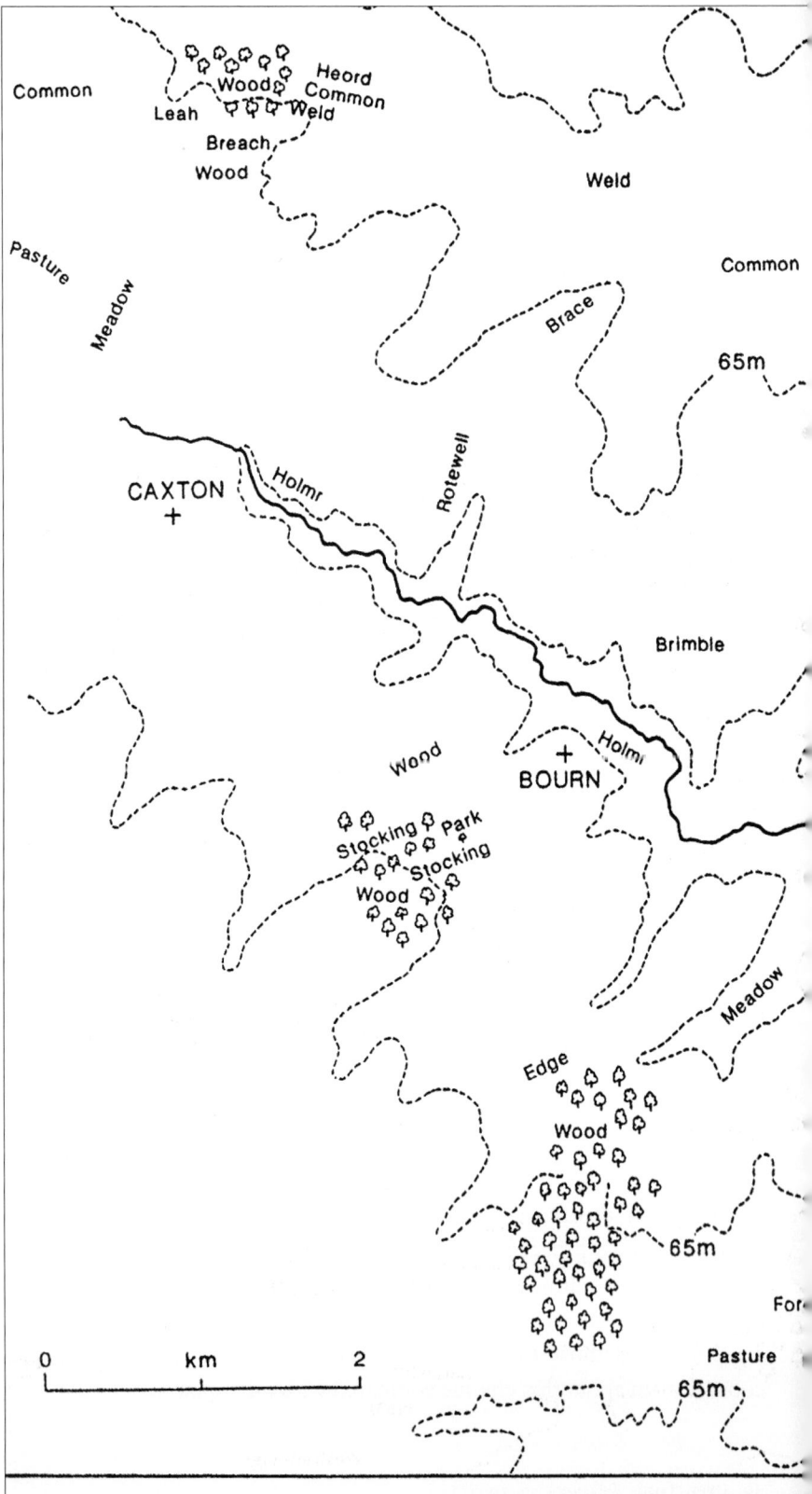

Figure 2.11 Land-use in the valley in the later Anglo-Saxon period. The distribution of field names across the valley records both the predominance of late Anglo-Saxon

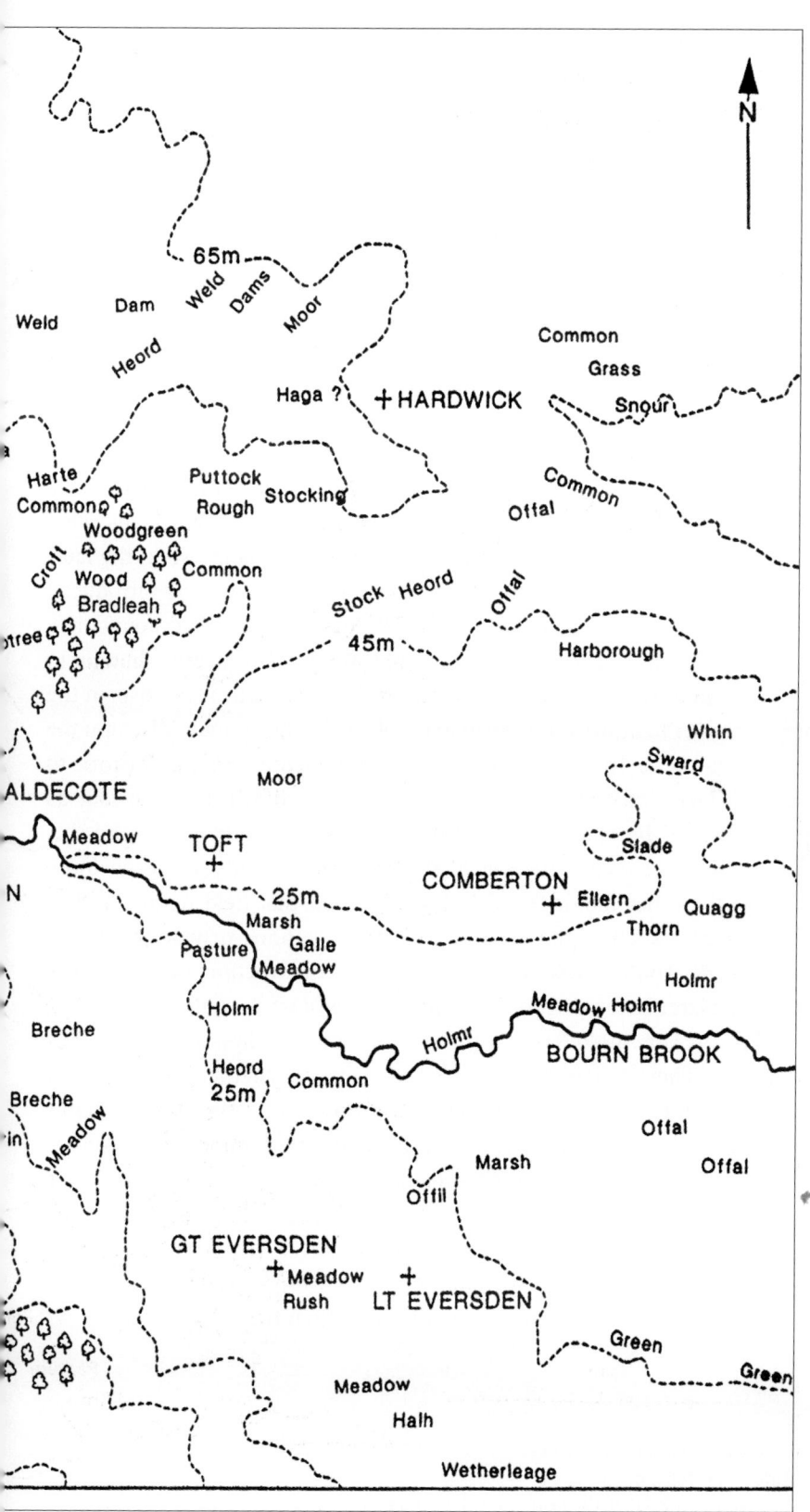

pasture and woodland across the middle and upper slopes, and meadow and marsh on the valley floor

Land use in the Bourn Valley in the later Anglo-Saxon period (Figure 2.11)

If prehistoric boundaries did survive to be reused in common-field layouts in the Bourn Valley, this survival may be expected to have been affected by land use at the time that the transition to common-field cultivation occurred. For example, ancient boundaries might be reused as common-field furlong boundaries where they were still visible as hedges, banks, ditches or earthworks in ploughland or pasture. They might, conversely, have been lost in areas of woodland and rough pasture, where they would be obscured by scrub or trees, and where the process of land clearance might be expected to have caused them further damage. In these areas furlong boundaries along completely new alignments would be more likely to have been created when these areas were included in the common fields. This hypothesis is examined below by reconstructing patterns of land use in the later Anglo-Saxon period, at about the time that common-field layouts were introduced into the Bourn Valley. If the hypothesis is correct, pre-common-field boundaries might be expected to survive in areas used as arable or intensive pasture, but not in areas of woodland or rough pasture, on the basis that 'once a feature exists in the landscape it is easier to utilise rather than eradicate it'.[17] This is not to discount the influence of economy, culture or tenure on the local transition from prehistoric to common-field agriculture. These factors may have been just as important as existing land use in the choice of common-field furlong boundaries, and this makes any attempt at reconstruction of the prehistoric landscape even more uncertain. On the other hand, David Hall has argued that field names 'reflect ancient topography, such as the presence of heaths, moors, or woodland' and 'with more work would allow a fairly precise reconstruction of a county's landscape in the later Saxon period'.[18] They provide almost the only evidence that has survived of any late Anglo-Saxon influence – cultural or physical – on the early common fields. Their reliability as evidence is based on their tendency for consistency over time. Puttokeswell in Kingston, for example, was mentioned in a charter of about 1189 and again in a terrier of the nineteenth century; Puttockesrou Field in Hardwick was noted in 1251 and had the same name in 1639.[19] The evidence is, however, fragmentary, and there are many examples of field and furlong names that have changed – often more than once – over the past 800 years. This evidence is therefore used, with caution, as a starting point for discussions about the landscape into which common fields made their first appearance.

---

17. McOmish et al., *Salisbury Plain*, p. 20.
18. Hall, 'Late Saxon Topography', p. 63.
19. Hassall, *Cartulary*, p. 81; CUL QC 17/16–22, G3/27 and EH1.

Woodland

Early field boundaries might disappear in areas in which woodland regenerated during the early Anglo-Saxon period, whereas they would be more likely to remain visible in areas of pasture or arable. Reconstructing the extent of woodland in the Bourn Valley in the late Anglo-Saxon period would therefore help to explain the differential survival of prehistoric boundaries in the common-field landscape.

The known medieval woods of the Bourn Valley – Bourn, Eversden, Hardwick, Kingston and Swansley (Caxton) Woods – generally lie on the flat, poorly drained boulder clay capping the southern and northern ridges. Only Hardwick Wood stands on the middle slopes of the valley, on a flat spur between two tributaries of the brook. Their locations confirm Rackham's generalisation that 'woods are not on land that was good for growing trees, but on land that was bad for anything else'.[20] Although there is no definitive evidence about the exact extent of woodland in the valley in 1086 something can be inferred from the distinction between the use of *silva* 'wood' and *nemus* 'grove' in describing woodland in Domesday Book (hereafter DB) and its contemporary texts, *Inquisitio Comitatus Cantabrigiensis* (ICC) and *Inquisitio Eliensis* (IE). Work in Warwickshire has suggested that *silva* may have been used to record woodland that was so extensive that it included areas of wood pasture for grazing, that is grassland scattered with pollard trees, while *nemus* was used for 'specific areas of [managed] woodland of limited extent' – typical of areas where woodland was a relatively scarce resource.[21] Of fourteen holdings in the Bourn Valley where woodland was recorded in DB, only one (part of Eversden Wood) was classed as *silva* by DB in 1086; Picot's woodland in Bourn was called *nemus* in DB and IE and *silva* in ICC.[22] All the other woodland holdings were *nemus*. The impression of managed woodland in the valley is supported by references in DB only to the provision of fencing, fuel or wood for houses from the woods in the valley – no wood was estimated in terms of the number of pigs which might pannage within it (Figure 2.12).[23] The apparent emphasis on managed woodland suggests that by the late eleventh century wood was already a relatively scarce resource within a largely cleared landscape.

The impression that the Bourn Valley was largely cleared of woodland by 1086 is confirmed by field names and the patterns of medieval furlong boundaries. Except in the immediate proximity of existing woods, there are few names

---

20. Rackham, *History of the Countryside*, p. 98.
21. Wager, *Woods, Wolds and Groves*, pp. 10–11; Hooke, 'Pre-Conquest Woodland', p. 121.
22. DB 32:23; IE pp. 88–9; VCH I, p. 425.
23. Pigs are unlikely to be pastured in managed woods because they eat new shoots sprouting from recently coppiced stools.

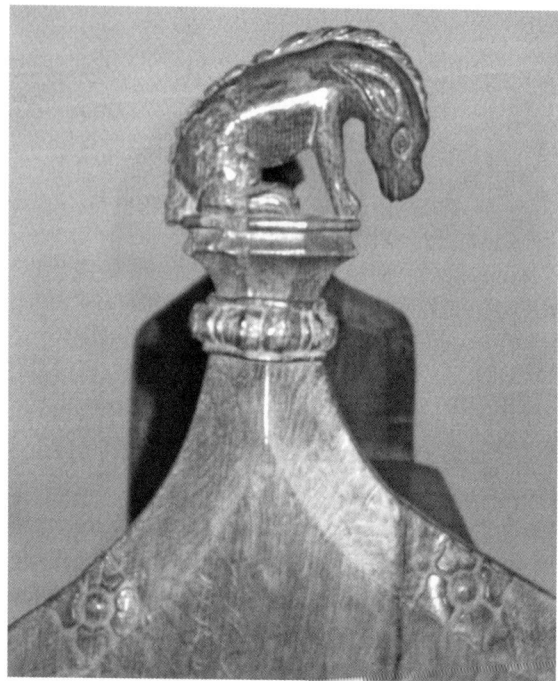

Figure 2.12 Medieval boar from a bench-end at Swavesey parish church, Cambridgeshire. There were relatively few pigs on the eleventh-century demesnes of the valley, but the fact that Eversden takes its name from these animals may mean that it provided a specialist render to the estate centre at Haslingfield during the middle Anglo-Saxon period. This would certainly be consistent with the field-name evidence for wood and wood pasture in the parish

indicating assarting or woodland clearance on these plateaux, and only three field names suggest possible reversion of arable land to scrub during the Anglo-Saxon period: Brace Dean (*brash* 'small branches, twigs', sixteenth century)[24] and Brimble Barrow Hill (*brïmel* 'brambles', sixteenth century)[25] might be indicative of neglected arable or overgrown ground in Bourn, and Snour Hill (*sno(w)e* 'brushwood', 1504)[26] in Comberton. This evidence is supported by the large and relatively regular shape and size of most of the furlongs which lie next to or near these ancient woods, which may show that they were laid out over cleared arable or pasture. If they had been cleared from woodland, they would be more likely to be small and irregular in shape (Figure 2.13). A careful analysis of the fields around specific woods, like Kingston, Hardwick and Eversden Woods, suggests that, even at their largest, these woods had never been more than about two or three times their present area, which they probably attained by the eleventh or twelfth centuries.[27]

Consecutive boundaries of Kingston Wood, preserved in footpaths and field boundaries to the east of the modern wood demonstrate that it, like the other

24. ChC 19thC; Gelling and Cole, *Landscape*, p. 69.
25. ChC P&M; Reaney, *Cambridgeshire*, pp. 313 and 342.
26. CUL EDR/H1; Reaney, *Cambridgeshire*, p. 333.
27. Rackham, 'Woodland in the Ely Coucher Book'.

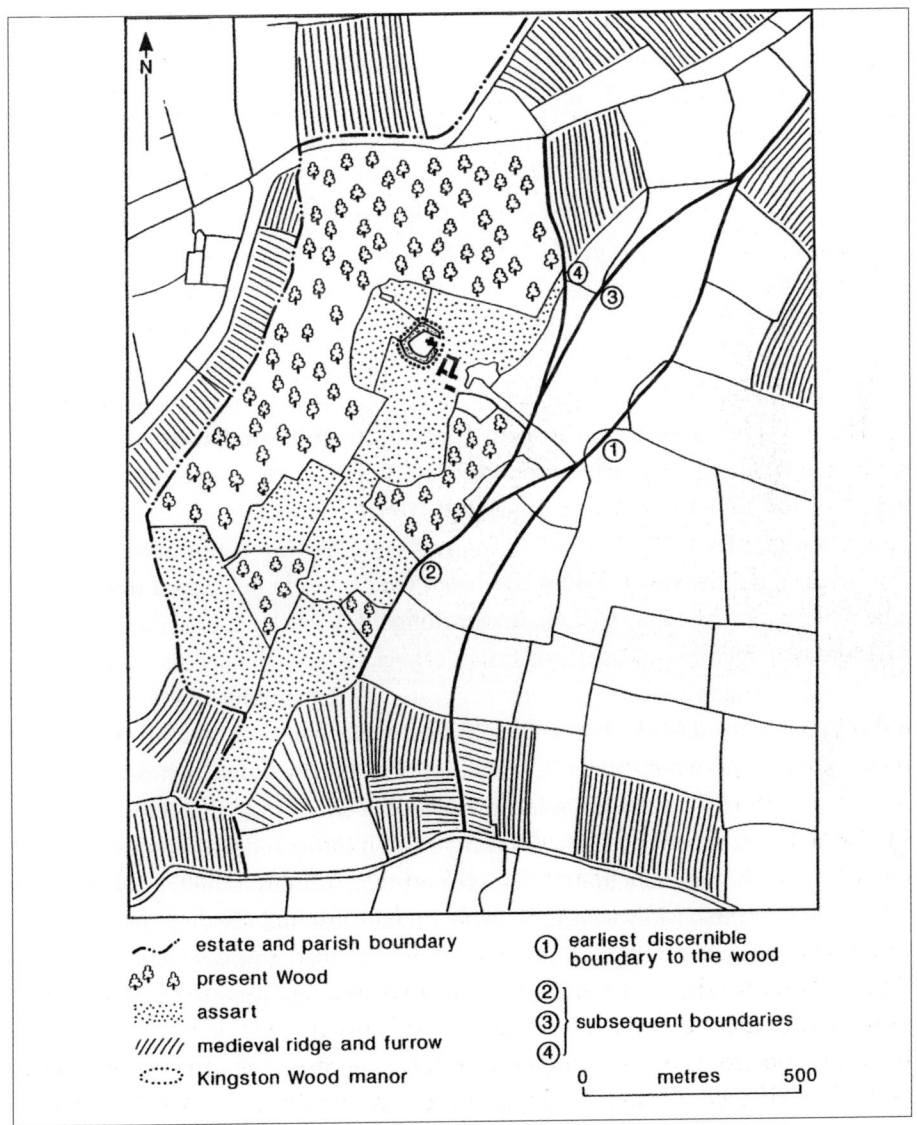

Figure 2.13 Kingston Wood in its wider landscape in 1720 (after CCRO R52/12/5/1)

woods of the valley, was probably never much more than about twice its eighteenth-century extent. There is little evidence of assart around the wood, except within the wood itself and on the high plateau immediately to the south. The large and regular medieval furlongs between Kingston Wood and Eversden Wood to the west suggest that these fields were laid out across open countryside

The character of the surviving late Anglo-Saxon woodland in the valley is sometimes illuminated by field names. Crabbyshe (Hill Furlong) (*crab* 'crab-apple', 1695)[28] lay in Wood Field, Caldecote, near Hardwick Wood and might suggest woodland assart since crab-apple trees are often found in woodland. Lime trees, frequently found in ancient woods, presumably grew in Linwood Close (*lind* 'lime-tree', n.d.)[29] also Caldecote. The proximity of these woods to grassland is suggested by the occurrence of 'puttock' (*puttockes* 'red kite') on both sides of the valley at Puttockdean (c. 1189),[30] the stream that runs northward from the western side of Eversden Wood, and Puttockrou (Field) (1251) in Hardwick,[31] just north of the wood. The name is derived from the buzzard or red kite, which had a preference for nesting in mixed deciduous woodland but hunted in grassland and, significantly, *-rou* means 'rough ground'.[32]

There is some evidence to suggest that hunting, a familiar aspect of high-status landholding, may have been associated with these woods in the Anglo-Saxon period. (Hedding) Hayes (Furlong) (1615)[33] in Caldecote – perhaps near Shorte Hartes Furlong (*hart* 'deer', 1597)[34] – and Hay (Common) (1251) in Hardwick[35] (neither very far from Hardwick Wood) might be derived from *haga* 'a type of fence that often seems to have run alongside woodland, possibly connected with the management of game animals', especially deer.[36] Successive intakes of woodland, perhaps an early park, are suggested by the sinuous roads that lie west of Bourn Hall, the site of a late Anglo-Saxon thegnly hall and Norman motte-and-bailey castle, and which include Stockings and Bourn Wood, where two mid-sixteenth-century field names, *pales hoke* and *palys hyl*,[37] may also refer to a park. Kingston is a name often attached to early royal hunting lodges and the existence of ancient woodland there underlines a tempting possibility.[38] Aelfric's huntsman brings these hunts vividly to life: 'I weave myself nets and set them in a suitable place, and urge on my dogs so that they chase the wild animals until they come into the nets unawares ... I catch stags and wild boars and roe-buck and does, and sometimes hares'.[39]

The evidence for Anglo-Saxon woodland in the Bourn Valley therefore

28. ChC Caldecot L; Field, *English Field-Names*, p. 66; Rackham, *History of the Countryside*, p. 212.
29. Reaney, *Cambridgeshire*, p. 366; Rackham, *History of the Countryside*, p. 102.
30. Hassall, *Cartulary*, p. 81; CUL QC 17/16–22; Colin Bibby suggested that these birds may have been buzzards although the derivation of the field name is from red kites.
31. CUL EDR G3/27 and EDR/H1.
32. Reaney, *Cambridgeshire*, p. 331; *ex. inf.* RSPB 16 March 2001.
33. CC Safe B 38/5.
34. CC Safe B 38/5 and 39/8; Reaney, *Cambridgeshire*, p. 323.
35. CUL G3/27 and EDR/H1.
36. Hooke, 'Regional Variation', p. 148 and *Anglo-Saxon England*, p. 154.
37. Both found in ChC Bourn M; Field, *English Field-Names*, p. 28.
38. G. Foard, personal communication.
39. Swanton, *Anglo-Saxon Prose*, p. 170.

indicates that those woods known to have existed in the medieval period may have been somewhat larger in the eighth or ninth centuries than they were by the high Middle Ages, but were not sufficiently different in scale to carpet the upper clay ridges of the valley. Instead, by the eleventh century, woodland appears to have been discrete and managed, with occasional enclosures for hunting. As a result, assarting appears to have been generally small-scale and fairly limited, and there are therefore relatively few areas in the Bourn Valley where earlier land divisions might be expected to have disappeared under woodland that regenerated in the early or middle Anglo-Saxon periods.

Pasture, commons and meadow

The middle and later Anglo-Saxon economy of the valley included a significant element of cattle and sheep farming, judging by the many furlong names referring to grazing of one kind or another. There was therefore considerable potential for prehistoric or Roman field or land boundaries to remain visible over much of the late Anglo-Saxon landscape of the Bourn Valley before the common fields were laid out.

By far the highest proportion of animals kept on the manorial demesnes in the valley in 1086 were sheep, despite the comments of the *Victoria County History of Cambridgeshire and the Isle of Ely* (hereafter VCH) that 'the heavy clay soil makes the land unsuitable for extensive sheep cultivation', and the fact that Hardwick (1086), Wetherley (1086) in Little Eversden and Sco(u)per (Dean) (possibly *sceap* 'sheep', sixteenth century) in Caldecote appear to be the only early place or field names referring specifically to sheep.[40] The variety of pastures that would have been available to these animals is extensive, demonstrating the existence of a complex and sophisticated management of a range of pastoral resources which were grazed in different months, as appropriate, by cows or sheep. First on the list is wood pasture, that is, areas of rough grazing studded with trees. An area called 'wetherley' (*wedra* 'sheep' + *lēah* 'wood pasture')[41] lay along the top of the southern ridge near the junction of the parishes of Orwell, Harlton, Little Eversden and Wimpole, perhaps on the edge of denser woodland. Its local importance is signified by the fact that it gave its name to one of the two hundreds into which the Bourn Valley was later divided. Another *lēah* lay around Hardwick Wood, whose earlier name was *Bradleh* (*brad* 'broad' + *lēah*, 1251).[42] It had once been larger and, perhaps, been part of a varied wood and grassland landscape: Puttockesrou (Field)

---

40. CUL EDR/H1; Reaney, *Cambridgeshire*, pp. 69 and 343; VCH 5, p. 101.
41. Reaney, *Cambridgeshire*, p. 69; Gelling, *Place-Names*, p. 198.
42. CUL EDR G3/27; Reaney, *Cambridgeshire*, pp. 331 and 316.

(puttockes 'red kite' + rou 'rough ground', 1251) lay north of Hardwick Wood.[43] Wood Green Common (1814) stood on the northern edge of Hardwick Wood, and Intercommon Furlong (1814)[44] – perhaps originally intercommonable wood or wood pasture – east of the wood. These areas of wood, wood pasture and rough ground may have extended further east to Stocking Close, which lay close to the village street at the time of parliamentary enclosure (stocc 'tree stump', 1837).[45] Stockwell (Dean Field) (stocc 'stump' + wielle 'spring', 1615)[46] lay just to the east.

Second, a huge grassland area called the We(a)ld extended westwards along the top of the northern ridge from Caxton (Caxtoneswald, c. 1150)[47] across Bourn (Burneweld, 1464)[48] and Caldecote (weld, 1597)[49] to Hardwick (The Well, 1639),[50] perhaps 'sheep pasture characterised by isolated stands of wood'.[51] There were still extensive common pastures in this area at the time of parliamentary enclosure in the early to middle nineteenth century, after a brief period under the plough during the high Middle Ages, and a further indication is derived from the moor (mor) recorded in the same areas of Hatchmore Dean Field in Hardwick (1639).[52] (Another moor lay under Moor Furlong in the northern part of Toft in 1815.)[53]

A third, perhaps differently managed, area of grazing lay across the central slopes of the northern side of the valley, characterised by names derived from heord ('herd'). Hardwick's own place name (heord + wic 'stock farm', 1086)[54] suggests an origin as a specialist farm for animals, and similar names are found across the valley from the northern part of Caxton and Bourn, across the central parts of Caldecote and Hardwick, to Comberton and Eversden. They include Heard Common (Caxton, 1661),[55] Herd Common and Hardman's Dean (Bourn, 1635, 1820),[56] the Cold Hard Common (Caldecote, 1854),[57] Hardle Dean (Hardwick,

---

43. CUL EDR G3/27 and EDR/1H1; Reaney, Cambridgeshire, pp. 331 and 316.
44. Both in PC H.1.1.
45. CCRO Q/RDc 51; Reaney, Cambridgeshire, p. 345.
46. Both CUL EDR/H1; Reaney, Cambridgeshire, pp. 345 and 350; Hooke, Anglo-Saxon England, p. 134.
47. G&CC XXXII.1.
48. Reaney, Cambridgeshire, p. 54.
49. CC Safe B 38/5.
50. CUL EDR/H1. There is no earlier version of this name, but its location in the same general area as the other weld names on top of the high clay plateau makes it likely that it was also originally one of these names.
51. Hooke, 'Early Cotswold Woodland', pp. 333–4.
52. CUL EDR/H1; Reaney, Cambridgeshire, p. 339.
53. CCRO 124/P80.
54. Reaney, Cambridgeshire, pp. 162 and 308; Hooke, Anglo-Saxon England, p. 134.
55. G&CC XXXII.29.
56. ChC Mun Ac.
57. CCC Safe B 39/8.

1602),[58] Harborough Field (Comberton, 1518),[59] and He(a)rd Common (Great Eversden, sixteenth century).[60]

Fourth, some of the oldest grazing land in the valley may have been the communally managed Offals/Offils (*ald* 'old' + *feld* 'an open space within sight of woodland', thirteenth century) at Comberton, Little Eversden, Harlton and Haslingfield (Chapter 3, below).[61] There may have been further very large, irregular commons immediately below the spring line, where there are many field names related to drainage and pasture in places where the land is relatively flat and difficult to drain. For example, Red Meadow (perhaps *hrēod* 'reed', 1811)[62] in Little Eversden lies just below the spring line and just west of Bullall (bull 'cattle' + *halh*, perhaps 'slightly raised ground isolated by marsh', early sixteenth century).[63] Other examples are described in Chapter 3.

Last in the list of varieties of grazing opportunity are the enormous number of meadows that lay along the banks of the Bourn Brook and its tributaries. In Great Eversden alone, a farmer could send his flocks and herds to Rounsells (1681), Chicken Pasture (1764), Paintells Meadow (1681), Bell Pit (early sixteenth century) and the Holmes (early sixteenth century).[64] Many, lying on the flat valley floor, were called names derived from *holmr* 'marshy meadow' which describes their character very well (Figure 2.6).[65] This damp grassland provided hay for winter and late summer grazing for the community livestock as well as grounds for hunting wild birds like crane, swans and teal. Although aerial photographs show that ridge and furrow had lapped into these meadows by the high Middle Ages, these lands appear to have been abandoned for arable quite quickly in the deteriorating climate of the early fourteenth century.

The variety and distribution of field names relating to pasture in the Bourn Valley demonstrate both how specialist and how extensive areas of grazing once were here. Many occur precisely in those areas in which Romano-British farmers were 'pursuing a stock raising economy' within a system of 'quite complex land

---

58. CUL EDR/H1.
59. Reaney, *Cambridgeshire*, p. 160.
60. CUL QC/15.
61. CUL QC 15/12, 15/36 and 15/52; Reaney, *Cambridgeshire*, pp. 74 and 78; O. Rackham, 'Trees and Woodland', p. 8; T. Legge, personal communication; Oosthuizen, 'Medieval Greens and Commons'.
62. CUL QC/15; Gelling, *Place-Names*, p. 26. The location of this name, close to the intersection between the Roman road (A603) and the main road along the southern valley, makes *ried* or *ryd* 'clearing' unlikely: Reaney, *Cambridgeshire*, p. 342.
63. CUL QC/15; Gelling, *Place-Names*, pp. 100–11; Mills, *Dictionary*, p. 270.
64. CUL QC 15/9 and 15/13.
65. Gelling, *Place-Names*, pp. 50–1.

management'.[66] The coincidence may just indicate that the Anglo-Saxon pastoral traditions of the Bourn Valley had their roots in much earlier agricultural practices.

Arable

The preceding survey of the distribution of field names relating to wood and pasture might indicate that arable cultivation in the Bourn Valley in the middle and late Anglo-Saxon periods, before the introduction of common-field cultivation, was limited to intensively cultivated infields around dispersed farmsteads and other interstices between areas of grazing. It is clear, however, from field names and the evidence discussed in Chapter 5 that arable cultivation was widely practised in the middle to late Anglo-Saxon periods, at very least in those parts of the valley that lay nearest to Bourn Brook. For example, arable cultivation of the lower slopes of the valley may be inferred from Ellon Furlong (*ellern* 'elder', 1723)[67] and Thornpitt Leys in Stallow Field, Comberton (1638)[68] and Thorns Furlong in Caldecote (1597),[69] since 'thorn ... and elder are especially associated with lack of woodland' and with arable cultivation.[70] Parish boundaries in the valley tend to follow a zigzag course between the furrows of medieval selions in the same parts of most parishes in which field names describing arable landscapes occur, apparently confirming that arable cultivation was already being undertaken on the lower slopes of the valley in the middle to late Anglo-Saxon period before parish boundaries became fixed.

Even so, arable cultivation was not without problems. Many field names record persistent difficulties with drainage, exacerbated by the numerous springs that ran into the arable lands. Waterlond Furlong and Slade Close (mid-sixteenth century and 1820),[71] both in Bourn, lay on the arable lands; Sowerditch Hill ('waterlogged, badly drained', 1615)[72] in Brook Field, Caldecote, may have been crossed by Polmorway (*pōl* 'pool' + *mor* 'marsh', sixteenth century);[73] Scumpitt Furlong (1615) lay in Toft.[74] The quality of the land was also often poor: Bellam Piece (Bourn, 1795)[75] may have been land that only a madman would cultivate, while

---

66. Wessex Archaeology, Report 45970, p. 3; Report 33220, p. 15.
67. CUL EDR/H1.
68. MRO H1/ST/E/107/1.
69. CC Safe B 38/5.
70. Rackham, *History of the Countryside*, p. 212.
71. CC Ac and Safe B 38/5.
72. ChC Add. 5; Field, *English Field-Names*, p. 42.
73. ChC Add. 5; Gelling, *Place-Names*, pp. 27–9 and 54.
74. CUL EDR/H1.
75. ChC Survey of Parsonage Farm 1795; Field, *English Field-Names*, p. 157.

every parish in the valley has field names referring to beans, which were commonly grown on poor soil for their nitrogenous qualities. Starvegoose Closes, on both sides of the valley in Great Eversden (1738), Comberton (1806) and Hardwick (1854), vividly characterise the soils near the tops of the ridges – the land in these areas did not produce enough to feed a goose.[76] Pudding Lane at Caxton End (Bourn, 1820)[77] referred to the heavy stickiness of the clay. Hardwick was known as 'Hungry Hardwick' in the nineteenth century, and the VCH notes the 'unyielding qualities of the heavy soil' and 'the infertility of the land' there.[78]

It is possible to attempt to quantify the extent of arable cultivation in the valley in 1086 on the basis that, unlike many parts of England where the precise meaning of data recorded in DB is unclear, in Cambridgeshire 'the record of [plough] teams provides a reasonable index of the arable land of the Cambridgeshire villages in the eleventh century',[79] particularly since the formula for the county (as for the rest of Circuit III) is quite precise: '*terra est x carucis*', 'there is (arable) land for *x* ploughs'. The method followed here has been to assign 60 acres to each plough-team on the basis of Darby's calculations for Norfolk in 1086, to multiply this by the number of plough-teams in each parish, and to take the result as a percentage of the modern acreage of each parish.[80] Small adjustments to parish boundaries, generally at enclosure, may mean that these figures are slightly inaccurate, but not by a significant order of magnitude. The results are shown in Table 2.1. These suggest that, generally, between about 30 and 40 per cent of the available land of each vill in west Cambridgeshire was under the plough by the late eleventh century. This is consistent with the figure of between 32 and 37 per cent for

---

76. CUL QC 15/36 and 15/40; CCRO Q/RDc 51. Although this is a modern name, soil that was poor in the nineteenth century was likely to have been poor in earlier centuries.
77. CCRO Q/RDc 35; Field, *English Field-Names*, p. 41.
78. VCH 5, p. 99.
79. Darby, *Domesday Geography*, p. 287.
80. Darby, *Domesday England*, p. 115. The figure of about 60 acres per ploughland in 1086 suggested by Darby for Norfolk and Suffolk is not very different from that suggested by Campbell, who concluded that 'there were on average 78.5 sown acres per demesne plough in the period 1250–1349 [when arable cultivation was at its most intense], which declined by 15.5 per cent to 66.6 sown acres per plough in the period 1350–1449' (when population pressure was less intense); Darby, *Domesday England*, p. 115; Campbell, *Seigniorial Agriculture*, p. 121. The 120-acre ploughland common in DB for other parts of England may have included the approximate third of arable that lay fallow each year. The ploughland in Dorset might have been 120 acres: Rackham, *History of the Countryside*, p. 333. However, a 120-acre ploughland would result in an arable acreage of 90.6 per cent for Toft in 1086, which is very high. This suggests that ploughlands in the Bourn Valley were more likely to be comparable to those of Norfolk and Suffolk, about 60 acres in size. There is no evidence to suggest that eleventh-century parish boundaries in the valley were very different from those of the nineteenth century and, in the absence of evidence to the contrary, it has been assumed here that the areas of these parishes remained roughly equivalent between these dates.

Table 2.1 Ploughlands and parish acreages in the Bourn Valley in 1086

Parish	No. of ploughlands	Parish acreage	Percentage ploughlands of total acres, if ploughland = 60 acres
Barton	12	1834	39.2
Bourn	23.5	3995	35.2
Caldecote	4	1007	23.8
Caxton	12	2169	33.1
Comberton	12	1954	36.8
Eversden	13.375	2190	36.6
Grantchester	12.875	2527	30.5
Hardwick	6.125	1438	24.6
Harlton	7	1261	33.3
Haslingfield	20	2573	46.6
Kingston	10.56	1907	33.2
Toft	10	1285	46.6
Mean: Bourn Valley			34.9
Mean: Cambs Hundreds			36.9

Source: DB; ICC; VCH 5, parish essays.

Suffolk in the same period.[81] It is important to remember that the eleventh-century portrait of arable farming in the Bourn Valley depicts a situation at or near the beginning of common-field cultivation. The severe pressures of population of the late twelfth and thirteenth centuries had yet to come. There is no evidence that the common fields of those parts of the Bourn Valley that lay at some distance from the brook were laid out in a single event, as appears to have occurred in Northamptonshire.[82] Indeed, many of the furlong names in Hardwick in 1251 suggest gradual conversion to arable from pasture or wood: *Haydole*, *Utfeld*, *Longedole* and *Puttokesroudole*.[83] The extent to which arable cultivation increased between 1086 and the mid-fourteenth century may be inferred from the growth of arable cultivation in Hardwick, whose fields covered only 24 per cent of the parish in 1086 but 54 per cent in 1251.[84]

The fairly typical character of agriculture in the Bourn Valley in 1086 is reflected in estimates of demesne sheep flocks in the same period: there were 62.9 sheep per 1,000 acres in the valley, just slightly above the average for the county of 60 sheep per 1,000 acres, suggesting that the balance between pasture and arable here was about the same as elsewhere in Cambridgeshire.[85]

In conclusion, it seems that much land in the Bourn Valley was still open

81. Hesse, 'Domesday Land Measures', p. 25.
82. Hall, *Medieval Fields*.
83. CUL EDR G3/27.
84. CUL EDR G3/27; VCH 5, p. 101.
85. M. Hesse, personal communication.

country in the later Anglo-Saxon period and still used for intensive grazing or rough pasture, just before or at the time that common-field cultivation was being introduced. Woodland was limited in extent, although it continued to be assarted throughout the high Middle Ages, fluctuating in size over the centuries. The most extensive areas of arable appear to have been limited to the lower slopes, although it seems probable that every farmstead in a pattern of dispersed settlement had its own heavily manured and intensively cultivated infield. Where earlier field boundaries survived, one reason for their retention in common-field layouts might have been their visibility as features in areas of arable or pasture, compared with their invisibility in areas of woodland assart. The high proportion of open ground inferred from field names leads one to suspect a substantial degree of persistence of ancient boundaries in the medieval landscape of the Bourn Valley, an hypothesis explored in Chapter 4.

3

The medieval landscape in about 1300

This chapter describes the medieval arable landscape of the Bourn Valley in 1300, when it lay at its greatest extent before being checked and fossilised by the climatic, demographic and economic changes of the early and mid-fourteenth century. It also examines the origins and development of the pastures and settlements that complemented these fields.

The common fields

By 1300 common-field cultivation was well established in the parishes of the Bourn Valley (Figure 3.1).[1] Arable lands covered most of the area of each parish. In Comberton, for example, 1,400 acres (71 per cent) of the parish was still cultivated as common-field arable in 1830;[2] field names, terriers and other documents, as well as air photographs recording medieval ridge and furrow make it clear that these fields were at least medieval in origin and once much more extensive, with ridge and furrow surviving in many meadows and leys into the mid-twentieth century. At Barton, arable covered at least 1,210 acres in 1279, about 65 per cent of the parish, while at Bourn there were at least 3,100 out of 3,955 acres of arable land at the same date.[3] Maps and surviving earthworks demonstrate that in medieval Caldecote almost the entirety of the parish lay under the plough.[4] The Coucher Book accounted for more than 50 per cent of the total acreage of Hardwick in its list of arable fields there in 1251.[5]

The arable was divided into two or three very large, common fields in most parishes. For example, Eversden, Kingston and Toft had just two fields each in

---

1. Much of the material in this section is derived from Postgate, 'Open Fields'.
2. CCRO R53/13/8; CCRO Q/RDc 57; VCH 5, p. 175.
3. Rot. Hund. ii, pp. 563–4; pp. 521–5; VCH 5, p. 10.
4. CCRO Q/RDc 76; CCRO R60/24/2/11; CC Safe B 39/8; CUULM.
5. CUL EDR G3/27.

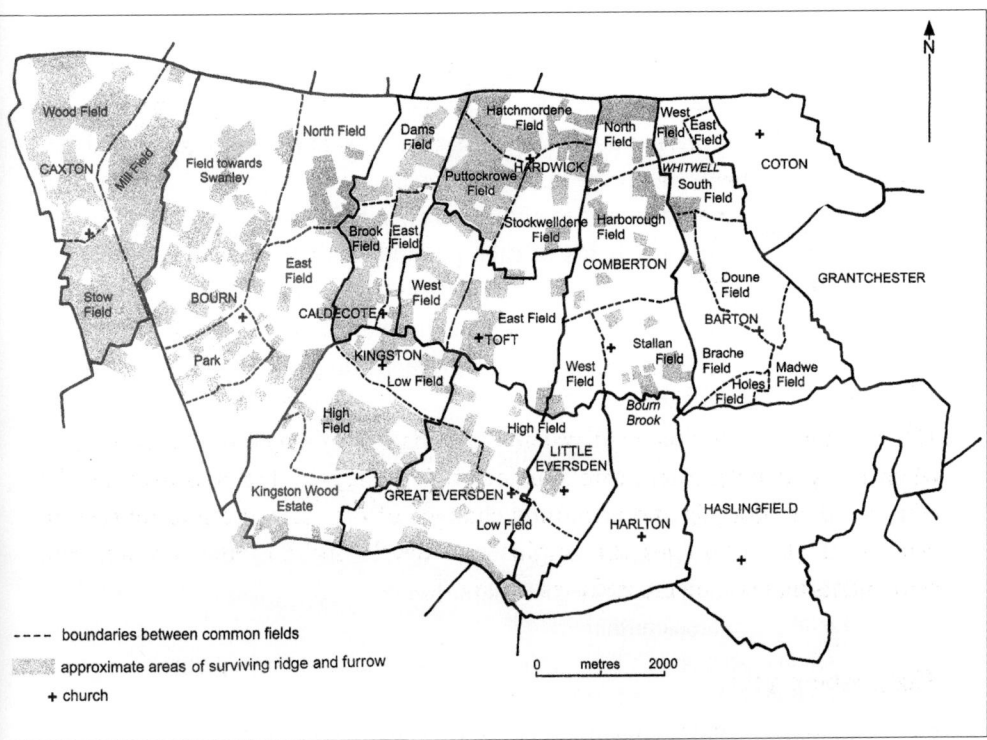

Figure 3.1 Common fields in the Bourn Valley in c. 1300 mapped against ridge and furrow shown on air photographs or still surviving on the ground. In many parishes medieval cultivation extended from valley floor to the tops of the ridges

1300. The fields in these parishes divided the arable lands between them fairly uniformly, with 'almost equal division of customary holdings between the "*campo australi*" and the "*campo boreali*"'.[6] At Bourn and Comberton, farmers partitioned their common fields into three.[7] These arrangements seem to have been very stable, since thirteenth- and nineteenth-century farmers in Comberton, Eversden and Hardwick each referred to many of the common fields and furlongs in their parishes with names that the other would have recognised.[8] Field names tended to be locational, directional or descriptive. In Barton in 1283, for example, the four fields were Madwe (meadow), Doune (down), Brache ('newly broken for ploughing') and Est (east); the lands of fourteenth-century Toft were divided between West and East Fields; while in Bourn thirteenth-century farmers went out

6. Postgate 'Open Fields', Fig. 7 facing pp. 25 and 17.
7. Ibid., Fig. 7 facing p. 25.
8. Ibid., p. 49.

to plough East Field, the Field towards Swanley (Wood) and North Field.[9]

On average, fourteenth-century peasants held between 25 and 30 per cent of the fieldland, and the manorial demesnes between 36 and 38 per cent, the remainder being in the hands of freeholders. The smaller lay manors had the highest proportions of demesne land and freehold tenants. Most peasants held half-virgate holdings of between 10 and 15 acres, subdivided into strips of an acre or less scattered across the fields of each parish.[10] This landscape of dispersed strips, near streams and on hills, identified by their relationships with trees, marshy meadows and pasture, is revealed in the many terriers listing these holdings (Figure 3.2). In 1589, for example, Robert King held the following lands in Low Field, Great Eversden:[11]

> j selion the east head butting on the common stream
> j selion in water furlong
> j selion in … fold furlong
> j selion in collewyllowes furlong
> j selion the north side butting on bourne brook
> j selion in fulbrook furlong
> j selion in stannards hill ye north head butting onthe common pasture
> jii selions between the homes [holmr]
> j selion in beanland furlong
> j selion in longewhitehill furlong
> xj selions in marsh furlong the south head butting on marshmeddowe

Most medieval fields in Longstowe and Wetherley Hundreds tended to be between 100 and 300 acres in extent, and furlongs usually covered between 5 and 15 acres.[12] There is evidence from Hardwick, Eversden and Bourn that local people referred to 'furlongs' (that is, subdivisions of the medieval common fields) and 'fields' interchangeably. For example, in Hardwick, six 'fields' were listed in 1251: Longedole had 29¾ acres, Haydole had 17½ acres, Hotefeld was made up of 42¾ acres in *diversis particulis* (that is, in strips) and so on.[13] The small areas of these 'fields' suggests that they were actually furlongs, dividing the arable into the three fields listed in the parish by 1615: Puttockrowe (called *Putokeshoudole* in 1251),

---

9. Ibid., Appendix 1.
10. Ibid., pp. 156–60.
11. CUL QC 15/2. A terrier (from *terra* 'land') was a list of the arable selions and other lands (closes and common rights) held by each farmer. Only a terrier describing all the land of a manor might record all the strips in a field system; however, most Cambridgeshire parishes had more than one manor, and so, even a manorial terrier would not present a complete list of all the arable and pasture land in a parish.
12. Postgate, 'Open Fields', Fig. 3; p. 50.
13. CUL EDR G3/27.

Figure 3.2 Common fields at Barton, 1819 (courtesy of the Cambridge Antiquarian Society). A rider and his hound pause on the crest of a hill in the early nineteenth century, the ridges of common-field cultivation clearly delineated in the landscape which lies between them and the parish church of St Peter at Barton

Stockwelldean and Hatchmoredean.[14] In Eversden eight 'fields' were listed in 1316, some of which – like Fulbroke and Chyrche – had the same names as furlongs ploughed 300 and 400 years later.[15] It is possible that local men used dynamic groups of furlongs rather than set areas of fields to decide which crops were to be planted in rotation each year.

Patterns of cropping appear to have remained fairly stable over the medieval period, reflecting the difficulties of the lower fertility and of working Grade 2 arable land on which marling had become commonplace by the thirteenth century. A three-course rotation seems to have been common. In 1251 John of Colne's

14. CUL EDR/H1.
15. Postgate, 'Open Fields', Appendix 1; CUL EH/1; CUL QC 13 and 15.

Figure 3.3 Waterlogged ridge and furrow on the valley floor at Harlton. The pressure on medieval farmers to find any land for cultivation is clearly demonstrated in these furrows on the Gault, where the crops they produced were always at risk from heavy or persistent rain. These lands were among the first to be abandoned in the fourteenth century and have never been ploughed since

estate in Caxton was made up of '72 acres of wheat, 10 acres of barley, 50 acres of dredge, 20 acres of oats and smaller amounts of beans and vetches'.[16] A lease of manorial demesne in Barton in 1261 stipulated that 24 acres should be sown with wheat, and 21 acres with barley, dredge and oats.[17] Sir William Castelacre, who owned most of Great Eversden in 1397, held the larger part of his wealth in his harvested crops: 300 quarters of wheat, 140 quarters of malt (barley) and 360 quarters of dredge.[18] In 1426 similar choices were apparent in Caxton, where there was slightly less wheat (27 per cent) grown than elsewhere in Cambridgeshire (32 per cent), and marginally more barley (25 per cent compared with 23 per cent elsewhere). There were also slightly fewer acres of oats (15 per cent compared with 17 per cent in other parts of Cambridgeshire). The introduction of peas in the late thirteenth century was enthusiastically taken up in the Bourn Valley: 26 per cent of the arable land in Caxton was under peas in 1426, compared with just 21 per cent elsewhere in the region. Dredge (7 per cent) made up the remainder.[19] Similar

16. VCH 5, p. 31.
17. VCH 5, p. 168.
18. Cal. Inq. Misc., vi, pp. 97–8.
19. Postgate, 'Open Fields', p. 189.

preoccupations with arable cultivation and its products were reflected in the surnames of many of those who paid the lay subsidy in 1327, like Agnes Breuster and John Molendarius (miller) in Kingston, Agnes Messor (reaper) in Eversden, and Walter le Hosebonde (labourer) and John Aylward (ensuring standards of ale) in Comberton.[20]

The documentary evidence for extensive medieval arable cultivation is supported by the survival of curving ridge and furrow of the same period across the valley, even on the waterlogged clay-tops of the ridges and the heavy Gault clays of the floodable meadows along the brook. Medieval farmers here were as land hungry as those anywhere else in the Central Province. The marginal character of some of the land taken into arable cultivation is demonstrated by the fact that many acres have never been ploughed again after their abandonment to pasture in the fourteenth century (Figure 3.3). Their exploitation for arable by about 1300 implies that the most easily ploughed lands of the parishes were already under cultivation by that time, and that the farmers of the valley were desperate enough to take the chance, for a long enough time to allow ridge and furrow to develop, of growing corn on land so vulnerable to waterlogging. By 1340 the heyday of arable cultivation had passed, and land in Kingston was lying *frisca et inculta* (rough and uncultivated) because it was so difficult to plough.[21]

Greens (Figure 3.4)

In the Bourn Valley, as in much of south Cambridgeshire, huge greens and commons (like the 'common pasture' familiar to Robert King) were as important in the medieval landscape as they had been in the Anglo-Saxon periods. They very often lay near springheads and close to streams where the ground, being poorly drained and difficult to cultivate, was easier to exploit as pasture than as arable. These areas were often the first to be enclosed in the later medieval period. Almost all lay on the heavy Gault clays of the flat valley bottom south of the Bourn Brook, just below the spring line. The combination of impervious Gault clay and flowing spring water in a relatively flat area made this land difficult to drain and almost impossible to plough – so difficult that even modern farmers find it hard to believe that this land could ever have been farmed. By the nineteenth century many of these areas of pasture were wholly or substantially bounded by roads, tracks or other rights of way, and property boundaries within them were often irregular, denoting piecemeal encroachment. Many were connected to one another by green

---

20. Evelyn-White, *Lay Subsidy*, pp. 53, 54, 29–30.
21. VCH 5, p. 115.

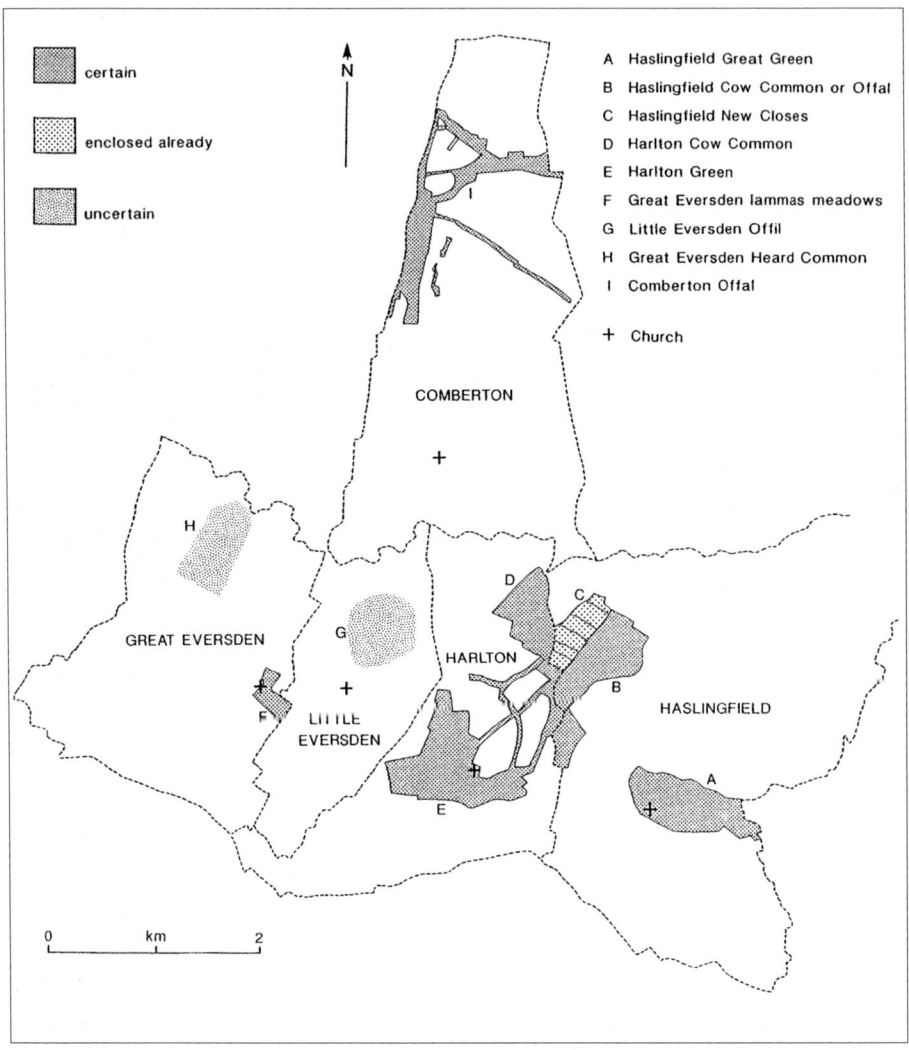

Figure 3.4 The Bourn Valley: greens and commons. The distribution of the Offals across the Gault clay of the valley floor is clearly demonstrated here, and reveals the extent of the early *feld*, which was the central feature of the territory of the *Hæslingas*

lanes. Almost all have disappeared since the mid-nineteenth century, some in the past thirty years (Figure 3.5).

The medieval open spaces of the Bourn Valley fall into two categories: those called 'green', 'common' or other names indicating pasture, and often associated with the main settlement of the parish, and those called 'Offal' or 'Offil' of which there is one in each of the three contiguous parishes of Haslingfield, Harlton and Eversden south of the brook, and a fourth at Comberton north of the brook.

Figure 3.5 Modern green at Haslingfield. At first sight, this small triangular space is the only modern survivor of the enormous Great Green which once underlay the medieval settlement (see Figure 3.6)

There were two enormous open areas of grazing in Haslingfield. Great Green, covering 100 acres, survived almost intact on the spring line under the present settlement until the mid-twentieth century (Figures 3.6 and 3.7). The oldest surviving map of Haslingfield dates from the early nineteenth century. By that date the green had been defined by roads and tracks, attaining a roughly oval outline, and encroached on by properties with irregular boundaries.[22] To the north-west lay a large common called the Offal (le Aldefeld[e] 1286: ald 'old' + feld 'field' or 'open country within sight of woodland') (Figure 3.8).[23] While it was evidently 'old' by the later thirteenth century, its use in that period is unknown, except that there is no evidence of ridge and furrow on it, which suggests that it has probably always been used for grazing. The use of feld in 'Offal' (ald + feld) and in 'Haslingfield' (Hæslingas + feld) indicates that the feld may date to the sixth or seventh centuries when place names ending in -ingas are believed to have been coined.[24]

At Harlton, immediately west of Haslingfield, there was another very large

22. CCRO Q/RDc 36.
23. Reaney, Cambridgeshire, p. 78; CCRO Q/RDc 36.
24. Dodgson, 'Significance of the Distribution', p. 19; Gelling, West Midlands, p. 110; Campbell, Anglo-Saxon History, p. 114.

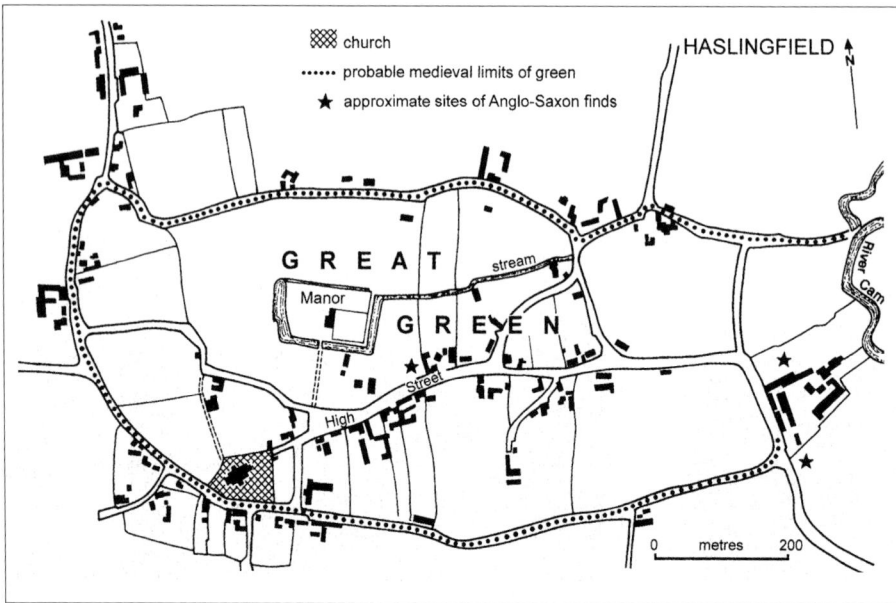

Figure 3.6 Great Green, Haslingfield (after RCHM(E), *West Cambridgeshire*, p. 136). By the early nineteenth-century the green was much encroached upon by settlement, including the sixteenth-century moated residence which lay at its centre. The location of the eleventh-century church on its southern perimeter, however, indicates that encroachment was only just beginning at the time that the church was initially constructed

Figure 3.7 Relic of Great Green, Haslingfield. Hidden along a minor lane in the village is a considerable fragment of the green, whose uneven hummocky character is still visible in the long grass

Figure 3.8 View across Haslingfield Offal. The radio telescopes of the Mullard Observatory stand on the flat valley floor, whose poor drainage and waterlogged soils best suited it to the *feld* preserved in the early and middle Anglo-Saxon Offals on the valley floor

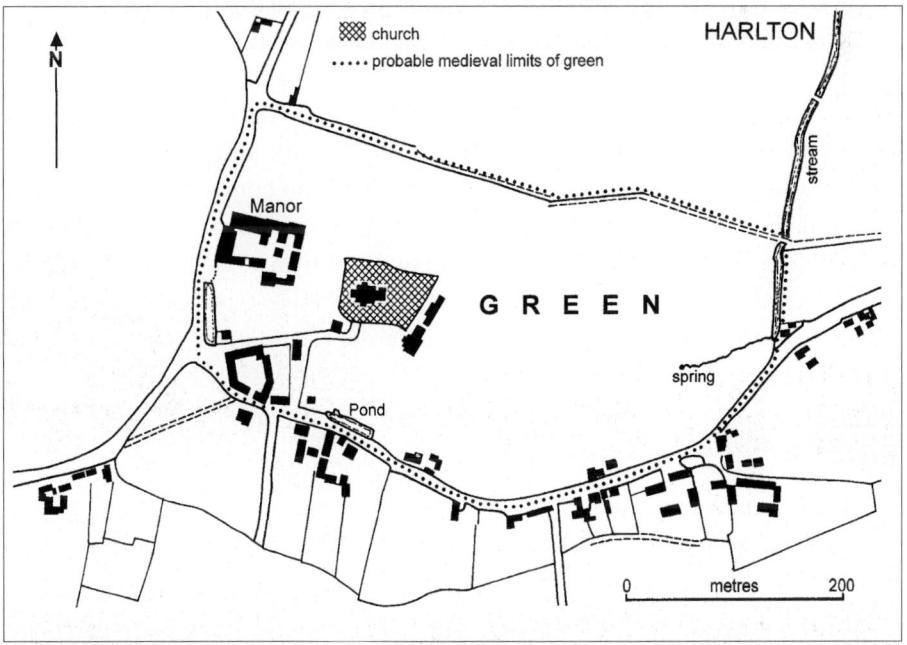

Figure 3.9 Harlton Green. As at Haslingfield, a large area of hummocky ground lying just below the spring line has been preserved in a substantial oval green, now defined by a road to the south and field boundaries to the north, and encroached upon by an eleventh-century parish church

green, also just below the spring line (Figure 3.9). It was bounded to the south by the present village street, and was encroached upon by the parish church, whose tithes were mentioned in the late eleventh century. North of the green lay Harlton Offil. Its site is not definitely known, but it probably lay in the north-east of the parish next to Haslingfield Offal, with which it formed a continuous area of pasture. Both were called Cow Common in the early nineteenth century, although by 1810 they had been separated by New Closes.[25] A third Offil, first documented in 1764, lay in the neighbouring parish of Little Eversden.[26] This Offil lay near the northern end of Little Eversden High Street where a low promontory of middle chalk met the Gault clay. It lay on poorly drained soil in an area just south of Marsh Close, which is still flooded by every winter's rains (Figure 2.6). It had become arable land by the time it was noted in documents. Another large area of pasture lay just below the spring line in the flat area surrounding Great Eversden parish church, where the waterlogged Gault clays are once again exposed (Figure 3.10). A number of pasture closes around the church formed continuous 'lammas' or hay meadows by the sixteenth century (Buck Rushing, sixteenth century, perhaps 'rushes'; *le cherchedole*, sixteenth century; and Ladymeadow, 1738).[27] He(a)rd Common (sixteenth century) was set on boggy ground north-west of Great Eversden church.[28] Adjacent furlongs were called Foulmire ('foul' + 'mud', 1681) and Betwixt the Holmes (*holmr* 'marshy meadow', early sixteenth century).[29]

Offal Common in Comberton was a large, broad swathe of pasture running along the parish boundary with Hardwick in 1839 (*le aldefelde, c.* 1250).[30] An extension called the Green reached southwards into the settlement, where *Nicolas ad le Grene* lived in 1279.[31] Starvegoose Furlong (1806), an irregular triangular furlong, was a late assart from the Offal, but there is no other evidence for arable cultivation on there.[32] Wide droves linked the Offal with Barton in the south-east and with substantial pastures to the north and north-east. Field names indicate that it was situated between areas of grazing to the west and east, connecting Stockwell Dean (*stocc* 'stump', 1615)[33] and Hardle Dean (*heord* 'herd', 1615)[34] in Hardwick to the west with Harborough Field (*heord*, 1518)[35] in the east.

25. CCRO 124/P52; CCRO Q/RDc 36.
26. CUL QC15/23.
27. CUL QC13/3 and QC15/22.
28. CUL QC 13 and 15; Reaney, *Cambridgeshire*, p. 332; British Geological Survey.
29. CUL QC 15; Reaney, *Cambridgeshire*, p. 336.
30. Reaney, *Cambridgeshire*, p. 74.
31. Rot. Hund. ii, p. 554.
32. CCRO R/53/16/20.
33. CUL EDR H/1.
34. CUL EDR/H1.
35. Reaney, *Cambridgeshire*, p. 160.

Figure 3.10 View towards the core of the extinct green at Great Eversden. The existence of a green around Great Eversden parish church is suggested by the many rights of way which meet in this area, by the communal buildings which clustered there – the church, a fifteenth-century guildhall (facing into the photograph) and the village pound which once lay to its right – and by the use of the medieval fields around the church as lammas meadows

The encroachment of Haslingfield and Harlton parish churches on their respective greens suggests that many of the less well-defined commons of the Bourn Valley were already in place by the eleventh century (Figures 3.6 and 3.9). The eleventh-century church at Haslingfield seems to have been one of the first encroachments on the green there, since it is situated just inside its southern edge. (If it had been a later encroachment, more properties between it and the edge of the green might be expected.) An even earlier date might be inferred from the discovery of Anglo-Saxon pottery both on the green itself, on its eastern edge, near the river, and the site of a substantial pagan Anglo-Saxon cemetery of the fifth and sixth centuries, less than 500 metres to the north.[36] Similar arguments apply to the siting of Harlton church, although there are no certain early Anglo-Saxon finds in the parish.[37] A pre-Conquest origin for these commons, hinted at by the archaeological evidence, gains strength from the name 'Offal' or 'Offil'. It is

---

36. Haigh, 'Archaeological Sites and Field-Names'; M. Coles, personal communication.
37. Finds from an early Anglo-Saxon cemetery recorded in the nineteenth century as coming from Harlton are of uncertain provenance and cannot be relied upon. The relationship between the similarly large green at Barrington and an early Anglo-Saxon cemetery there should, however, also be noted: Oosthuizen, 'Ancient Greens'.

derived from le *Aldefeld(e)* – the old *feld* whose mid-thirteenth-century documentary reference indicates that the Offals were already 'old' by that date.[38] *Feld* can be interpreted in two ways. The more common, and later, meaning indicates an arable field.[39] This definition seems unlikely in the context of the Bourn Valley, since one would need to explain why very early arable fields would have been set out on the heavy and waterlogged Gault clays at a time when population pressure on land was relatively light and more tractable land was available elsewhere. A reference to *brach* ('newly broken land') on Harlton Offal in 1332 and 1349 implies that at least some of this area was still pasture at the time, and supports the case against the view that the Offals originated as early arable fields.[40] This doubt is reinforced by the use of three of the four Offals as common pastures well into the nineteenth century. It is possible that they were land that had been ploughed in the high Middle Ages and then returned to pasture, but two pieces of evidence, neither conclusive, suggest that this was not the case. The first is that Haslingfield and Harlton Offal/Offils were described as 'commons' in the early nineteenth century, whereas arable converted to pasture in Cambridgeshire was usually, but not invariably, called 'leys'. The second is that there is no aerial photographic or other evidence for medieval ridge and furrow on Haslingfield, Harlton or Comberton Offals. Against this should, of course, be set the evidence from Little Eversden, where the Offil had been completely incorporated into the common fields by the early nineteenth century. The balance of the evidence therefore suggests that the Offal/Offils were areas used for grazing.

This conclusion is more appropriate to the second meaning of *feld*, which is both earlier and more unusual, dating from the sixth or seventh centuries: 'open country in sight of woodland'.[41] It seems to have described uncultivated land that was generally open, in the same sense as the modern Afrikaans word *veld* (familiar from the well-known novel, *Jock of the Bushveld*). This would make good sense in the context of the Offals, as it refers to land available for pasture, and would also explain why the *feld* was already 'old' by the thirteenth century. As remarked above, the survival of an early meaning of *feld* and its association with the place name at Haslingfield implies that these pastures may have been extant as early as the seventh century. The Offal/Offils appear to be the relics of a very large area of *feld*, the distinctive feature of the territory of the *Hæslingas*, and it seems that they covered most of the south-eastern valley floor from Haslingfield to Eversden in the sixth and seventh centuries, extending north of the Bourn Brook into Comberton.

38. Reaney, *Cambridgeshire*, p. 78.
39. Gelling, *Place-Names*, p. 236–7.
40. VCH 5, p. 221; Reaney, *Cambridgeshire*, p. 313.
41. Rackham, 'Trees and Woodland', p. 7.

Offal is a distinctive and unusual name. It may be related to the *ofaldfal* of Lincolnshire which was land that was 'not manorial but communal in origin' in the thirteenth century.⁴² There, it was land that was very carefully surveyed and measured, down to the last foot, and distinct from the assessed lands of each parish. The assessed lands were usually arable, those that in Cambridgeshire were measured in hides and virgates, and this suggests that the *ofaldfal* may have originated as pasture, whatever its use by the thirteenth century. If the *ofaldfal* and the Offals of the Bourn Valley have a common origin (by no means certain), then the communal ownership and control of the former may just imply that the Offals/Offils originated as distinctive areas of communally-held pasture appropriate to middle Anglo-Saxon clan territories.⁴³

It is significant that these commons and greens lie within the Central Province, an area in which large areas of 'indigenous' pasture are generally rare (although there is plentiful evidence for small, planned, post-Conquest greens laid out for settlement as, for example, in the late eleventh-century resettlement of north-east England and the many places in Cambridgeshire with medieval markets).⁴⁴ Commons are not usually associated with 'classic' two- or three-field landscapes. This is because it is usually expected that the growth of the common fields gradually obliterated the large pastures of the middle and later Anglo-Saxon periods, and that the pasture thus lost was replaced by allowing between half and a third of the arable to lie fallow each year for grazing, and by allowing the animals of the community onto the stubbles after harvest. The occurrence of these large greens and commons in the valley is anomalous in the Central Province, a point to which we return in Chapter 7.

Settlements in the valley

The plans of medieval settlements have been extensively studied over the past thirty years, and a number of models for the origins of medieval settlement have been developed.⁴⁵ In essence, a distinction is generally drawn between the dispersed settlements of 'ancient' countryside, where a number of hamlets and farmsteads lie scattered about a parish, and the nucleated settlements of the 'champion' landscapes of the Central Province where the population of a parish occupies a single settlement. There are variations on this model, including

---

42. Hallam, *Settlement and Society*, pp. 159–60.
43. Oosthuizen, 'Medieval Greens and Commons'.
44. Taylor, *Village and Farmstead*, pp. 133–8; Beresford and St Joseph, *Medieval England*, pp. 164–6; Taylor, 'Medieval Market Grants'.
45. Taylor, *Village and Farmstead*; RCHM(E), *Central Northamptonshire and North-West Northamptonshire*.

'polyfocal' settlements where a number of foci were set relatively close together, with small open spaces between them, but nonetheless still essentially offering just one settlement in the parish.[46]

Settlement in the Bourn Valley was strongly nucleated throughout the medieval period. It was often situated just below the spring line, at the junction between arable and meadow or pasture. Two examples, Toft and Hardwick, are explored here, to illustrate the relationship between settlement and the wider agricultural landscape within which they were set. These examples are particularly apposite since an estate called 'Toft' but incorporating both Toft and Hardwick had been acquired by Wulfnoth before 975, when he sold his 10 hides there, with 'all the stock, living and dead' to the Abbey of Ely.[47] The division of Toft and Hardwick into separate units can be traced to the mid-eleventh century. Between 1029 and 1035 Abbot Leofsige claimed a week's food-farm (*feorm*) from the Abbey's estate at Toft (still including Hardwick).[48] However, only Hardwick was confirmed to the Abbey between 1042 and 1057, suggesting that by that date most of Toft had been granted away.[49] By 1066, the Abbey had established a demesne manor at Hardwick.[50] This chronology implies first, that by the mid-eleventh century the Abbey had lost the larger part of its arable in the two parishes (since most lay in Toft, see Chapter 5); and second, that its manorial centre had moved from Toft to Hardwick, thus explaining the unusual occurrence of this secondary place name as a manor. This chronology provides a framework for the development of settlement in the two parishes. Although settlement at Toft is nucleated, there is no evidence there for any formal planning of properties or streets in any period (Figure 3.11). Aerial photographs show the earthworks of house platforms bordering the meadows that separate the Bourn Brook from common-field furlongs; the eleventh-century church is also situated on the edge of the meadow, along Stockwell Dean (a tributary of Bourn Brook).[51] From this it might be inferred that, in the medieval period, nucleated settlement at Toft was sited on pasture. By the early modern period, significant shifts in settlement had occurred. The village was still nucleated, but settlement had moved northwards onto enclosed parcels of common-field selions. The grid-like plan to the settlement so apparent to modern eyes results from the fossilisation of medieval and earlier fieldways and furlong boundaries which crossed the parish from north to south and from west to east

---

46. Taylor, 'Polyfocal Settlement'.
47. LE, p. 100; Hart, *Early Charters*, p. 221.
48. Hart, *Early Charters*, pp. 49–50.
49. Ibid., p. 50.
50. IE, pp. 152–3, VCH 5, pp. 101–2, DB 5:36–7.
51. CUULM AIR 91–3; CCRO Q/RDz 8; CCRO Q/RDc 23.

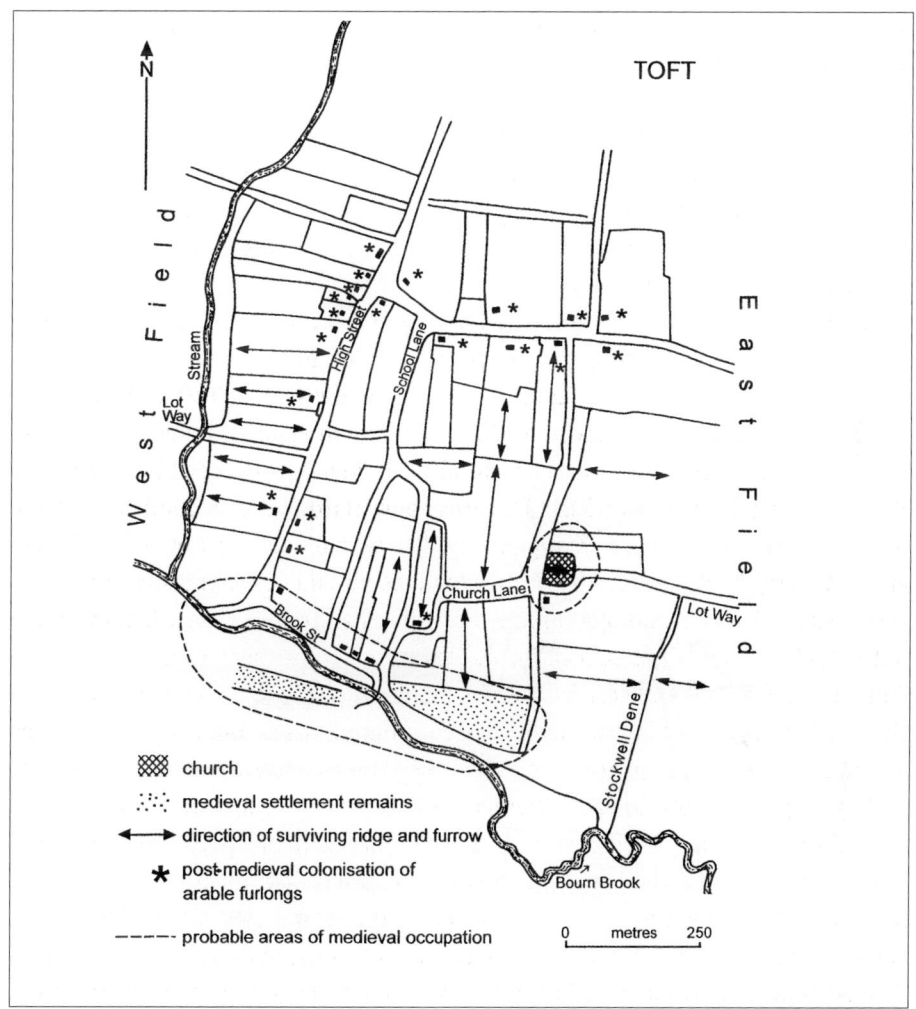

Figure 3.11 Plan of settlement at Toft in 1815 (after CCRO Q/RDc 23). The regular plan of the settlement at Toft reveals its origins in colonisation of arable land which lay in geometric divisions, framed by prehistoric alignments running from south-west to north-east, transected at right angles by the long, narrow commons of the eighth-century proto-common field

(see Chapters 4 and 5 below).[52] The distance of the church from both the deserted and the modern settlements, and the separate location of these two latter elements suggest that several shifts of settlement have occurred at Toft, although it is possible that the church may always have been isolated. The important features of settlement at Toft are the continued nucleation of its settlement in the medieval

52. Oosthuizen, 'Medieval Settlement Relocation'.

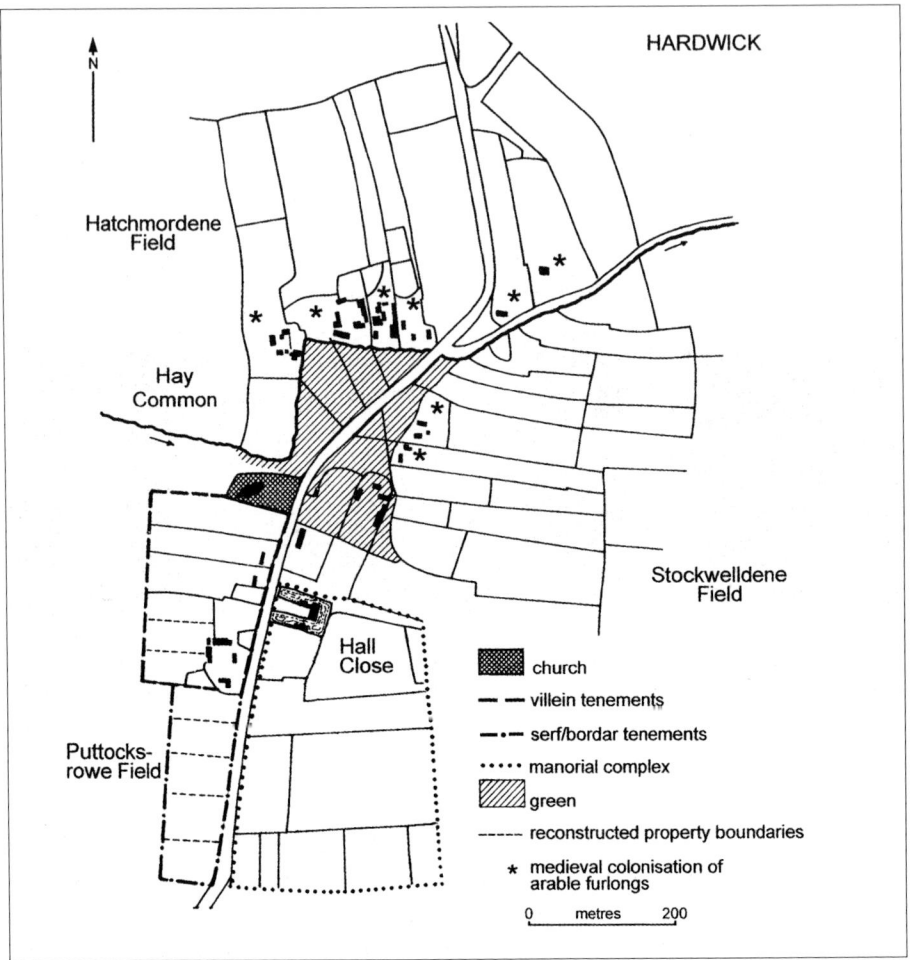

Figure 3.12 Plan of the medieval settlement at Hardwick (after PC H1.1). In the eleventh century, the settlement was laid out south of a planned green enclosed from Hay Common. The manorial complex lay to the east of the main street (q on Figure 4.1), faced by the tofts and crofts of the villeins and bordars on the west

period, and the integration of the settlement into the pattern of the medieval common fields. The field system appears to be earlier than the settlement, which has accommodated itself to the layout of furlongs and selions (Chapter 5).

Although also nucleated, Hardwick has a very different plan.[53] The spine of the village is a major route that ran from the valley bottom at Toft to the plateau on the northern ridge, and the settlement appears to have been laid out to the south of a planned rectangular green which had been carved out of Hay Common at its

---

53. This interpretation of Hardwick owes much to the insights of Harold Fox.

Figure 3.13 View south-west across the green, Hardwick. Although the parish church still provides a communal focus to the green, and a nineteenth-century well stands nearby (just off the right of the photograph), other communal facilities have disappeared, like the pound whose only relic is a stone in the modern base of the village sign

junction with the spinal road (Figures 3.12 and 3.13). The church was probably built in the late Anglo-Saxon period, since it contains a consecration cross of that date. It is sited at the northern end of, on the same alignment as, and on a site of the same width as, a block of planned tenements lying to the south, indicating that it is probably contemporary with them.[54] There appear originally to have been six properties in this block, comparing favourably with the seven villeins listed on the manor in 1086, and suggesting that this period of planning may have occurred in the eleventh century.[55] Further south another planned block with shorter plots may have been divided into five properties, perhaps relating to the four serfs noted in DB. The seigneurial compound appears to have lain east of the main street. A moat was constructed at its north-west corner (Hall Close) in the late twelfth century, and was occupied at least until the end of the following century.[56] Taken together, this suggests that the Abbey laid out a planned settlement at Hardwick in the late tenth or early eleventh century. North and west of the green, common-field

54. CCRO Q/RDc 51; CUL Ms Plans 582; CCC HER.
55. DB 5:36–7.
56. Haselgrove, 'Hardwick', pp. 49–50.

furlongs were colonised over subsequent centuries, perhaps in the period up to 1300 when the number of tenants quadrupled to about forty-three.[57]

The massive increase in arable at Hardwick from about 24 per cent of the available land of the parish in 1086 to perhaps as much as 54 per cent in 1251 graphically demonstrates the extension of the common fields across the parish, influenced by rising profits from grain and the fourfold increase in population between much the same dates.[58] It vividly illustrates the shift on the northern slopes of the valley from a predominantly pastoral to a predominantly arable landscape between about 1000 and 1300. The planned development of the settlement at Hardwick at the same time as the extension of arable cultivation in the parish is demonstrated by the close relationship between the settlement plan and the field pattern of the parish. Of all the settlements in the valley, only Hardwick has a radial plan, its lanes and tracks integrating the settlement with the common fields unlike the grid-like plans of the other settlements which reveal their accommodation to a pre-existing field layout.

By 1300 the process of settlement nucleation in the valley was complete. In some cases, like Haslingfield and Harlton, the houses of the parish were sited around the edge of – or beginning to encroach upon – the hummocky pastures lying just below the spring line. In other cases, settlement had moved onto arable strips, as at Toft, Hardwick, Caldecote, Comberton and, perhaps, the Eversdens.[59] The process of settlement nucleation in the valley seems in most cases to have been undertaken in several phases which were complete by the thirteenth century. In almost all cases this process was informal, with only occasional evidence for formal planning. Hardwick seems to be the exception, the village there resulting from just one intense phase of settlement planning, possibly related to the introduction of common-field layouts in the parish.

Moated settlement (Figure 3.14)

A common feature of the fourteenth-century landscape of the Bourn Valley was its moated sites. In the Central Province, moats are infrequently found, except on its eastern borders, and most of those moats are commonly associated with manor houses within nucleated settlements.[60] In the 'ancient' landscapes of East Anglia, by contrast, there was a proliferation of moats during the period between 1100 and 1300, constructed for medieval freemen who created new holdings in isolated areas of rough pasture or woodland.

57. Rot. Hund. ii, pp. 538–9.
58. IE, pp. 152–3; VCH 5, pp. 101–2.
59. Oosthuizen, 'Medieval Settlement Relocation'.
60. Roberts and Wrathmell, *Region and Place*, pp. 57–8 and 160.

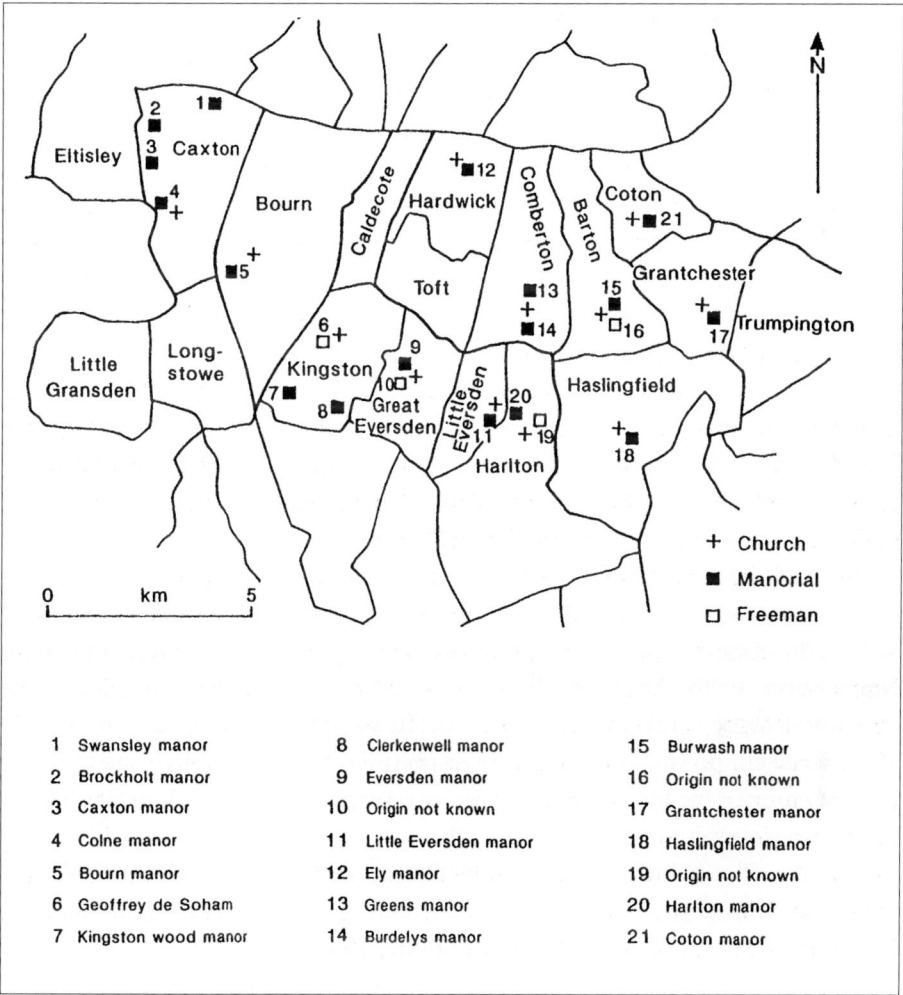

Figure 3.14 Distribution of moats in the Bourn Valley. Most moats, whether manorial or constructed by freemen, lie within the nucleated settlements of the valley. Those outside the nucleations, like Swansley and Kingston Wood Farm, were isolated manors with no associated settlement, founded after the Conquest on pasture or waste

The moats of the Bourn Valley fall into two groups. Those created by wealthy and aspiring freemen were set exclusively in the nucleated settlements of the valley – emphasising both the strong pull towards nucleation and the lack of large areas of assartable land. They conform well with expectations that settlement in the Central Province would be nucleated, even though they were not manorial (Table 3.1). The second group contains all the outlying moats in the valley. It is more problematic, since all these moats were manorial in origin, rather than those of freemen. Every one is the site of a manor first founded, or created by

Table 3.1 Characteristics of moated sites in the Bourn Valley

Settlement	No. of moats	Moats within settlement		Moats outside settlement	
		Manorial	Freeman	Manorial	Freeman
Barton	2	0	2	0	0
Bourn	1	1	0	0	0
Caxton	4	1	0	3	0
Comberton	2	2	0	0	0
Grantchester[1]	2	1	1	0	0
Gt Eversden	2	1	1	0	0
Hardwick	1	1	0	0	0
Harlton	2	0	2	0	0
Haslingfield	1	1	0	0	0
Kingston	3	0	1	2	0
Lt Eversden	1	1	0	0	0
Total	21	9	7	5	0

Source: RCHM(E), *West Cambridgeshire*, parish essays.
Notes: 1. Including Coton.

subinfeudation after 1066, and they have no Anglo-Saxon antecedents.[61] They lay on portions of demesne given to religious houses during the twelfth and thirteenth centuries, like the Scalers demesne in Bourn and Caxton granted to St Neots Priory, or the Mortimer demesne in Eversden and Kingston given to the nuns of St Mary, Clerkenwell. These moated manorial sites seem to have been constructed simply to administer their respective estates, and there is no evidence that they formed the focus for any settlement. On the contrary, they appear to have been quite isolated.

All the evidence indicates that settlement in the Bourn Valley has been highly nucleated at least since the late Anglo-Saxon period, perhaps roughly since the common fields were introduced. The attribution of the Bourn Valley to the Central Province is therefore apposite, at least in terms of settlement nucleation and the character of its common fields, but the survival of large greens and commons into the medieval period and beyond hints at problems with the characterisation of 'ancient' and 'champion' landscapes to which we will return in Chapter 7.

Conclusion

By 1300 the landscape familiar to the farmers and labourers who cultivated the Bourn Valley was generally that of the big villages whose 'predictable land of wide views [and] sweeping sameness' was familiar to the inhabitants of other parts of the Central Province.[62] Houses lay in nucleated settlements, some planned, some

---

61. VCH Cambridgeshire 5, parish essays.
62. Rackham, *History of the Countryside*, pp. 4–5.

with the appearance of planning derived from their colonisation of field land. In those parishes with larger areas of woodland or pasture, blocks of demesne land had been granted to minor religious houses which built small, often moated, domestic complexes where a bailiff could live and manage the holding. Peasant farmers and their labourers left their homes on fine days in the autumn and spring to drive their ploughs or harrows to near or distant selions, in common fields that covered most of the land of each parish. In season, tenants were allowed into the woods to collect their allotment of coppice and underwood. Boys took cattle and sheep to graze on the meadows by the brook and its tributaries, or on the large common pastures of the Offals and greens whose use was regulated by the community. That communal control was one of the few remaining vestiges of the freeholders and warlords of the sixth- and seventh-century clans who had once used these grasslands to raise cattle and sheep, and the following chapters attempt to unravel the processes through which these landscapes, familiar to the Hæslingas, Earningas and Grantasæte, evolved into the large arable fields of the Middle Ages.

4

Ancient fields into medieval furlongs

In the Bourn Valley, fragments of a regular system of land division which predates the medieval common fields appear to have been fossilised within the furlongs and strips – selions – of the medieval landscape (Figure 4.1). A significant number of these early land divisions in the Bourn Valley remained in use until parliamentary enclosure, and some survived as earthworks into the modern period (Figures 4.2 and 4.3). The importance of this evidence is that it comes from an area which lay within the planned, 'champion' countryside of the Central Province, rather than in the zones of 'ancient' countryside of the other two provinces where most of the evidence for early landscapes has been found. It is particularly significant since the most extensive work on medieval field systems has demonstrated that the introduction of medieval common-field agriculture in the Central Province utterly erased these earlier boundaries.[1]

The wider context

There is now a great deal of evidence for the survival of prehistoric boundaries in areas of 'ancient' countryside outside the Central Province where medieval fields were not laid out on any large scale. They survive particularly well in areas marginal for arable cultivation, where they were often reused in the boundaries of medieval fields. For example, Christopher Taylor has noted that

> in Wessex, there are, and were, vast areas of these [prehistoric] fields, overlain by later, short-lived, medieval ridge and furrow. Though the ridge and furrow is or was only temporary and not part of a fully developed open- or common-field system, it does show well how pre-existing field systems often controlled the layout of the later ridge and furrow … even though many of their boundaries are ploughed away.[2]

1. Hall, 'Origins of Open-Field Agriculture', pp. 37–8; Hall, *Medieval Fields*, p. 46; Brown and Foard, 'The Saxon Landscape', p. 91; Bryant et al., 'Relict Landscape'.
2. C. Taylor, personal communication.

This ridge and furrow is generally interpreted as the final reaches of medieval cultivation 'moving on to land furthest from the main settlements and presumably at a late date'.[3] The integration of prehistoric or Romano-British field boundaries into medieval cultivation preserves the short-lived attempts by medieval farmers between about 1100 and 1300 to expand cultivation onto marginal soils, as at central and southern Overton in Wiltshire, a good illustration from outside the Central Province of the persistence of these boundaries in medieval landscapes.[4] In the South-East Province, too, examples of the incorporation of earlier fields into surviving medieval fields have been found at Scole-Dickleborough, Norfolk and Yaxley, Suffolk, and in numerous examples in Hertfordshire.[5] A regular Romano-British field layout which survived into the Middle Ages and beyond has been identified at Asheldham, Essex.[6]

However, even in the Central Province itself, there may have been more survivals of pre-medieval land and field boundaries in common-field boundaries than has previously been realised, even though the evidence is often limited to areas enclosed before parliamentary enclosure and not therefore at the heart of common-field arrangements. The evidence includes such influential studies as those of rectilinear field layouts transected by Roman roads at Lichfield in Staffordshire and Goltho in Lincolnshire, and more recently at Haddon in Northamptonshire.[7] 'Sinuous linear features' originating in the Iron Age and forming the basis of more modern land divisions survive at Horsley and Harlow Hill, across Hadrian's Wall, about 9 miles (14 kilometres) west of Newcastle upon Tyne.[8] There seems to have been reuse of Romano-British ditches within the medieval settlement at Wharram Percy in Yorkshire,[9] and Romano-British field layouts have been shown to have influenced the orientation of medieval furlongs on Lambourn Down, Berkshire.[10] Della Hooke has gone so far as to suggest that, on the edges of the midland region, common-field layouts may sometimes 'represent a process of adaptation to an earlier field system'.[11] The question of whether or not a pre-medieval field layout may have been fossilised within the furlong boundaries and headlands of the Bourn Valley is not therefore as outlandish as it may first appear.

3. Taylor and Fowler, 'Roman Fields', p. 161.
4. Fowler, Landscape Plotted, Figure 6.11.
5. Williamson, 'Early Co-Axial Fields', pp. 425 and 428–9; Williamson, Hertfordshire, pp. 150–1.
6. Drury and Rodwell, 'Asheldham'; Rippon, 'Early Planned Landscapes'.
7. Bassett, 'Lichfield' and 'Goltho'; Upex, 'Landscape Continuity'.
8. Tolan-Smith, 'Romano-British and Late Prehistoric Landscape'.
9. Beresford and Hurst, 'Wharram Percy', p. 79.
10. Ford et al., 'Berkshire Downs', p. 405.
11. Hooke, 'Early Forms', p. 123.

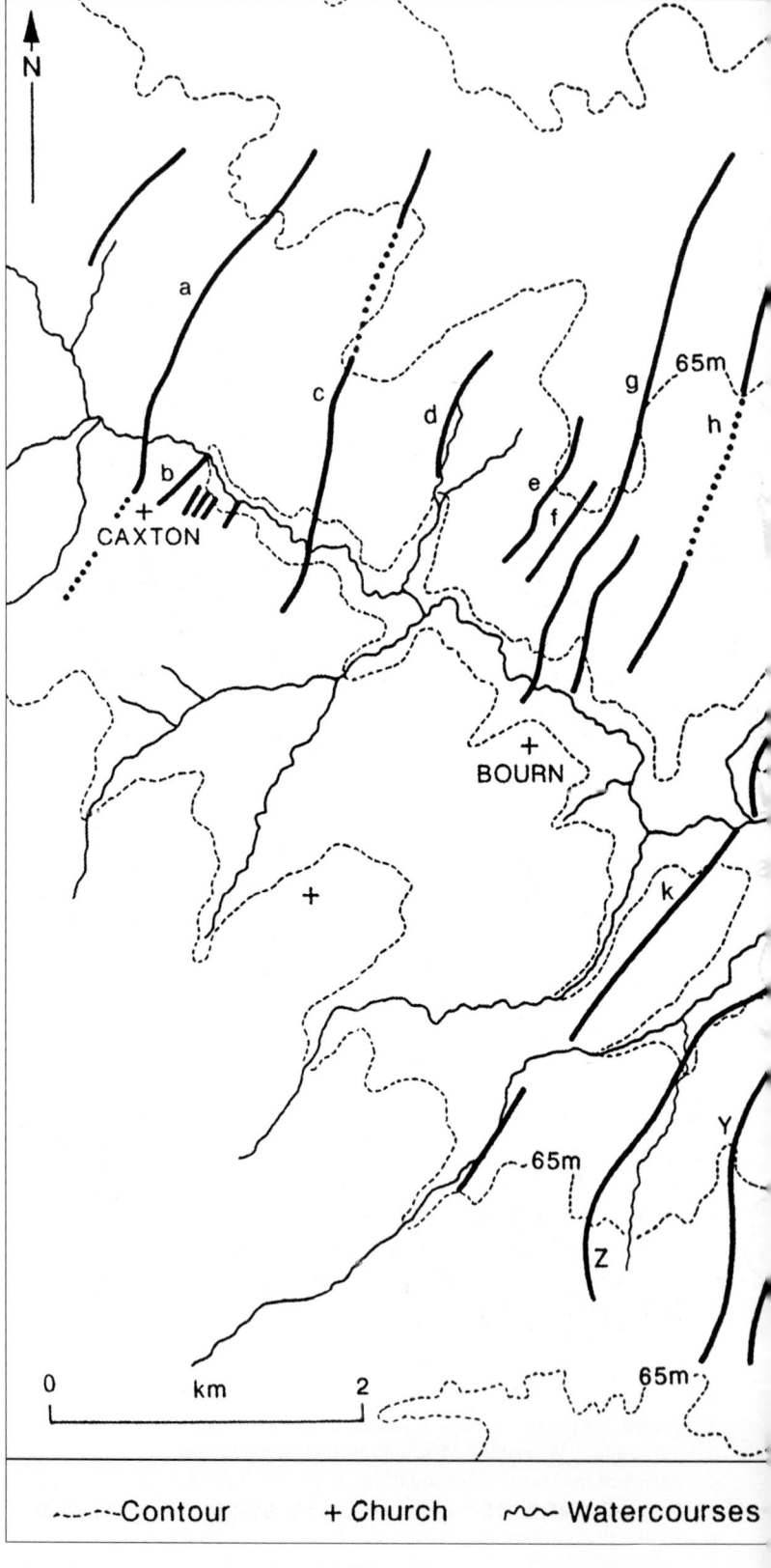

Figure 4.1 The Bourn Valley: ancient alignments (see Appendix A for Key)

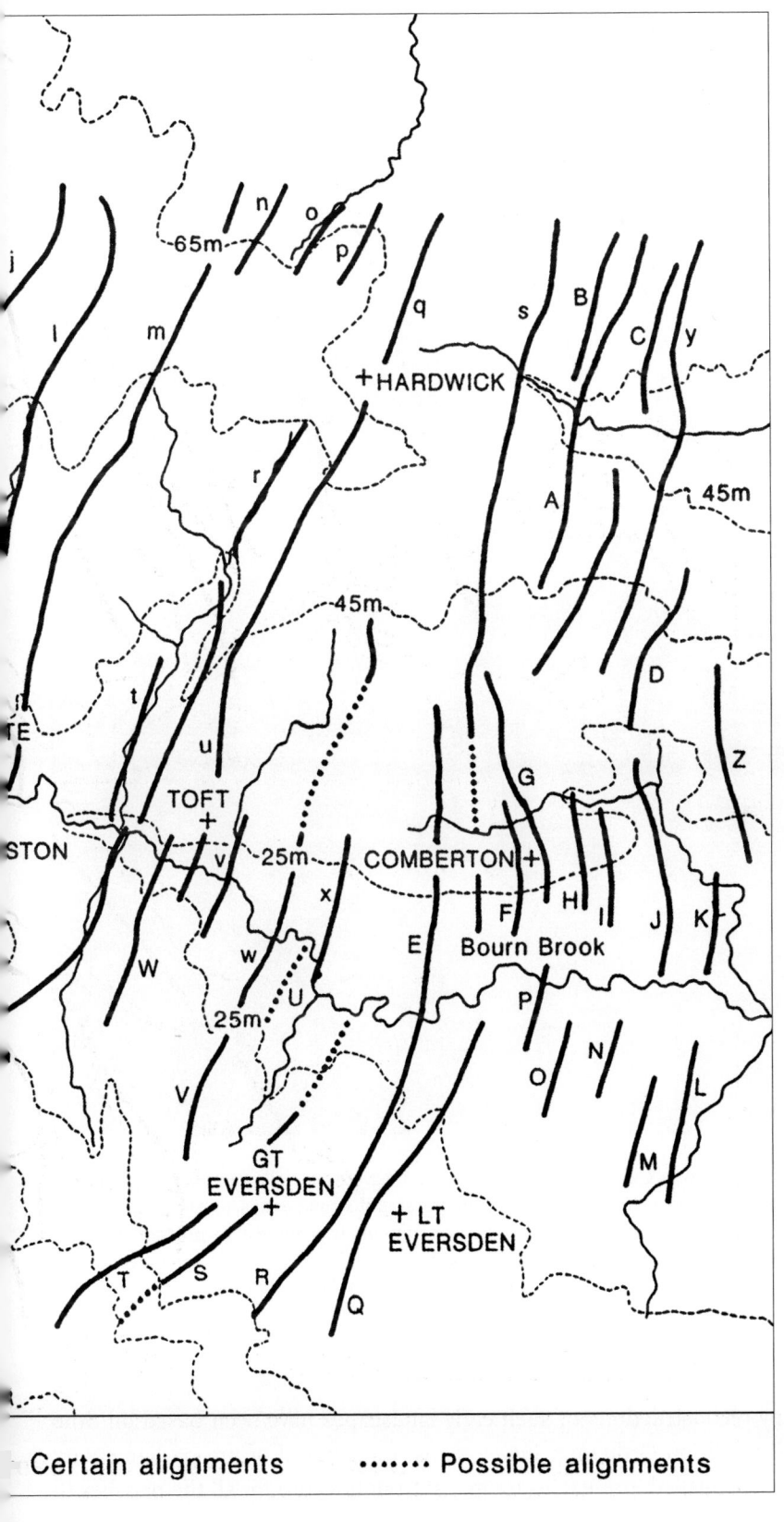

Certain alignments   .... Possible alignments

Figure 4.2 Strympole Way, Caldecote (l on Figure 4.1). A 'cavernous holloway' whose high banks suggest that it may be many hundreds of years old. Its sinuous course runs at least from the Bourn Brook to the northern ridge, where a late Iron Age coin was found at its junction with the trackway which followed the watershed. Holloways are generally thought to be restricted to areas outside the Central Province, but they are not unusual in the Bourn Valley

Sources

While many reconstructions of such early landscapes have been based on tithe maps or first edition Ordnance Survey maps, the survival of pre-parliamentary enclosure maps (called 'pre-enclosure maps' from now on) for all the parishes in

Figure 4.3 Looking south-west along Broadway, Bourn (g on Figure 4.1) where, once again, high boundaries on either side betray the ancient origins of this alignment

the study area, except Kingston and the Eversdens, means that the former become supplementary. They provide a good example of the effects of differential creation and survival of documents for different parts of Britain. Pre-enclosure maps are augmented by parliamentary enclosure maps and awards, estate maps and Ordnance Survey maps of different periods as well as by documentary sources, in particular terriers, and aerial photographs and extensive, systematic fieldwork. The uneven survival of early documents means that most sources for the landscape history of the valley are post-medieval and a large percentage date from the late eighteenth or early nineteenth centuries.

There must be some reservations in attempting to reconstruct a medieval and pre-medieval landscape from such late evidence, although other scholars have also accepted the usefulness of these sources for this purpose. For example, Carenza Lewis, Patrick Mitchell-Fox and Christopher Dyer (who used similar evidence for their survey of the history of eleventh- and twelfth-century settlement in the east midlands) have commented that 'in general the maps reflect an earlier situation'.[12]

12. Lewis et al., *Village, Hamlet and Field*, p. 120.

David Hall has taken a similar view, noting that 'a communal field system with complex and seasonally variable access rights has every chance of being unchanged because it is difficult to effect any alteration in a conservative agricultural community, especially where legal rights are involved'.[13] This view is particularly important in the Bourn Valley where parliamentary enclosure did not take place until well into the nineteenth century, almost within living memory.

There is physical evidence, too, to support the view that the landscapes documented in post-medieval maps and terriers were essentially those that had been laid out in the medieval period. For example, property boundaries within settlements seem to be very stable as long as they are in continuous use or remain as earthworks in the landscape. While most of the evidence for the longevity of property boundaries comes from urban sites such as Cambridge, Norwich and York, where some Anglo-Saxon property boundaries are still in use today, the boundaries of rural tofts and crofts seem to be equally long-lived.[14] There does not seem to be any reason why the selions of the common fields upon which each household's survival depended should not remain equally stable. Aerial photographs of ploughed-out ridge and furrow – where the furrows are visible as soilmarks – show that the furrows between selions were ploughed in almost exactly the same place year after year (e.g. Figure 4.6). The furrows show as dark lines in plough soil, and these lines are fairly sharp; if the furrow between selions had 'wandered' from one year to the next, these dark lines would be 'fuzzy' from the air. This precision is also apparent in the exact correlation between sixteenth-century strip maps and remains of arable cultivation on the ground.[15]

The information provided by pre-enclosure maps is remarkably full. For example, that of Comberton (1839) clearly delineates and names common-field furlongs and balks; that for Caldecote (c. 1854) shows each holding, many still in curved, single strips.[16] The accuracy of the detail on these maps can be confirmed by field observation and by aerial photographs of the alignments of surviving headlands and of ridge and furrow. It should be noted, though, that these maps simply show land use within the common fields in the early nineteenth century and therefore do not necessarily show the full extent of arable land in the high Middle Ages. Aerial photographs and field observation, for example, have

---

13. Hall, 'Late Saxon Countryside', p. 108.
14. Craig Cessford, lecture to Cambridge Antiquarian Society autumn conference, November 2005; Hall, *Viking Dig*, p. 49; Roberts, *Rural Settlement*, p. 41; Oosthuizen, 'Medieval Settlement Relocation'.
15. Beresford, *Lost Villages*, p. 50. Stephen Rippon has expressed a dissenting view, 'relatively few field boundaries will remain stable after their initial laying out': 'Early Planned Landscapes', p. 49.
16. CUL Ms Plans r.a.2; CCRO R60/24/2/11.

demonstrated that in many cases land shown as meadow or pasture on nineteenth-century pre-enclosure maps carried the remains of medieval ridge and furrow, and had clearly once been under the plough. At its peak in about 1300, medieval common-field cultivation in the Bourn Valley was more extensive than all arable cultivation in the early nineteenth century.

Other documentary sources have generally corroborated these maps, but the limit to their utility is underscored in the three parishes without pre-enclosure maps where the reconstruction of the pre-enclosure landscape in any more than the broadest detail has not been possible (the Eversdens and Kingston). Eighteenth- and nineteenth-century estate maps are of limited use in reconstructing the medieval furlongs of these parishes since they do not show the detail of the common fields. The surveyors' sketches for the first Ordnance Survey map of 1810 predate parliamentary enclosure in all eight parishes, but comparisons between this draft, the final map, and the parish enclosure maps, raises considerable doubts about their accuracy since neither tracks nor closes on the draft bear much relation to those on the other maps.[17] The final published version of the Ordnance Survey map coincides in many points with information shown on the parliamentary enclosure maps and that of Baker's map of Cambridgeshire, dating to 1820.[18] Parliamentary enclosure maps and awards exist for all eight parishes, but do not generally show very much detailed evidence relating to the pre-enclosure landscape of the arable fields, in particular the alignment of common-field furlong boundaries, although they do sometimes show the limits of the main pre-enclosure fields.

In the absence of other evidence for the location of common-field furlong boundaries and strips in the Eversdens and Kingston, it might be possible to reconstruct the medieval field layouts of these parishes from terriers and other documentary evidence, using the methods pioneered by David Hall.[19] Hall uses field books (lists of ownership of land in pre-enclosure furlongs) as a sort of verbal jigsaw puzzle. The number and acreage of strips in each furlong is used to calculate the probable dimensions of the furlong, assuming a length of 220 yards for each strip or selion. Directions in the documents about the relationships between strips and furlongs and their neighbours are used to infer the relative siting of different furlongs. These, together with observation in the fields of the remains of medieval ridge and furrow (the physical manifestation of the strips) and their headlands (which formed the furlong boundaries), can then be used to recreate a map of the pre-enclosure landscape. Unfortunately, there are no

17. Copy of surveyors' sketches in CCRO.
18. Ordnance Survey 1884, 1 inch to the mile; CUL Maps.aa.53 (1).82.1.
19. Hall, Northamptonshire, Ch. 3.

fieldbooks for the Bourn Valley. In the three parishes in the Bourn Valley that lacked a pre-enclosure map, the terriers of individual holdings and other documents recording the pre-enclosure landscape do not list more than a few strips in each furlong, nor is there any indication of the number of strips in each furlong. Information about the relationship between furlongs is also sparse and vague. For example, in 1589 one of the more detailed entries in a terrier for the Eversdens describes 'one selion in stannards hill furlong ye north head butting on the common pasture'.[20] Although it is possible, on the basis of other evidence, to say roughly where this furlong lay, this record is of little help in the identification of the boundaries of the furlong or the common pasture, as might be possible if information about the number of selions in Stannards Hill Furlong and its neighbours were available.

Aerial photographs taken by the RAF in 1946–7 show the remains of ridge and furrow where land taken out of arable cultivation in the north and south of each parish in the later Middle Ages was still pasture, but most ridge and furrow in the arable fields of the parishes had already been ploughed out by 1947, although headlands often survive as low banks even in modern arable (Figure 4.9).[21] Further information on the extent of medieval ridge and furrow is available in photographs in the collection of the Cambridge University Unit for Landscape Modelling (CUULM) and is also available in the records in the Cambridge County Council Historic Environment Record (CCC HER). Although some has been ploughed out over the past thirty years, there is enough ridge and furrow still standing as earthworks or as traces of earthworks to allow inferences to be made about the original extent of the medieval common fields of the valley.

Finally, field boundaries characteristic of medieval agriculture on parliamentary enclosure maps and on the first edition Ordnance Survey 6-inch map (1886) with the reversed C- and S-shapes, are assumed to have a medieval origin.[22] These field boundaries are not always recorded on parliamentary enclosure maps, which simply show allotments to different landowners and not subdivisions within them. It seems likely that, in subdividing new allotments, new hedges were often laid along pre-existing field divisions where older alignments continued to be useful in the creation of the post-enclosure landscape. Similarly, near Hadrian's Wall, many eighteenth-century private enclosure boundaries 'were constructed on the same lines as the earlier medieval furlong boundaries or their headlands'.[23]

20. CUL QC 15/2.
21. RAF air photographs 106G/UK/1490 and CPE/UK/2024.
22. OS 1886 XLVI, all sheets.
23. Tolan-Smith, 'Romano-British and Late Prehistoric Landscapes', p. 72.

Analysis and results (Figure 4.4)

Topographic and cartographic deconstructive analysis were used to examine the pattern of pre-enclosure furlongs and other field divisions in order to explore the extent to which pre-medieval field patterns could be discerned within the medieval landscape. Two independent methodologies were used in order to try to avoid the possibility that subjective assessments might influence interpretation: retrogressive analysis and deconstructive analysis of abutting boundaries.

The first method, that of retrogressive analysis, was first explored in print by Flinders Petrie who suggested that the relationship between Roman roads and, for example, hedges or ditches might enable the unpicking of the chronological relationship between these features.[24] Petrie's suggestion that maps of different periods might be compiled on the basis of this methodology was used and developed by others from the 1970s onwards.[25] In essence, the method consists of reconstructing the pre-enclosure landscape, as far as possible, by using one or more of the following six techniques. First, by the successive removal of post-medieval and then medieval features on a map (where their date can be established by documentary or cartographic evidence, by field names or by stratigraphic relationships), as well as of any boundaries that lie perpendicular to or parallel with these features. Second, the shift of settlement in the post-medieval period towards areas of grazing means that minor boundaries around houses, gardens and farms can also be removed. Encroachments on common grazing, woodland and waste offer a third opportunity for deconstruction; these can sometimes be recognised by their field names, but can as often be identified by a 'pattern of irregular infilling which has disturbed the characteristically continuous and often convex outline of the common'.[26] A fourth technique is to exclude field boundaries (but not roads) that do not conform to the general framework.[27] Fifth is the retention as a 'major element' only of those boundaries that continue along at least three fields or furlongs. And finally, although not a technique, changes in the alignment of dominant features in the landscape may mean that an apparently unified, regular landscape might be made up of features of different periods.[28] This methodology is now well established although it still gives rise to some uncertainties about its objectivity, particularly the difficulties of applying

---

24. Petrie, 'Proceedings of Meetings'.
25. Rodwell, 'Relict Landscapes in Essex'; Smith, 'Alrewas, Fisherwick and Whittington'; Bassett, 'Lichfield', 'Goltho'; Williamson, 'Settlement Chronology'; Rippon, 'Early Planned Landscapes'; Tolan-Smith, 'Romano-British and Late Prehistoric Landscapes'.
26. Williamson, 'Early Co-Axial Fields', p. 424.
27. Bassett, 'Lichfield', p. 95.
28. Rippon, 'Early Planned Landscapes', p. 49.

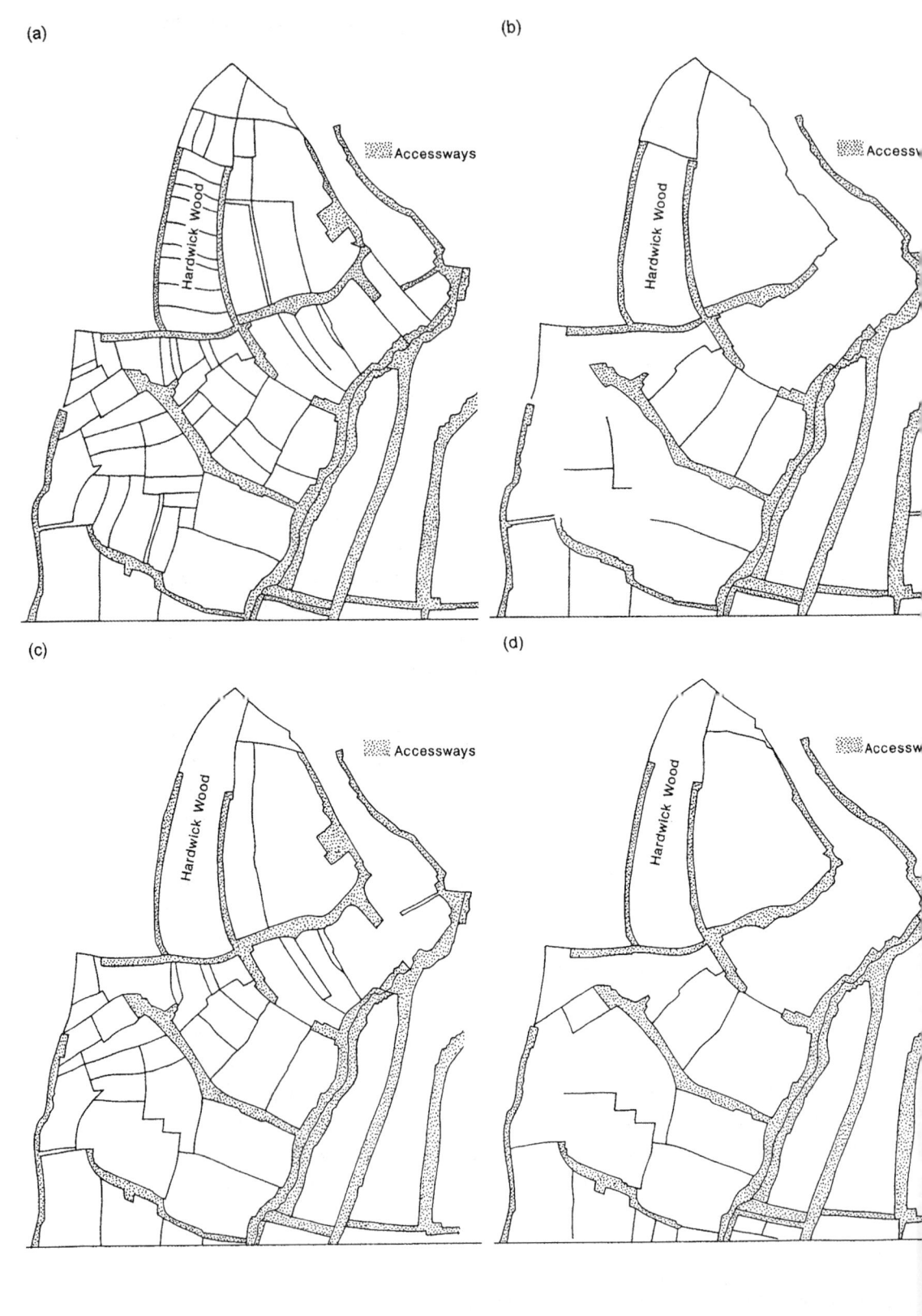

Figure 4.4 Retrogressive and deconstructive analysis in the discovery of early field boundaries: case study of pre-enclosure fields in the north-western part of Toft in 1815 (after CCRO 124/P60). In (a) the fields in part of Toft are reproduced as they were at parliamentary enclosure in 1815. (b) shows the result of applying the first method, retrogressive analysis, to (a), in order to try to reconstruct the earliest field boundaries in this area. (c) and (d) demonstrate successive stages of applying the second method, deconstructive analysis (removing boundaries which meet at T-junctions), to the map shown in (a). That both methods (b) and (d) result in more or less the same conclusion suggests that these may indeed be the earliest field boundaries

the creation of these strips, since the strips respect the parish boundary rather than the other way around.[33] If the strips had been created before the parish boundary, the latter would have been indented around the ends of the furlongs, for which there are many precedents (Figure 4.5).[34]

The only one of these long, cross-valley alignments that can be dated is the parish boundary between Hardwick and Comberton, which was both a tenth-century estate boundary and is still a hundred boundary, perhaps of early tenth-century date (Figures 2.7 and 5.3). The cross-valley alignments seem likely, therefore, to have been in place in or by the tenth century. Aerial photographic and archaeological evidence, however, suggests that they were already in use in the Roman period, and that they may be of Roman or even prehistoric origin. Figure 4.6, for example, shows a system of parallel, rectilinear ditches surrounding a small rectangular farmstead at TL 379 592 in Hardwick, which field-walking has demonstrated to be Romano-British. Overlying the ditches, and on the same alignments, are the soilmarks of medieval ridge and furrow, whose curving headland – running from the lower centre of the photograph to the top left – follows an earlier Romano-British ditch (lying east of and parallel to q on Figure 4.1). The headland is still visible as a low bank, curving across the modern arable. Here medieval farmers have clearly reused an earlier land division, perhaps surviving as a grassy ditch, when laying out their new furlongs. This is not an isolated example – the boundaries and enclosures of two other Romano-British farmsteads, one in Caldecote and one in Hardwick, also on the high ground in the north of the valley, lay under, and on exactly the same alignment as, medieval ridge and furrow. And a late Iron Age coin of Cunobelinus was found in Caldecote at the junction of Strympole/Broadway (l on Figure 4.1) with the St Neots ridgeway.[35]

One way of testing the possibility that the cross-valley alignments might be Roman or earlier is to examine their stratigraphic relationship with the two Roman roads (Ermine Street and the present A603 between Wimpole and Barton)

---

33. CUL Ms Plans r.a.2; Figure 4.4.
34. For example, Taylor, *Fields*, p. 76.
35. Oakey, *Highfields, Caldecote*, p. 28; CCC HER; CUULM ABX14.

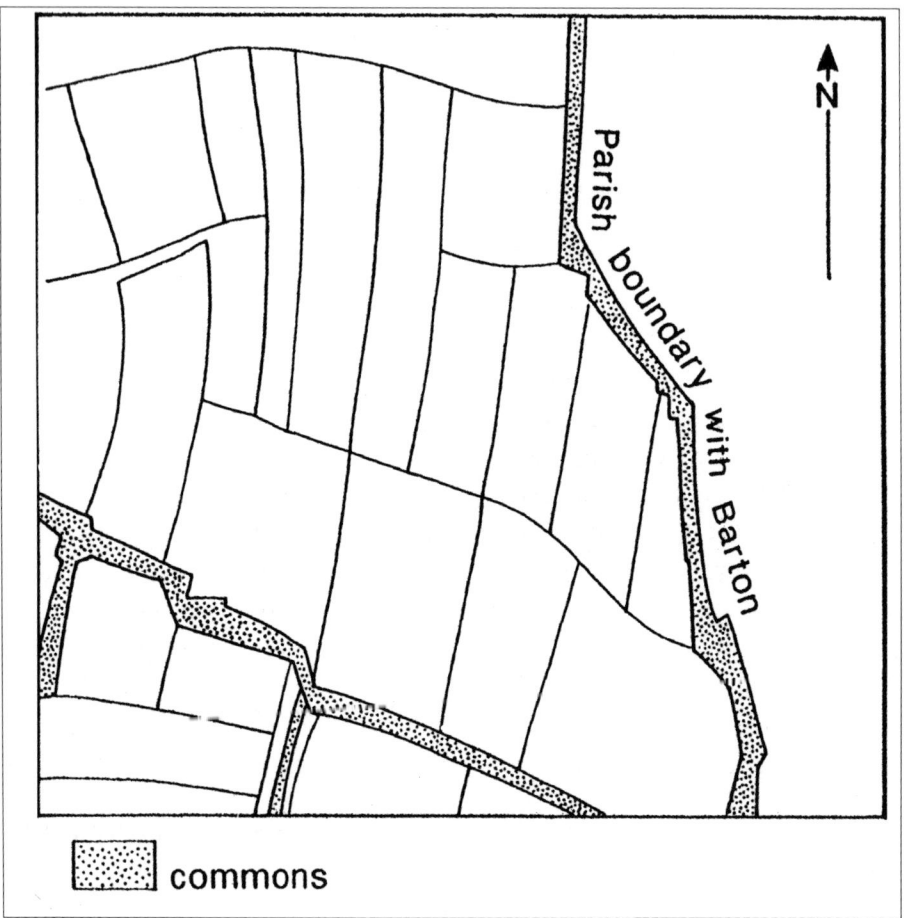

Figure 4.5 The relationship between a prehistoric alignment, reused in the northern section of the parish boundary between Comberton and Barton, and selions in Harborough Field, Comberton, in 1839 (at about TL 395 575; after CUL Ms Plans r.a.2; A on Figure 4.1). The ends of the selions 'bite into' the fieldway which runs along the parish boundary, their encroachment demonstrating that the fieldway was there before the selions were laid out

which respectively cross the western and eastern ends of the valley. If the alignments were Roman or later, they might be expected to lie parallel to or at right angles to the Roman roads; if they predate the Roman period, then the Roman roads might be expected to cut across them. This would create triangular fields, like those resulting from the interaction of rectangular fields laid out during parliamentary enclosure by nineteenth-century railway lines or modern motorways. In the west of the valley, at Caxton, the south-westerly/north-easterly furlong boundaries that perpetuate these earlier cross-valley alignments ran parallel to each other across the central fields of Caxton. The land between them

Figure 4.6 Curved furrows between medieval ridges revealed in plough-soil at Hardwick at TL 379 592 (CUULM ABX14). Underlying the medieval furrows are the dark lines of Romano-British ditched field boundaries and the ditches surrounding a small, rectangular farmstead. The medieval features lie on precisely the same alignments as their Romano-British predecessors. In fact careful examination reveals that the medieval ridge and furrow stops and begins again on either side of the Roman ditch which runs from bottom right-centre towards the upper left-hand side of the photograph. This marks the site of a medieval headland, which still survives as a long bank curving across the field (Copyright reserved Cambridge University Collection of Air Photographs)

lay in long, if slightly irregular, rectangles. These rectangles have been bisected into triangles by Ermine Street, suggesting that the road is later than the cross-valley alignments (Figure 4.7).[36] The triangles along Ermine Street at Caxton might just be 'accidental' if the rectangles of which they are part were confined simply to the fields immediately adjacent to the road. This is not the case – other boundaries extend the parallel field layout some distance to the west and east of the road (Figure 4.8). It appears that the cross-valley alignments in Caxton are just a part of a wider pattern that extends across the valley to Barton in the east and the Mare Way in the south. The relationship between these alignments and Ermine Street at Caxton therefore indicates that the cross-valley alignments predate the Roman road – they must be pre-Roman, laid out at some point in the prehistoric period.

36. Oosthuizen, 'Caxton'.

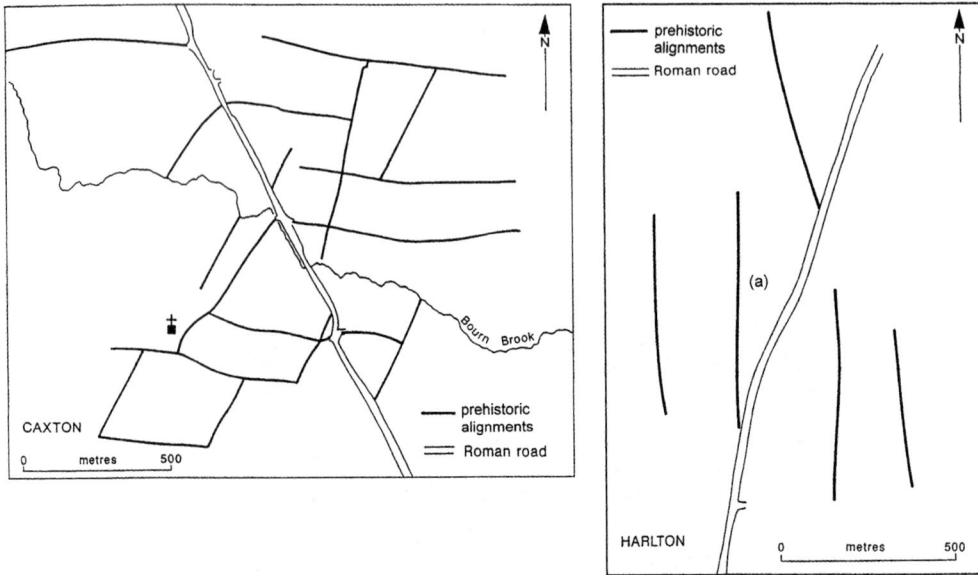

Figure 4.7 Relationships between Roman roads and medieval furlong boundaries at Caxton and Harlton (c. TL 304581, after CUL Maps r.b.10; c. TL 390540, after CCRO 124/P?). In both places, the Roman roads cut across the alignment preserved in the later furlong boundaries, demonstrating that the latter fossilise pre-Roman alignments. (a) is the headland shown in Figure 4.9

A similar conclusion can be drawn from the relationship between these cross-valley alignments and the Roman road between Wimpole and Barton (the present A603) at the eastern end of the valley at Harlton. There, too, the road cut across pre-enclosure furlong boundaries to create triangular subdivisions. As the Roman road approaches Bourn Brook along the flat, poorly drained valley floor, it divides the furlongs on either side of the road into triangular halves of a larger rectangle. Other furlong boundaries to west and east lie on the same alignment. Some of these boundaries survive as long, low banks in the modern fields, and they can be seen diverging from the Roman road, demonstrating the triangle on the ground, as one travels along the A603 (Figure 4.9).

If the long, cross-valley alignments had been laid out after the Roman roads were constructed, they would have been more likely to have been laid out parallel to the Roman roads (as can be seen in the southern part of Caxton). Instead, each road appears to bisect the land lying between the long, parallel alignments into triangles which *together* make rectangles. While it is possible that early farmers may have preferred to align their fields on the brook even if it meant the creation of a triangular field, the coincidence of two pairs of triangles, one at Caxton and one at Harlton, each pair of which fits together to create a rectangle, is more difficult

Ancient fields into medieval furlongs 85

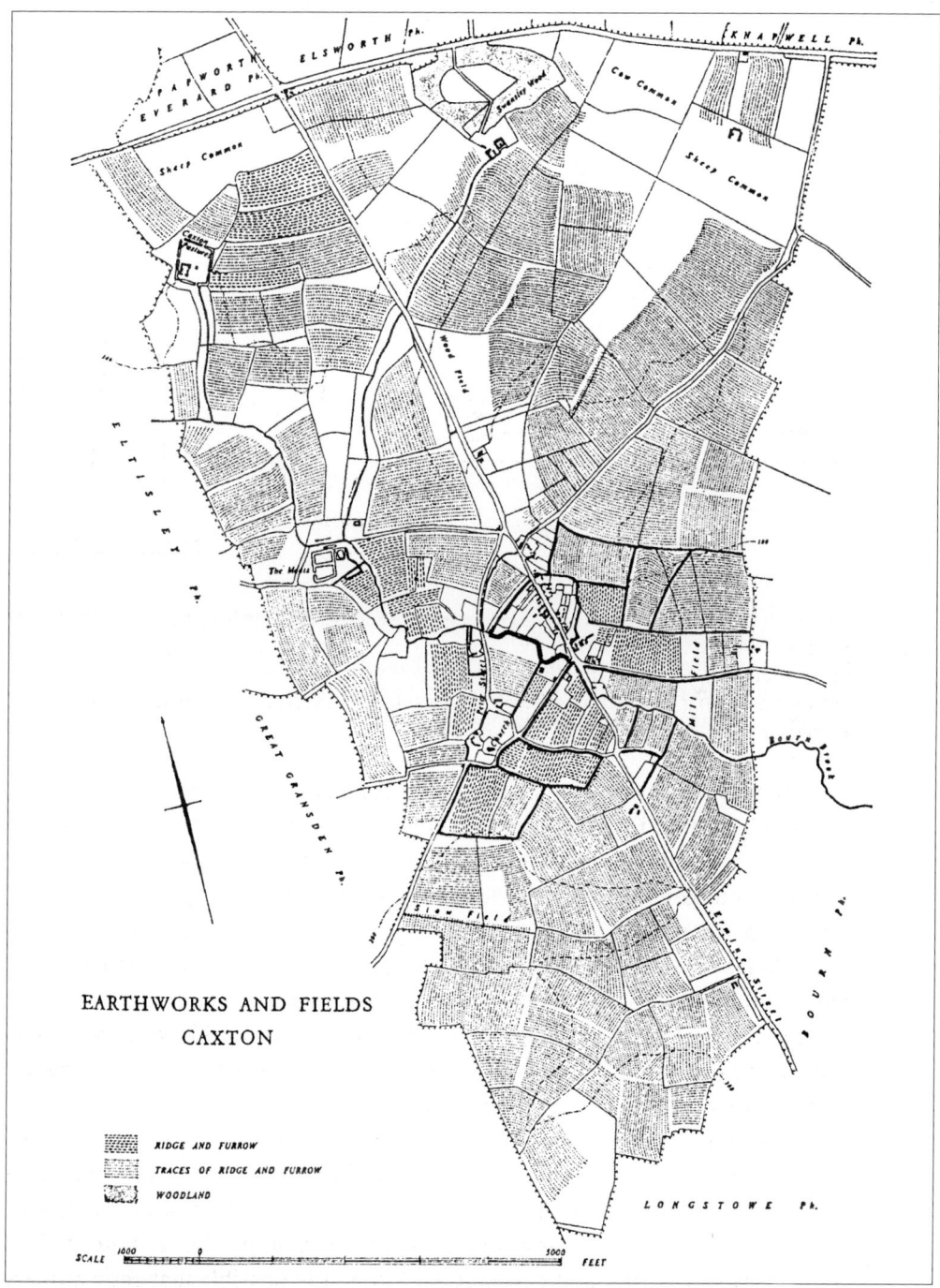

Figure 4.8 Field boundaries and the Roman road at Caxton (reused with permission from RCHM(E), *West Cambridgeshire*, p. 43), with the additional emphasis of some field boundaries, showing how Ermine Street cuts across a system of parallel field boundaries

Figure 4.9 A medieval headland survives as a low bank in modern fields (c. TL 388540). The medieval furlong of which it was part was assarted from Harlton Offal, preserving the alignment of a prehistoric land-division (*a* on Figure 4.7)

to explain. As Tom Williamson has commented about another locality: 'Although the presence of the road has ... strongly influenced the development of those boundaries which lie in its immediate vicinity, the general organisation of the landscape over a wider area, and of the major landscape elements in particular, is non-conformable and evidently earlier'.[37]

The relationship between the Roman roads and these boundaries is analogous to the relationships between such roads and earlier fields as, for example, at Dickleburgh, Norfolk, and Yaxley, Suffolk, where the way in which the Roman road cut across rectangular fields, reducing them to triangles, suggested that the fields predated the construction of each stretch of road.[38] There is a similar example of the same process at Bullocks Haste, Cottenham in Cambridgeshire, where the first century AD Car Dyke transects an earlier rural settlement, also laid out on regular principles.[39] In both cases, the relationship between a major route

37. Williamson, 'Early Co-Axial Fields', p. 425.
38. Ibid., pp. 24–8.
39. Oosthuizen, *Cambridgeshire*, p. 18.

and field boundaries implies that the latter were already in existence before the roads were built. Both in the west and in the east of the Bourn Valley the relationship between the cross-valley alignments and the Roman roads implies that these land divisions already existed at the time of the Roman conquest in 43. They seem very likely to be prehistoric and appear to have survived either in use or as earthworks long enough to be reused as furlong boundaries in the medieval period.

How much earlier these long, cross-valley alignments are than the Roman period is suggested by their character. They seem more like the Iron Age 'spinal' and 'subsidiary linears' of Salisbury Plain than like the co-axial layouts of Bronze Age Dartmoor (Chapter 1). The parish boundaries of the Bourn Valley, running along the Mare Way and St Neots ridgeways, resemble 'spinal linears' since they run along watersheds, while the cross-valley alignments are similar to 'subsidiary linears': they are slightly sinuous in character, they lie about just over 200 yards (200 metres) apart, and they divide the landscape up into strips which incorporate all the environmental differences of the valley bottom, slopes and top pastures. As in Suffolk,

> it is as if a net were lowered gently over the landscape so that where it fell on flat ground the linear pattern of the net remains more or less unchanged, but where it fell on uneven ground the pattern of the net became deformed or distorted by the topography.[40]

The survival of the alignments in the Bourn Valley as substantial holloways like Strympole Way in Caldecote or Royston Way in Little Eversden (respectively l and Q on Figure 4.1) might mean that they originated as double banks separated by ditches, recut repeatedly or scoured through long use as trackways.[41]

It seems likely that before the introduction of common fields in the later Anglo-Saxon period, the cross-valley alignments were particularly well preserved in areas of open pasture or arable in the valley. Their survival across so much of the valley means that the landscape of the Bourn Valley was probably more or less continuously exploited by farmers, throughout the Roman and Anglo-Saxon periods, supporting the argument advanced in Chapter 3 that the valley had relatively limited amounts of woodland throughout the Anglo-Saxon and medieval periods. As in nearby East Anglia, 'intensive grazing of large areas must have

---

40. Warner, *Suffolk*, pp. 49–52.
41. It is difficult to explain why such substantial structures might have been needed. On Salisbury Plain, these alignments seem to have originated as territorial divisions (McOmish et al., *Salisbury Plain*, p. 61), and it is possible that this tenurial origin may justify the large scale of this work in the Bourn Valley too.

continued through the post-Roman centuries' even if some Romano-British farms were abandoned.[42] The inference of extensive areas of open grazing in which older field boundaries remained visible is supported by the analysis of faunal remains from early Anglo-Saxon sites in East Anglia, which showed that there were relatively few deer in this period and there was extensive sheep grazing.[43] Agricultural landscapes can be used in many ways: arable, pasture, meadow, marsh or wood. Land that may appear archaeologically to have been abandoned may nevertheless have had a use – for example, as pasture – that is not visible to later generations, as land that is 'set aside' in the modern period might demonstrate. For example, there are good grounds for suggesting that the area along the brook in Caxton, where Ermine Street transects the long alignments into triangles, may have been in continuous use as arable or intensively grazed pasture since the prehistoric period. It lies along the Bourn Brook on some of the more tractable land in the parish, and field names in this part of the parish carry no suggestion of woodland clearance. Certainly, as far as medieval common-field farming is concerned, 'arable cultivation predominated in Caxton from an early date'.[44] These fields may have been converted directly from pre-common-field to common-field agriculture without any break in cultivation, other than that necessitated by the imposition of new patterns of cropping and tenure.

The function of the cross-valley alignments

It seems most likely that the point of these alignments, at the time that they were laid out, was to divide the valley into relatively equal segments, each including the meadow of the valley bottom, the arable lands of the central downs, and the pasture-topped plateau at the top of the ridge. If this is the case, then the reason behind this division may have been the relatively equitable apportionment of the environmental resources of the valley between extended family groups, as on Salisbury Plain, where it was concluded that 'the sheer scale of construction of the linears and their distribution suggests that the primary function was a form of socially determined land division'.[45] This explanation lies in contrast to those who explain these landscapes in terms of of seasonal transhumance, as herders led their flocks and herds to upland grazing in the spring, returning to their permanent dwellings in the autumn.[46] Similar long alignments and rectilinear

42. Williamson, 'Settlement Chronology', p. 171.
43. Crabtree, 'Animal Exploitation', p. 43.
44. VCH 5, p. 31.
45. McOmish et al., Salisbury Plain, p. 64; see pp. 11–12 above.
46. Williamson, Hertfordshire, p. 147; Bryant et al., 'Relict Landscape', pp. 14–15.

5

A proto-common field

Footpaths, drifts and stretches of long banks underlying the modern fields run from east to west along the lower contours of the northern slopes of the Bourn Valley from Grantchester to Toft, at right angles to the prehistoric alignments discussed in the previous chapter (Figures 5.1 [Appendix B] and 5.2). Early nineteenth-century pre-enclosure maps show that these features are the relics of long, narrow commons (also used as headlands) dividing common-field arable into furlongs. They imply that these four parishes were included within a single field system and appear to be the remains of a very large, proto-common field.[1]

Medieval common fields and their origins

Common fields are generally considered to have been laid out between about 850 and 1150 in a process that saw them completely replacing earlier field arrangements, whose alignments they utterly ignored. Although different forms of open-field system are found in many parts of England, the 'classic' characteristics outlined in Chapter 1 are restricted to the Central Province. Until recently, the most commonly accepted explanation for the process by which common-field cultivation was introduced into each parish in the Central Province has been that the earliest common fields were relatively small, often placed in a relatively central position within a parish. Over time, new furlongs were added to these early fields as arable was cleared or assarted from the surrounding woods and pastures. When so much land had been converted to arable that there was no longer enough pasture to feed the animals of the parish, a crop rotation was introduced, which meant that a sizable proportion (very often about a third) of the arable fields was left fallow each year to supplement the remaining grazing.[2]

---

1. The reasoning for this interpretation can be found in the subsection to this chapter entitled 'Explanation'.
2. Hall, *Medieval Fields*, p. 44.

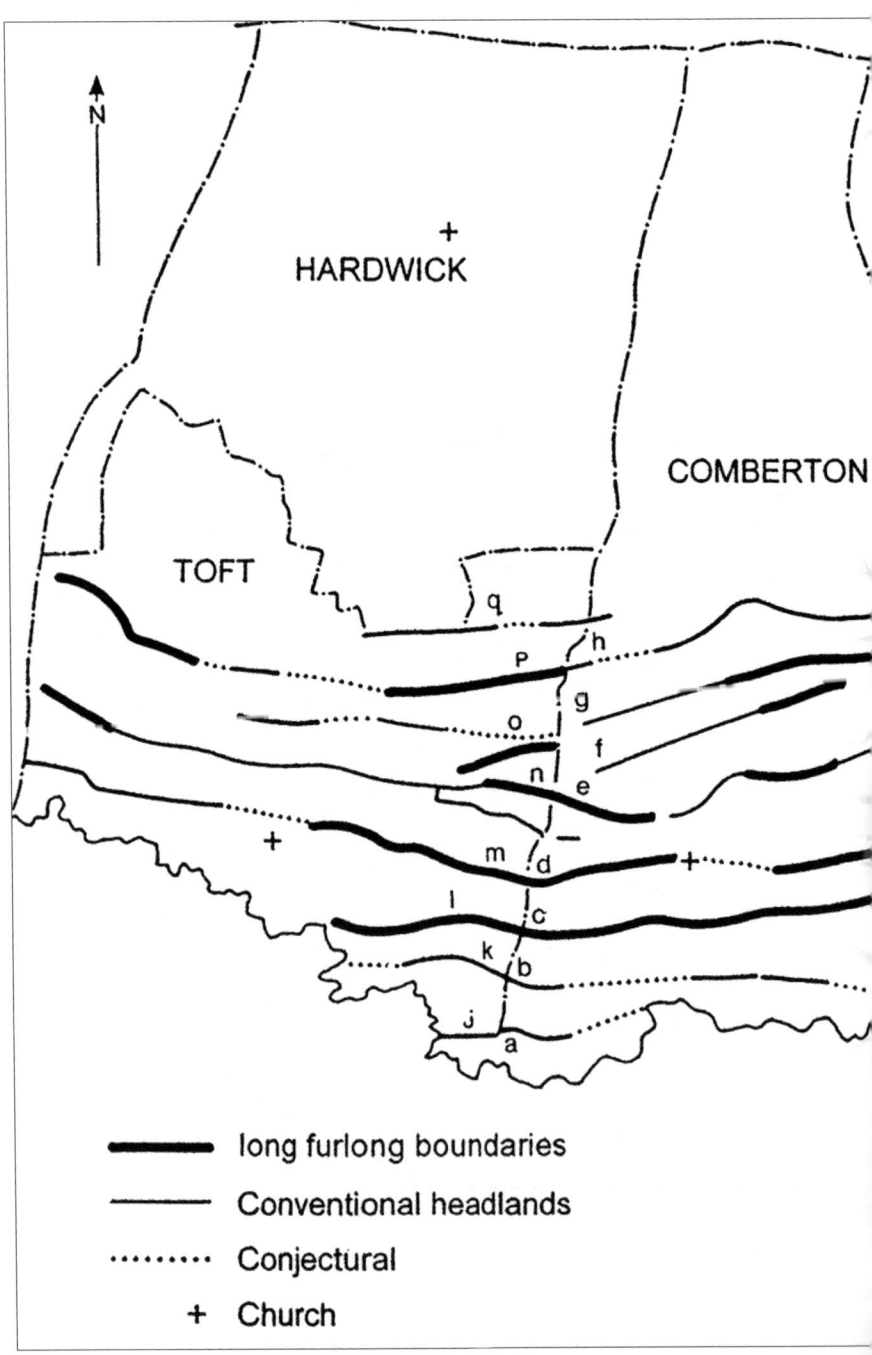

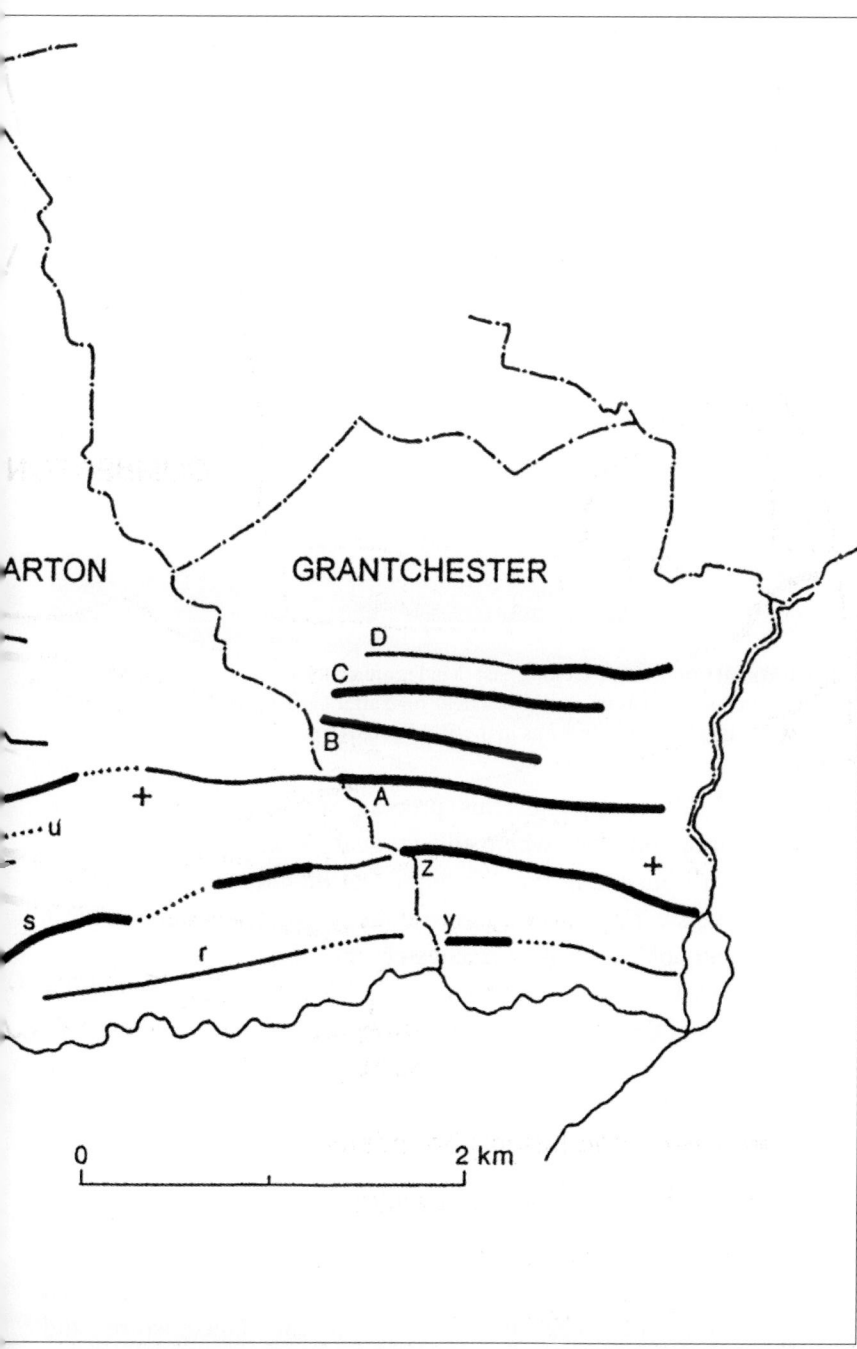

Figure 5.1 The proto-common field lying across the northern slopes of the Bourn Valley (see Appendix B for Key)

Figure 5.2 Stallan Way at Comberton, looking east (b in Figure 5.1). Part of one of the long, narrow commons, Stallan Way was preserved as a field-road after parliamentary enclosure in 1839. It is now less than half as wide as it was in the Middle Ages – a shadow of its former self

A beautifully argued example of this process can be seen at Leighton Bromswold in Huntingdonshire, where the gradual increase in numbers of farmers in the parish is visible in the distribution of holdings in the common fields.[3] The few farmers with the oldest farms in the parish held selions in most furlongs because, their holdings being present since the inception of the common fields, they had acquired strips in every furlong and were dominant in the smaller furlongs; the holdings of those with the newest farms were concentrated in fewer and larger furlongs. The oldest furlongs were small and irregular in shape, while the later furlongs were larger and had a more regular appearance. This method of common-field creation may be typical of areas in which there was a significant amount of woodland in the late Anglo-Saxon period and in which farmers gradually cleared each furlong from wood or wood pasture over a relatively long period of time.

A second model has been suggested by David Hall and others for areas – such as Northamptonshire, the Yorkshire Wolds and the Lincolnshire and Cambridgeshire fens – where arable cultivation seems to have been continuous since the Roman period, and where the landscape was kept relatively open before

3. Roberts, *English Village*, pp. 49–51.

the introduction of common fields by its use for pasture. Hall's model is characterised by common fields – made up of enormous furlongs up to a mile long – which were laid out across the greater part of a parish in one single event.[4] He has suggested a mid-ninth-century date for this process in Northamptonshire, because he found no evidence for settlement later than about 850 from beneath these common-field systems. As the number of farmers within the parish increased, so these huge furlongs were subdivided to create smaller furlongs, thus increasing the number of selions available for distribution among the growing number of farmers in each parish. At Wollaston in Northamptonshire, for example, the strips in 'no less than 14 furlongs form a continuous alignment, 12,500m long', indicating their origin in a single furlong which had later been divided and subdivided until it contained fourteen segments, each fraction becoming a furlong in its own right.[5] The divisions of these earlier huge units into smaller furlongs seems generally to have occurred by the eleventh century in Northamptonshire and appears to have been undertaken to ensure that arable was fairly distributed among the growing population of the vill.[6] At Raunds, for example, 'six furlongs in North Dale field, with strips oriented in the same direction, make up one massive furlong with lands 1,000 metres long'.[7] This model describes the creation of common fields in a single event, where the earliest furlongs were very long, and where they were later subdivided into the smaller furlongs with which we are more familiar.

This chapter describes and then discusses evidence that appears to offer a third model for the origins of common fields in the Bourn Valley which, by 1300, extended over most of the area of each parish.

Describing the proto-common field

Long alignments, occasionally fragmentary, following the contours from east to west, cross four contiguous parishes – Grantchester, Barton, Comberton and Toft – across the lower, northern slopes of the Bourn Valley. They can be observed on the ground along tracks, field boundaries, hedges, roads and low ridges in the fields, but the detail of pre-enclosure maps reveals that they were once continuous across the four parishes, making up a uniform arrangement of boundaries which ran uninterruptedly for up to 5.7 miles (about 8½ kilometres) across an area over a mile (2 kilometres) wide. They survived almost intact until parliamentary

---

4. Hall, *Medieval Fields* and *Northamptonshire*; Harvey, 'Planned Field Systems'; Hall, 'Distribution and Change', p. 45.
5. Hall, 'Field Work', pp. 115–32.
6. Hall, *Northamptonshire*, pp. 135–6.
7. Hall, *Medieval Fields*, p. 48.

enclosure in these parishes swept the common fields away between 1795 and 1839.[8] This regular pattern was made up of at least seven very long strips of land called 'commons' at the time and which were an integral part of the common fields of these parishes. They ran roughly east–west along the contours and parallel to the Bourn Brook, dividing the arable land between them into furlongs whose subordinate strips or selions ran at right angles to the brook. They tend to be placed about 220 yards (200 metres) apart, so that the length of the strips between them was about 220 yards, although this varied with the topography as streams and valleys also influenced their alignment.[9] They were up to 54 yards (50 metres) wide – relatively narrow for commons. The proto-common field was laid out over some of the best farming land in the valley. It lay close to the brook, where gravel and alluvium had ameliorated the worst of the boulder clays and on a definite, but gentle, slope which assisted with drainage.[10] There are other such slopes further north, but they lack these better soils.

A detailed extract from the Comberton pre-enclosure map shows the character of these long commons in more detail (Figure 5.3). Although they were called 'commons' by the early nineteenth century and it seems unlikely that they were ever ploughed, they were also used as headlands for turning the ploughs of the blocks of selions they defined,[11] They were exceptionally wide for headlands, being up to 54 yards (50 metres) in width, compared with the usual Cambridgeshire headland of 11 to 13 yards (10 to 12 metres) in width. While it is not unusual to find headlands grassed over as balks in common fields in the late medieval period and after, it is unusual to find such very wide headlands and for them to be called 'commons'.

The representation of the long, narrow commons on the pre-enclosure maps seems likely to be accurate. They might be dismissed as a local parochial eccentricity if they had been found in just one parish, but they are found on all four maps. They are unlikely to reflect a personal idiosyncrasy on the part of an individual surveyor because neither Grantchester (1795), Barton nor Comberton

8. CCRO 152/P11, 152/P2, 124/P80; CUL Ms. Plans r.a.2.
9. See 'Medieval Common Fields' in Chapter 1, pp. 12–14.
10. P. Tebbitt, personal communication.
11. The headland of a furlong was a strip of land, usually 11 to 13 yards wide in Cambridgeshire, which bounded the top or bottom of a furlong and which usually ran at right angles to the prevailing axis of the selions it contained. Before the mid-fourteenth century, headlands were usually cultivated, but thereafter sometimes left as a grassy balk or access way. They were most commonly created where the selions of one furlong ran on the same orientation as those in its neighbours. The headland gave the plough teams a space on which to turn without encroaching on the selions of the next furlong. In the Bourn Valley, the selions within the arrangement described in this chapter all ran at right angles to the Bourn Brook and therefore 'needed' headlands between them to provide a turning space for their plough teams.

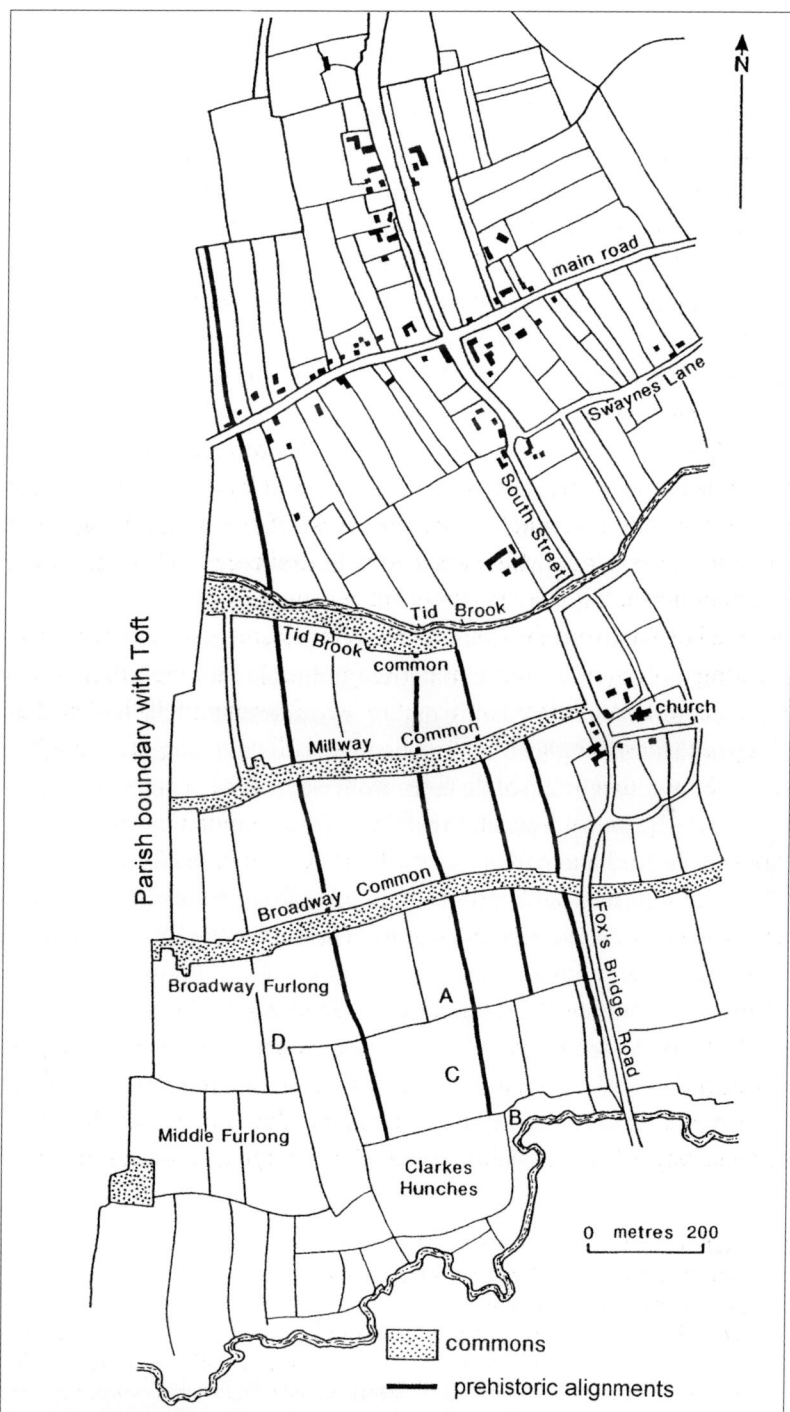

Figure 5.3 The south-western common fields of Comberton in 1839 (detail after CUL Ms Plans r.a.2). Prehistoric alignments preserved in selion boundaries have been highlighted in this map, but the dominance of the long, narrow commons running from west to east is nevertheless clearly demonstrated – they weave over the prehistoric land divisions

(both 1839) were surveyed by the same man, and it is unlikely that the anonymous surveyor of Toft was involved in the survey of these other parishes, since Toft was enclosed in 1815, more than twenty years earlier than Barton or Comberton, and twenty years later than Grantchester. It is also unlikely that the four surveyors did not know the way in which headlands between furlongs were conventionally represented on maps. A glance at Figure 5.3 shows, for example, that headland A between Broadway Furlong in Comberton and the unnamed furlong to its south follows the usual convention in being represented simply by a single line, unlike the depiction of Broadway or Millway Commons. Finally, the accuracy with which the pre-enclosure surveyor represented the actual landscape on the map itself is probably reliable, since his work formed the basis of a substantial realignment of properties and the establishment of future legal responsibilities relating to those properties. So there seems little reason to doubt the accuracy of the representation of the long, narrow commons on these early nineteenth-century maps.

The regular, unitary arrangement of the proto-common field across an area of over 7 square miles (17 square kilometres) indicates that the arrangement had been planned, rather than occurring organically, and that it had been laid out in a single phase. This is suggested by the roughly parallel alignment of the long commons, their generally equal distance from each other of about 220 yards (200 metres), and by the way in which their character as commons was also relatively continuous from parish to parish. It seems very likely that the long commons once extended continuously across all four parishes and were all once up to 50 yards wide. None of these characteristics is likely to be the result of accretion over time.

Nonetheless, the proto-common field differs in four important ways from the many examples of massive furlongs found in Northamptonshire, Cambridgeshire, Lincolnshire and Yorkshire. First, the alignments within it continued across four parishes, uninterrupted by parish boundaries, one of which was also a hundred boundary. As far as is known, this is unprecedented. Furlong boundaries usually stop at parish boundaries. Second, the long, narrow commons were exceptionally long: extending more than 5 miles (over 8 kilometres), they were between seven and eight times longer than most of the furlongs (and, hence, headlands) of Northamptonshire referred to above and in Chapter 1 (pp. 17–18). Third, they were also exceptionally wide for headlands – at up to 50 yards in width, they are between four and five times the width of a conventional headland. And finally, they run along the contours rather than at right angles to them, unlike those in the examples cited above where the furlongs generally led from lower to higher ground. An apparently similar landscape near Polesden, Surrey, is made up of lynchets that run for about a mile (1.6 kilometres) along the contour, and are crossed by medieval manorial, parish and hundred boundaries. They may be a fragment of a much larger arrangement, and 'it seems possible that the lynchets surveyed in this valley result from arable cultivation of a "Polesden" estate during the Saxon period prior to the full development of the hundredal administrative system'.[12] However, the lynchets at Polesden represent selions (tenurial units), whereas the distinctive feature of the Bourn Valley is that the long commons seem to have originated as divisions between furlongs, that is, units of cropping.

The date at which the proto-common field may have been created

At first sight, the extraordinary arrangement of the proto-common field could have been laid out at almost any date. However, there is some evidence that enables a tentative date to be ascribed to it. The long, narrow commons overlie, and therefore post-date, the prehistoric cross-valley land divisions described in the previous chapter. Figure 5.3 shows that, although traces of the prehistoric alignments have been preserved as the boundaries of some selions, the long, narrow commons run continuously across them. Broadway Common, for example, makes no concessions to the prehistoric alignments that are preserved underneath it. The dominance of the long, narrow commons over the prehistoric boundaries suggests they are later than the latter. If, as argued in the previous chapter, these cross-valley alignments were laid out in the Iron Age, the long, narrow commons must be Roman or later.

At the other end of the time frame, the subdivision of the proto-common field by parish boundaries indicates that the long, narrow commons and the fields between them were probably in place before parish boundaries were agreed. This argument is supported by the way in which the parish boundaries follow a zig zag course through these furlongs, following the furrows of individual selions in an indented line, which usually indicates fields that were created before parish boundaries were agreed (Figure 5.3).[13] North of the field system, parish boundaries are sinuous and smooth, following the prehistoric alignments, perhaps preserved in an area of grassland pasture. If the parish boundaries had predated the proto-common field, they might be expected to be as direct and continuous inside the field system as they are outside it, that is, they would simply follow the prehistoric alignments to the brook. The later proto-common-field layout would simply have been made to conform to these existing boundaries. It would not have been difficult to arrange this: selions are usually only 9 to 11 yards (8 to 10 metres) wide, and it would have been straightforward to lay out a field system within a boundary such that the selions respected the boundary (e.g. Figure 5.3).

12. English and Dyer, 'Polesden', pp. 4–6.
13. Taylor, Fields, p. 76.

The date of the parish boundaries is therefore crucial. Most parish boundaries are notoriously difficult to date and could have been agreed at any date from the ninth century up to about the twelfth or thirteenth centuries.[14] Therefore, it would be quite possible for all four parishes to have been part of an extensive estate which was not fragmented until after the Norman Conquest. There is, however, no record of any manorial or tenurial link between these four parishes – they did not share a common manorial lord in 1066 or later, nor is there any evidence that any one of them was a chapelry of one of the others, nor that the farmers of one parish shared rights in the fields of one of the others. DB records that all four parishes were independent of each other and held by different lords by 1066. This suggests that, whatever the date of the parish boundaries, they are likely to have been in place by the mid-eleventh century. A little more precision about the date of the parish boundaries may be obtained by examining that between Toft/Hardwick and Comberton. By the mid-tenth century, Toft and Hardwick together made up a single estate, independent of their neighbours. This 10-hide estate was given to the Abbey of Ely in 975 by Bishop Æthelwold, who had bought it from a man called Wulfstan. It was argued in Chapter 2 that all the parishes of the Bourn Valley had once been part of an extensive estate whose *caput* was at Haslingfield. Wulfstan's ownership of 10 hides at Toft and Hardwick indicates that this estate had already started to break up by the mid-tenth century and perhaps before. Even if Wulfstan was the first owner of the 10 hides after they were granted away from Haslingfield, he had obviously received it before 975 and could have held it for as many as thirty years previously. The proto-common field must have been laid out in or before the mid-tenth century.

However, the parish boundary between Toft and Comberton is also the boundary between Wetherley and Longstowe Hundreds (Figure 5.3). The hundred boundary was as likely as parish boundaries to have been conservatively maintained as holders of land would have needed to have known to which hundred their land was liable for tax (*geld*). Cyril Hart has suggested that hundred boundaries in Cambridgeshire were laid out in about 917, immediately after the conquest of this part of the Danelaw by Edward the Elder, and this suggestion has generally been accepted.[15] The histories of Wulfstan's estate and the hundred boundary both suggest that the boundary between Toft and Comberton was in place by the tenth century. The indented character of that boundary, picking its way across the alignment of long, narrow commons and the furlongs between

---

14. Pounds, *English Parish*, pp. 3 and 67–9.
15. Hart, *Hidation of Cambridgeshire*.

them, indicates that this field system must have been created in or before the tenth century, as it was already in place before the boundary was agreed. This probably indicates that the proto-common field was almost certainly laid out in or before the early tenth century.

Narrowing down the date

So far, it has been argued that the proto-common field was laid out between the first and tenth centuries. This broad range can be narrowed further by a more detailed examination of the relationship between the proto-common field and other landscape features of known date.

A number of Roman sites lie within or intersect with the proto-common field and can be used to explore the possibility that it might be Romano-British in origin: the Roman road between Wimpole and Cambridge (the present A603), and two Romano-British settlements, both in Comberton. The Roman road from Wimpole to Cambridge leads into Barton from the south-west along a predictably straight alignment. However, it is diverted eastwards onto Stallan Way, one of the long, narrow commons (k, b, s and z on Figure 5.1; see also Figure 5.4), from the point of its intersection with Stallan Way. The original course of the Roman road towards Cambridge has been lost in the common fields of Barton north of this point. The contemporary importance of the Stallan Way and the irrelevance of the Roman road at the time that the field system was created is underscored by the way in which the medieval main road from Wimpole to Cambridge (still the course of the modern road) followed Stallan Way rather than the Roman road from that point at which the two intersected. This suggests that Stallan Way, and hence the proto-common field, is post-Roman. This impression is supported by the shallow angle of intersection between the respective alignments of Stallan Way and the Roman road. If the Roman road had been an important feature at the time that Stallan Way and the rest of the field system originated, it would have been preserved within the proto-common field and it is likely that the latter would have been laid out in a way that allowed the two to intersect in a more regular way. The shallow angle at which the two meet suggests that the Roman road may already have been almost or wholly out of use at the time that the proto-common field was laid out.

The impression that the proto-common field is post-Roman is sustained by its relationship with the two known Romano-British settlements in the area. The first settlement, the Roman villa in Comberton, lay just north of the Bourn Brook and east of Fox's Bridge Road on the boundary between meadow and arable (Figure 5.5). Some of the walls of the villa appear to be preserved in the lynchet and hedge which together form that boundary. It was a substantial building with such high-

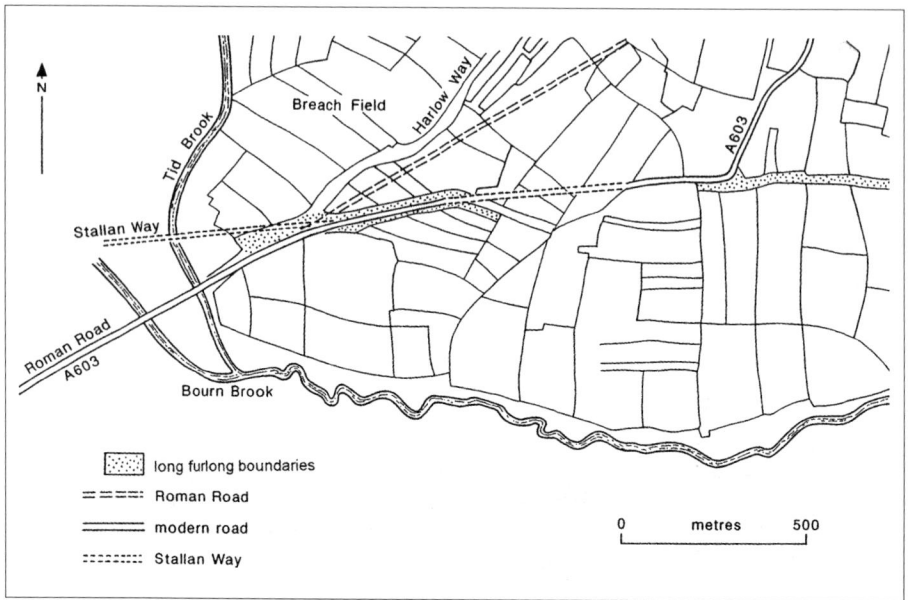

Figure 5.4 North of its intersection with Stallan Way (b and s in Figure 5.1), the alignment of the Roman road (A603) is lost in Barton's fields, and the medieval (and modern) road follows Stallan Way, suggesting that this stretch of the Roman road was already out of use when Stallan Way was constructed

status fittings as painted walls, a hypocaust and a bath suite.[16] Aerial photographs of other Romano-British villa sites show these buildings were often set in designed landscapes defined by walls or ditches, perhaps identifiable as gardens or 'demesne farms'.[17] Such boundaries are unlikely to remain south of the villa, which lies on the northern meadows of the Bourn Brook, but they might be preserved in furlong boundaries further north. There is, however, no indication that the alignment of furlongs or selions in the proto-common field was influenced by earlier boundaries, and it seems more likely that they were created after the villa site had been abandoned in the late fourth century. That is, they are most probably post-Roman.

This conclusion is supported by the relationship between the proto-common field and a second Romano-British settlement: an extensive 'native settlement' against the Barton parish boundary at TL394561, where field-walking has found large quantities of Romano-British pottery (F on Figure 5.6).[18] It lies at the southern end of, and on the same alignment as, Whitland Furlong, overlapping

---

16. VCH 7, p. 45.
17. Frere and St Joseph, *Roman Britain*, pp. 188–9 and 196.
18. CUULM BCK41; CCC HER; CUL Ms. Plans r.a.2.

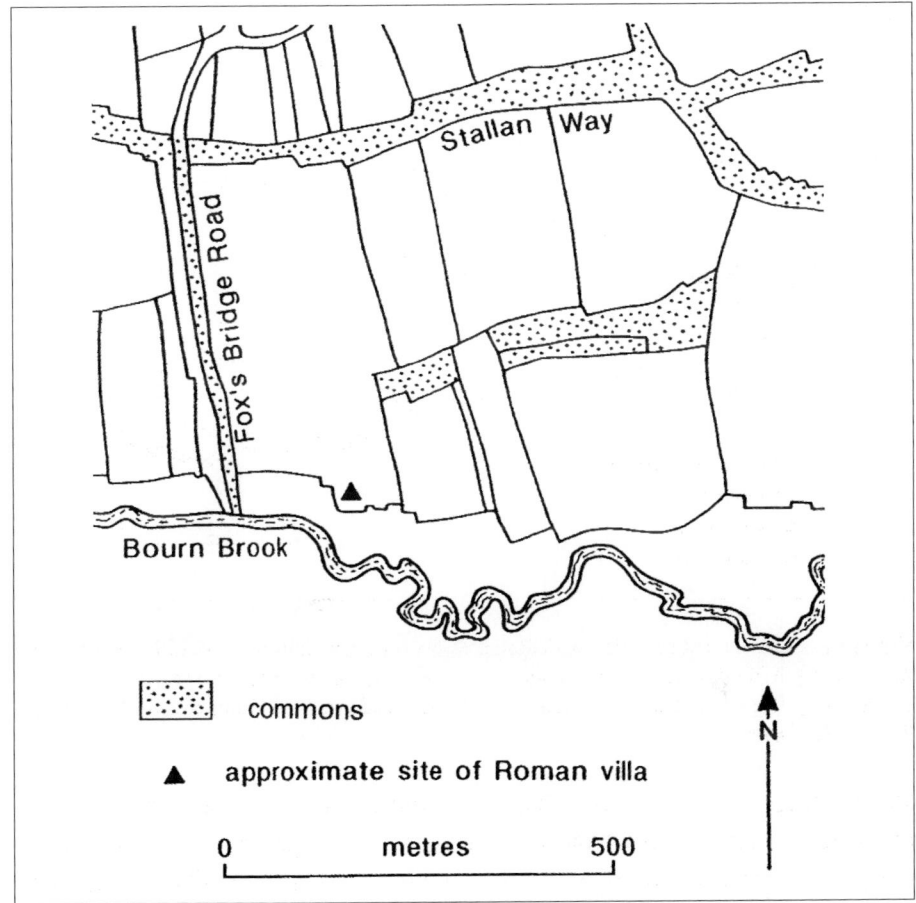

Figure 5.5 There is no apparent relationship between the long, narrow commons or other boundaries within the common fields of Comberton in 1839 and the site of the Roman villa there (after CUL Ms Plans r.a.2)

Red Ditch Meadow. The alignment of Whitland Furlong is distorted towards the east, away from the general north-easterly direction of the rest of the arrangement of the proto-common field. The distortion is emphasised by the way in which the north-eastern corner of Whitland Furlong projects into Barton across the line of the parish boundary. It gives the orientation of the furlong the appearance of having been rather uncomfortably included in the common-field layout. The discontinuity in alignment suggests that the Romano-British settlement and the furlong boundary are of different dates. If the furlong boundaries were contemporary with the settlement, it would be expected that they might be more easily aligned upon it. The uneasy relationship between the alignment of the north-eastern boundary of Whitland Furlong, which appears to have been

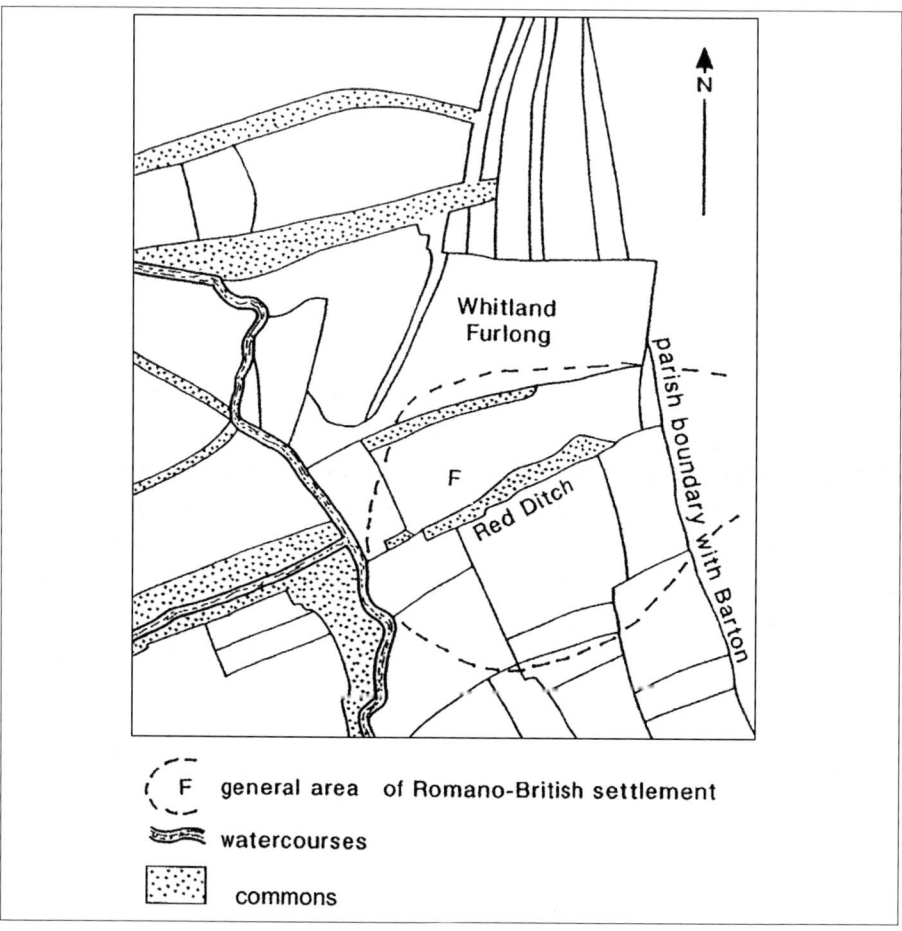

Figure 5.6 Whitland Furlong in Comberton (c. TL 396560) was one of the subdivisions of the common field in 1839 (after CUL Ms Plans r.a.2). The long, narrow commons forming the framework of the proto-common field form a regular geometric relationship with the parish boundary between Comberton and Barton. The regularity is disrupted by the northern and eastern boundaries of Whitland Furlong

influenced by the layout of the Romano-British settlement, and the general alignment of the proto-common field may indicate that the settlement predates the latter, which is probably post-Roman.

All the evidence discussed so far therefore suggests that the proto-common field was probably laid out after the late fourth or early fifth centuries, but before the imposition of hundred boundaries in the early tenth century. This broad period of about 500 years can be narrowed down further, but with less certainty, since the arguments that follow are more generalised.

If the proto-common field was laid out before 917, then it is possible that it was created during the Scandinavian occupation of Cambridgeshire between about 870 and 917. However, Debby Banham, in a recent examination of the evidence, has concluded that the case for a Scandinavian introduction of common-field cultivation in England is unproven and suffers from two major disadvantages. The first is that the limits of common-field cultivation (coincident with the Central Province) do not correspond with the area of the Danelaw, hence 'if common-field cultivation was introduced by Scandinavian settlers, they didn't introduce it everywhere they lived, and someone else must have introduced it to other areas'.[19] The second is that strip cultivation appears to have been introduced in Scandinavia in the twelfth century, two or three centuries after it is first believed to have been introduced in England. The case for a Scandinavian introduction of common-field agriculture seems at worst unlikely, and at best unproven. More locally, the Scandinavian impact on the Cambridgeshire landscape seems to have been remarkably muted. There are only six Scandinavian or part-Scandinavian place names in the county, and relatively few field names.[20] Scandinavian archaeology is almost entirely absent. If anything, the history of the landscape in Cambridgeshire seems to indicate that the period of the Danelaw was one of stasis, in which there was little obvious social or landscape change, perhaps because there were relatively few Scandinavian peasant settlers and the immigrant lords who took over Anglo-Saxon estates were content to manage their lands in traditional ways. The negative impact of the Scandinavian settlement on Cambridgeshire monasteries, for example, appears to have been exaggerated.[21] It is this relative conservatism that appears to have preserved patterns of landholding in the southern Danelaw that looked old-fashioned in other parts of England by the time of the conquest of Cambridgeshire by the kingdom of Wessex in the early tenth century.[22]

In all, it seems unlikely that the field system of long, narrow commons and the furlongs between them was created during the period of the Danelaw. The evidence for Scandinavian settlement of the area is sparse, and there is no evidence to suggest that the field system is Scandinavian in character. Furthermore, this period appears to have been one of relative conservatism, in which the creation of a new and unusual field system would have been atypical. This suggests that we should be looking for a date between the end of the Roman period in about 410 and the Scandinavian invasions of 870 for an origin for this layout.

The period between 400 and 870 is generally divided into two: that between

---

19. Banham, forthcoming.
20. Caxton and Croxton combine Scandinavian personal names with Anglo-Saxon tūn; Toft and Bourn are certainly Scandinavian: Reaney, *Cambridgeshire*, p. xix.
21. Oosthuizen, 'Anglo-Saxon Minsters'.
22. Faith, *English Peasantry*, p. 122.

400 and about 700, when political organisation was fragmented, and that between about 700 and 900, which saw the emergence of the seven major Anglo-Saxon kingdoms (Chapter 1). There are two reasons why it seems unlikely that this unusual field layout was created between about 400 and 700. First, it was a period of political, economic and social instability, in which shifting local and regional allegiances were unlikely to provide either the authority or the organisation within which such a massive reorganisation of the landscape might have taken place. It was a period in which the Bourn Valley was apportioned between different clans, like the *Grantasæte* and the *Hæslingas*, not all of which may have been able to control the whole of the northern slope of the valley. Second, pollen evidence and faunal remains demonstrate that the period is characterised by an increased emphasis on pastoral cultivation. Pollen analysis from Hockham Mere, west Norfolk, has been interpreted as showing a shift to pastoralism between about 340 and 650; the wetter, colder conditions of the late sixth and seventh centuries may have made ploughing the clay fields of the Bourn Valley additionally difficult, prolonging the emphasis on stock farming into the late seventh century.[23] This makes it difficult to see the impetus for the introduction of an extensive and intensive arable field arrangement over such a large area between 400 and 700. The only archaeological evidence from excavation supports the suggestion of a middle Anglo-Saxon origin for the proto-common field. A small, early Anglo-Saxon settlement at Grantchester, and its associated cemetery, lay at the far eastern end of Mere Way (A on Figure 5.3), at the boundary between the arable in the west and the meadows along the Cam. The excavators commented that 'the earliest of three successive phases of the east-west hollow road [Mere Way] was found. Its ruts were cut deeper into bedrock than later roads and the sherds from it suggest that it was in use at this time'.[24] Later phases were dated to the middle Anglo-Saxon period.

The period between about 700 and 870 seems the more likely period for the construction of the proto-common field, and this is a feasible suggestion. It was a time of greater political and economic stability, increasingly centralised administrative control and the rapid development of complex and sophisticated trading networks which connected large emporia with the rural areas around them. There was a concomitant emphasis on agricultural specialisation, very often in grain (see pp. 9–10 below).[25] Cambridgeshire, which appears to have been politically fragmented before about the mid-seventh century, was incorporated into the Mercian kingdom at about that time and came under direct Mercian

---

23. Murphy, 'Breckland', p. 203; Bell, 'Environmental Archaeology'; Crabtree, 'Animal Exploitation', p. 43.
24. Alexander and Trump, 'Grantchester', n.p.
25. Palmer, 'Three Southern English *Emporia*'.

jurisdiction. The clan territories of the Bourn Valley seem to have been incorporated into an extensive royal estate, however loosely managed, and centred on Haslingfield. The royal manor there still provided a render of three days' food (*feorm*) to the king in honey, corn and malt in 1086 together with a commutation, which implies that the render in kind was once larger.[26] Honey is generally taken as indicating at least a ninth-century date for the *feorm*.[27] It is possible that the proto-common field was a communally cultivated arable area, part of an extensive estate centred on Haslingfield and to whose *feorm* it contributed. It appears to have been laid out from scratch in a single phase, perhaps between about 700 and 870. There is nothing within it to indicate that it is made up of the amended fields of any other kind of cultivation regime or of different periods. The planned, unitary character of the long, narrow commons and the furlongs they separated, across four parishes, suggests that their plans were initiated by a central authority that controlled at least all four parishes rather than by each community within the layout. Nevertheless, while all the conditions needed for its creation were present in the eighth and early ninth centuries, that is a long way from conclusive proof.

Explanation of the layout of the proto-common field

It is difficult to explain why seven or more continuous alignments, lying about 220 yards (200 metres) apart, should run for over 5 miles (8½ kilometres) along the contours of the valley, or why it was important that they should be commons. For example, if they were laid out as droveways to allow the movement of stock across arable fields to or from a central place, then those central places have been lost. The commons are aligned neither on Cambridge (to the north-east) nor on Haslingfield (to the south-east). Nor does this explain why it was necessary for so many droves to lie so close to one other, when one or two would have done just as well.

The arrangement seems to have been created for a system of arable cultivation from the outset. This is implied by three features: first, the way in which the hundred boundary between Comberton and Toft respects the furrows of individual selions as it crosses the layout. Second, the absence of any field names referring to pasture or grassland within the long, narrow commons and their fields, in contrast to the large area immediately to the north. The third feature is implied in the long, narrow commons themselves, so different from the more usual headlands that divided common fields into furlongs. Perhaps they were included in the field layout to provided a 'bank' of additional nutrients that could be added

26. DB 1:7.
27. Stafford, 'Farm of One Night', p. 497.

to the arable fields they separated. Sheep grazing on the commons by day could be folded onto the stubbles at night, where they added the additional nutrients gained during the day. Sheep grazing only on the stubbles would simply be recycling existing nutrients within the field. 'Additional grassland at the field-edge reduced the demands which the system placed upon its environment. More livestock could be kept and the furlongs which remained ploughed benefited from the transference of nutrients, through animal manure, from those left under grass'.[28] The extensive pastures on the middle and upper pastures to the north imply that the middle Anglo-Saxon farmers of the valley did not need the long, narrow commons to feed their herds and flocks. The benefit must have been for the arable rather than for the animals. If this explanation for the long, narrow commons is correct, it may mean that the arable furlongs they separated were designed for intensive cultivation without a fallow period, and so needed to be enriched by intensive manuring. If the fields had been designed for fallowing, the commons would have been unnecessary, since cattle and sheep would have grazed on the fallows for a substantial part of the year. The integrated relationship of long, narrow commons and arable furlongs suggests that intensive corn cropping may have been a central part of the proto-common field from the outset. Barton's very name suggests a food render (*bere* 'barley' + *tūn* 'barley farm' or 'outlying grange').[29] The resultant benefits for productivity may explain why grazing on the long, narrow commons was retained once common-field cultivation had spread across the remainder of the four parishes.

The geographical relationship between the proto-common field on the lower slopes of the Bourn Valley and areas of intensive and rough grazing and woodland on the central and upper slopes suggests the characteristics of the agricultural regime known as 'infield and outfield', where the 'infield' is intensively cultivated for arable and the 'outfield' is primarily used for grazing, but brought into cultivation for short periods interrupted by long periods of fallow. Common grazing beyond the limits of arable fields of all periods is still visible in those parts of Britain in which it was not replaced by the introduction of common-field production. For example, 'beyond the [Bronze Age] terminal reave [at Mountsland Common, Exmoor] would have been open grazing land, perhaps common land shared by several communities'.[30] In many places, particularly where pastoral husbandry remained dominant, a clear division between those areas under intensive, permanently cultivated arable and those used for common grazing persisted into the Middle Ages. At Badgworthy on Exmoor, for example,

---

28. Fox, 'Social Relations', p. 111.
29. Hooke, 'Regional Variation', p. 125; Mills, *Dictionary*, pp. 25–6.
30. Riley and Wilson-North, *Exmoor*, p. 102.

intensively cultivated medieval arable lands lay below 'a managed system of grazing for livestock'.[31] Infields and outfields in this sense are not usually found in the Central Province, where the extension of the medieval common fields across almost all the available land of each parish has obscured or destroyed any evidence of such arrangements, if they ever existed. If the interpretation of the distribution of furlong names in the Bourn Valley is correct, then this, together with the very unusual character of the proto-common field, offers one of the first instances of preservation of infield and outfield cultivation to have been recognised within the physical remains of 'classic' common fields.

How was this eighth- or ninth-century proto-common field managed? The stepped character of the parish and hundred boundary between Toft and Comberton (Figure 5.3) suggests that the communities of each later parish were already identifiable when the field was first laid out, and that selions, or some similar form of field division, were an integral part of the arrangement from its inception. This is because the parish boundary seems to have been laid out in a way that respects and distinguishes between tenurial realities. Some selions belonged in Comberton and others in Toft, and the strips belonging to each parish were geographically clustered. If this were not the case and the land cultivated by the farmers of each later parish was indiscriminately mingled at the time that the boundary was set out, then it would have been straightforward to reorganise the arable lands in such a way that the boundary would not have needed to be indented. This may indicate that some elements (selions and furlongs) of common-field arrangements had evolved within this layout by the mid-ninth century. There is, though, no way of knowing what the cropping arrangements were – that is, whether these fields followed any crop rotation, or how the crops were divided among them. Was the whole layout laid down to a single crop each year (unlikely) or were several grain crops grown in different parts of the field (more likely)? And if several grain crops were grown, it would be useful to know whether each grain was grown in a discrete part of the field, or whether each community cultivated only one.

The most likely interpretation of the layout of long, narrow commons and the furlongs between them is that it was a middle Anglo-Saxon proto-common field intended for the intensive production of grain. If this is correct, then the Bourn Valley provides the earliest physical evidence for the date at which common-field agriculture was first introduced in the Central Province. The earliest previously known ridge and furrow (the physical manifestation of a selion) dates from the late eleventh century at Hen Domen, Montgomeryshire, where the remains of common-field cultivation are overlain by a Norman motte-and-bailey castle; the

---

31. Ibid. See also Hooke, *Anglo-Saxon England*, p. 115.

earliest 'firm written evidence' of common-field cultivation in the Danelaw comes from Brandon and Livermere, both Suffolk, where 'every eighth acre' was sold to the Abbey of Ely between 939 and 949.[32]

The physical cohesion of the proto-common field in the Bourn Valley, combined with its significant extent, indicates that it was probably laid out before parishes had evolved into independent communities. This implies that, whether or not local people took an active part in its planning and implementation, it was instigated by some higher authority that had the power to combine communities in a project in which their own landscapes played just a part. If this is correct, then the proto-common field is also the first physical evidence for the working of those extensive estates inferred by historians and geographers from documentary evidence, place names and parish boundaries.

How did this work on the ground? The proto-common field seems likely to have been farmed by men living in dispersed farmsteads across the valley. The survival on the high clay plateau at Cambourne of a 'sizeable assemblage' of early to middle Anglo-Saxon pottery, early Anglo-Saxon cemeteries at Haslingfield and Grantchester (and, perhaps, Harlton and Barton) and an early to middle Anglo-Saxon settlement at Grantchester all confirm the existence of settlement across the valley during the Anglo-Saxon period.[33] A charter of 672–4, which granted an estate to Chertsey Abbey that included Chertysey, Thorpe, Egham, Chobham, Molesey and Woodham as well as *Getinges* and *Hunewaldesham*, implies that many communities which only achieved administrative independence much later were nonetheless recognisable in this period.[34] The archaeological evidence suggests that the Bourn Valley was no different. The relationship between the proto-common field and settlement in the four parishes in the middle Anglo-Saxon period is, however, tantalising and obscure. The only evidence of settlement comes from Grantchester, where an early and middle Anglo-Saxon settlement, and its associated cemetery, lay where Mere Way (A on Figure 5.1) met the meadow bordering the River Cam.[35]

In all, the long, narrow commons and their associated furlongs across the four parishes of the Bourn Valley may indicate the first *physical* manifestation of the earliest common fields, and provide an insight, however tentative and obscure, into the workings of middle Anglo-Saxon extensive estates.

32. Barker and Lawson, 'Hen Domen'; C. Hart, personal communication.
33. Cambourne: Wessex Archaeology, Report 45977.1, p. 11; Haslingfield, Harlton and Barton: Fox, *Archaeology of Cambridgeshire*, pp. 255–59; Grantchester: Haigh, 'Archaeological Sites and Field Names'.
34. EHD 1, pp. 479–80. I am indebted to Stephen Bassett for this reference.
35. Alexander and Trump, 'Grantchester', Period II comment; Brown and Foard, 'Saxon Landscape', p. 76.

Explaining the origins of the proto-common field and its demise

A possible explanation for the origin of the proto-common field may lie in the agricultural, cultural and administrative histories of the two centuries before 700 that preceded the likely date of its middle Anglo-Saxon construction. As previously discussed, the sub-Roman and early Anglo-Saxon periods appear to have seen some shift to pastoralism, with some arable lands being converted to grass.[36] Farming appears to have concentrated on produce derived from cattle and sheep, and arable was converted into areas of intensive or rough grazing according to need.[37] The proportions of cattle, sheep and pigs varied from place to place according to the agricultural conditions of each locality and according to the social status of the inhabitants of a site. There were more sheep on low-status sites, and this probably includes the Bourn Valley.[38]

Traces of a tradition of value placed on cattle are preserved in the speeches attributed to the tenth-century shepherd and oxherd of Ælfric's *Colloquy*. The shepherd described how 'In the early morning I drive my sheep to their pasture, and in the heat and in cold, stand over them with dogs, *lest wolves devour them*; and I lead them back to their folds and milk them twice a day; and move their folds', while the oxherd explained that 'I lead ... [the oxen] to pasture, and I stand over them all night *watching for thieves*; and then in the early morning I hand them to the ploughman well-fed and watered'.[39] Ælfric clearly believed that sheep were less at risk from theft than cattle, and this emphasis on the value of cattle is echoed in Athelstan's laws, promulgated in the early to mid-tenth century, which refer to the man 'who tracks cattle into the land of another', in references to cattle-raiding in the Hundred Ordnance (c. 939–c. 961),[40] and the assignment of monetary compensation for damage even to the eyes and tails of cattle.[41] Archaeological evidence of the social importance of cattle includes the large percentages of cattle and pig bones found at high-status sites like Icklingham in Suffolk and Wicken Bonhunt in Essex, which seem to have been related to feasting – that is, to conspicuous consumption. This seems also to be the implication of early Anglo-Saxon decorated drinking vessels made from cattle horns, such as those from Little Wilbraham in Cambridgeshire, Sutton Hoo in Suffolk and Prittlewell in Essex, which were part of feasting assemblages (Figure 5.7).[42] An economy in

---

36. Murphy, 'Breckland', 'Anglo-Saxon Landscape'; Bell, 'Environmental Archaeology'.
37. Hooke, 'Regional Variation', p. 137; Austin et al., 'Tin and Agriculture', p. 225.
38. Rippon, 'Landscapes in Transition', p. 57; Crabtree, 'Animal Exploitation', p. 42.
39. Swanton, *Anglo-Saxon Prose*, p. 170, my emphasis.
40. EHD I, pp. 423 and 430.
41. EHD I, pp. 404–6.
42. University of Cambridge Museum of Archaeology and Anthropology; Carver, *Sutton Hoo*, p. 132; Blair et al., 'My Lord Essex', p. 13.

Figure 5.7 Reconstruction of an Anglo-Saxon drinking horn, made from a cattle horn (in the University of Cambridge Museum of Anthropology and Archaeology). The metal decorations and fittings were found in an Anglo-Saxon cemetery of the fifth or sixth centuries at Little Wilbraham, Cambs

which cattle and sheep herding were the dominant forms of agricultural activity may have led to the emergence of social values that placed as much emphasis on these animals as symbols of status and wealth as on their economic or productive potential. The size, quality and even colour of a herd of cattle – like the 'vast royal herds, each bred to a single colour' of the Zulu kings – and the amount of fodder needed to keep them over the winter, might be expected to reflect the status of their owner.[43] It is difficult to believe that cattle were the only or most frequent objects of theft in late Anglo-Saxon England and yet they are almost the only examples cited in the laws.[44] The implication is that cattle remained dominant symbols of status, long after their pre-eminence in the agricultural economy had disappeared.

The use of cattle as signifiers of wealth and status in Anglo-Saxon England probably came under increasing pressure from the end of the seventh century onwards. A burgeoning and increasingly sophisticated network of local and regional trade linked large trading centres with their rural hinterlands, fuelled by and fuelling local lords' and regional kings' demands for food renders in grain

43. Murphy, 'Breckland', p. 194; Morris, *Washing of the Spears*, p. 79.
44. EHD I, pp. 423 and 430.

from their estates for both trade and subsistence.⁴⁵ At Old Windsor, in Berkshire, for example, large-scale assarts of woodland and a large three-wheeled watermill in the late eighth and ninth centuries demonstrate an almost industrialised approach to grain production in this period.⁴⁶ It is this change from an economy focused primarily on pastoral farming to an economy increasingly directed towards arable cultivation that forms the basis for a conjectural argument, offered here only tentatively and in the absence of other explanations, for the creation of the proto-common field over a large area of the lower Bourn Valley. Was the proto-common field laid out as part of a strategy intended to resist pressures leading to a shift to wholesale arable cultivation by accommodating these strains to the smallest possible extent? If so, the strategy had three interdependent strands: to preserve as much of the common pastures on the middle and upper slopes as possible; to concentrate arable in one place; and to attempt a system of intensive, infield cultivation. It was only when the proto-common field eventually failed several generations later to meet its objective to produce sufficient grain, that conventional common-field agriculture was more generally introduced into these parishes, perhaps in or after the late tenth or eleventh centuries. After this time the place of cattle as important signifiers of status could not be sustained.

Common fields may therefore have been introduced into the Bourn Valley in at least two, perhaps three, phases. In the first phase, occurring perhaps at some time in the eighth or early ninth centuries, a proto-common field was laid out across the southern third of at least four parishes on the northern slopes of the Bourn Valley. In the second phase, between the tenth and twelfth centuries, 'classic' common fields were extended over a wider area within each parish by each community working independently of its neighbours. By the thirteenth century at the latest, so much arable had been taken into cultivation that it was organised into the mature two- or three-field system familiar to us today and mapped in Figure 3.1. The implications for this conclusion are explored in Chapter 7.

---

45. Palmer, 'Three Southern English Emporia'; Carver, 'Kinship and Material Culture', p. 142; Murphy, 'Breckland', p. 203; Moreland, 'Significance of Production'.
46. Palmer, 'Three Southern English Emporia', p. 57.

6

Landscape and society in the eleventh century

The conservatism that saw the retention of older field boundaries in the common fields of the Bourn Valley might be the physical expression of a society in which tradition was particularly important and, if this were the case, it is possible that the men who laid out new fields in the valley in the Anglo-Saxon period held their land and managed their relationships with each other in ways that were becoming progressively more old-fashioned. This proposition can be explored through the status and patterns of tenure of the men who farmed the Bourn Valley in the later eleventh century and who, with their descendants, extended common-field cultivation across the slopes of the valley between about 1000 and 1300.

Most of the men who held land in the valley in 1066 belonged to a class of freemen called 'sokemen' in the Cambridgeshire folios of DB. Although sokemen were found across Cambridgeshire at that date, there were more of them in the Bourn Valley than almost anywhere else in the county. It used to be believed that sokemen were the descendants of Scandinavian immigrants of the ninth and tenth centuries, since their distribution across eastern England in 1086 appeared to coincide with the area covered by the Danelaw. This view is no longer held by most scholars who now consider that sokemen were probably peasant farmers, the 'descendants of the broad mass of the semi-free cultivators of the great Middle Saxon estates'.[1] In the ninth century, 'the terms on which Scandinavian landholders took over land seems, in some way not yet understood, to have preserved many aspects of a comparatively free peasantry', perhaps in the Bourn Valley the descendants of the clans of the Hæslingas, Grantasæte and Earningas, men with largely Romano-British ancestry.[2] If some elements of the relationships between middle Anglo-Saxon freemen and their lords, and the forms of tenure by which they held their land, survived in the Bourn Valley in the eleventh century, then this persistence might shed some light on the processes through which later

---

1. Hadley, 'Multiple Estates', p. 3; Williamson, Norfolk, p. 94.
2. Faith, English Peasantry, p. 122.

Anglo-Saxon and early medieval farmers developed the proto-common field which matured into the common-field landscape of about 1300.

The evidence of Domesday Book

The major source for the investigation of social conditions in the Bourn Valley in the eleventh century is, of course, the Cambridgeshire folios of DB.[3] There are, however, two other texts dating from approximately the same period, which cover much the same ground as DB, sometimes offering a little more detail. The *Inquisitio Comitatus Cantabrigiensis* (ICC) and the *Inquisitio Eliensis* (IE) often name sokemen who are anonymous in DB and also record the numbers of animals on Cambridgeshire demesnes.[4] Because these documents offer information about landholding in Cambridgeshire in 1066 ('in the time of King Edward') as well as in 1086 ('in the time of King William'), it is possible to use them – with caution – to explore land tenure in the county on the eve of the Norman Conquest.

The problems associated with the use of these sources are well known. The most obvious is the difficulty of being sure what the exact meaning is of the terms that are used to categorise data, especially the men referred to as *sochmanni*, who are translated as 'freemen' in the Phillimore Edition.[5] 'Sokemen' were so called from rights over land known as soke (*soca*) and sake (*saca*).[6] *Saca* referred to specific rights over land: to grant and sell land freely, and to labour and income from unfree tenants. *Soca* referred to rights of jurisdiction over land – the obligation to attend the soke-lord's courts and to pay some dues and services to that lord; it did not necessarily have any connection with *saca*. Most of the Cambridgeshire men whose holdings were recorded in DB had jurisdiction (*soca*) over their own land, that is, they were not subject to the manorial court of any higher lord. They also had the right to sell or grant their land freely and had rights to any services owed from the tenants upon it (*saca*). In this, they appear to have had the same status as men often called freemen (*liberi homines*) in Suffolk, and that is how they will be referred to here.[7] Almost all Anglo-Saxon freemen commended themselves to a higher lord for patronage and protection. In DB this

---

3. Rumble, *Domesday Book: Cambridgeshire*.
4. VCH I; IE.
5. DB.
6. Roffe, *Domesday*, pp. 30–2. This is not the same as the more common definition of a sokeman as a man or woman over whom or over whose land a higher lord had rights of jurisdiction and service (*soca*). This was common in the Danelaw, but there is little evidence that many higher lords had soke rights in Cambridgeshire in 1066.
7. A man's status was determined by the status of the land he held: he might be a freeman in some contexts and a sokeman in others depending on how he held his land.

is noted in the formula that he was 'the man of n'. Commendation did not grant the lord any rights of *soca* or *saca* over his liegeman or over that man's land, and it was often the case that even where a man was subject to the soke of one overlord, he was commended to another. The relationships between sokemen and higher lords in the Bourn Valley in 1066 seem generally to be of commendation rather than soke, since it is the formula of commendation rather than of soke that is mostly used in DB.

Freemen and their holdings in the Bourn Valley in 1066[8]

The Bourn Valley was one of the most densely populated areas of Cambridgeshire in 1086 with sixteen to twenty people per 1,000 acres in Longstow and Wetherley hundreds respectively.[9] At about seven men per 1,000 acres, the valley had the second highest density of 'sokemen' in Cambridgeshire in 1066,[10] making up around 42 per cent of the total population, just over twice the mean of 20 per cent for the county as a whole, and well above the 30 per cent generally selected as significant.[11] Seventy-three per cent of the 146 men in the Bourn Valley whose rights over land were documented in DB were able to grant and sell their holdings, and a further 23 per cent were able to withdraw from their holdings or from the soke of their overlord. All these men should probably be regarded as *liberi homines*.[12] Only 3 per cent were unable to withdraw from their holdings and probably really were *sochmanni* whose persons and land were subject to the *soca* or *saca* of another.

8. Twelve parishes in the Bourn Valley are used in this analysis of DB: Barton, Bourn, Caldecote, Caxton, Comberton, Eversden, Grantchester (including Coton), Hardwick, Harlton, Haslingfield, Kingston and Toft.
9. Darby, 'Domesday Geography of Cambridgeshire', Fig. 3.
10. The assumptions underpinning this calculation may be contentious. First, it has been assumed that each unnamed man listed in DB is a unique individual who did not have more than one holding in the valley. In fact, as will emerge, this seems very unlikely. The second problem relates to the way in which DB accounts for tenants. On the one hand, no *villani*, *bordarii*, *cotarii* or *servi* are listed for 1066; on the other, few sokemen are listed in 1086. This, together with the frequent coincidence in many parishes between numbers of *villani* in 1086 and numbers of sokemen in 1066 has led many historians to conclude that pre-Conquest sokemen were demoted to villein status after the Norman Conquest. Whether or not this is the case, it is still likely that those sokemen who held larger holdings before 1066 also had tenants and demesne workers on their land. And finally it assumes that, even if the *villani* of 1086 are broadly the same people as the sokemen of 1066, the numbers of people in the valley did not change very much between those two dates.
11. Dodgshon, 'Early Middle Ages', Fig. 4.2 left. All those men called sokemen in the Cambridgeshire folios of DB are included here in order to compare them with these more general figures.
12. The rights in relation to their land of twenty-nine of the 175 sokemen in the Bourn Valley were not noted in DB.

The freemen of the Bourn Valley seem to have been independent farmers with full rights over their land. The fact that there were so many here in the mid-eleventh century suggests a landscape of many small farms, whether dispersed or nucleated, whose owners co-operated with each other in the management of communal resources, such as the Offals and those arable fields, like the proto-common field, that were cultivated in common. The size of their holdings varied from just a few acres to several hundred; some had just one holding, others a clutch; some held freely and some on lease. Aelmer, a thegn whose seat was at Bourn, held a number of holdings amounting altogether to over 15 hides. At the other end of the scale his namesake Aelmer, son of Goding, held just two small holdings of 20 and 10 acres respectively at Kingston.[13]

The high percentage of *liberi homines* in the population of the Bourn Valley in 1066 does not, of course, necessarily imply that these men also held an equivalent proportion of the land in the valley. While DB does not list the actual acreage of land in the hands of freemen in 1066, it does record the proportion owed by each man towards a general tax (the *geld*) which was assessed in 'hides'.[14] The precise relationship between the hidage and the actual size and composition of a man's holding is not known, but is believed to 'reflect the economic potential of each estate' based on its arable land, whatever its additional resources of wood, meadow, marsh or pasture.[15] The hidage assessments owed by the freemen in the valley may reflect the relative acreages of arable land that they held, given that most land is Grade 2, except for the Gault clays on the valley floor which are Grade 3 agricultural land. The value of each holding can probably therefore be taken as a rough index of the actual size of the holding for comparative purposes.[16] Of the 101 hides 3 virgates at which the twelve parishes of the valley were assessed in 1066, 51 per cent was held by freemen, who had full rights over their land. This is probably a fairly reasonable measure of the actual proportion of the land that they held.

The high density of population in the valley in 1066 was reflected in a high number of holdings: there were more holdings per 1,000 acres there than

13. DB 14:49–50, 32:23, 33:1; 13:12 and 25:8.
14. Each county received a tax assessment which was shared between the hundreds in the county, then between parishes in each hundred, and then between landholders in each parish, in proportion to the percentage of the economic resources of the parish that they held: Faith, *English Peasantry*, p. 114. The tax was levied on a unit known as a hide, made up of 120 'fiscal' acres which could also be measured in fractions of hides called virgates (a quarter of a hide in Cambridgeshire).
15. Roffe, *Domesday*, p. 59.
16. In other counties 'inland', the core lands of large estates, did not pay the *geld*, nor did the demesne lands of the king; nevertheless both were assessed in terms of hides in the Cambridgeshire folios of DB: Faith, *English Peasantry*, pp. 49–51.

anywhere else in Cambridgeshire (with the exception of Wetherley Hundred with which the valley overlapped).[17] More than half of the fifty-eight holdings were held individually – a proportion rising to 68 per cent if ten holdings with five or more holders are excluded. Many of these holdings seem to have been quite small – for example, 57 per cent of the 175 freemen in the valley each held fewer than 30 hidated acres.[18] There is something odd about this calculation, however, since about 100 of these 175 men were concentrated on only 22 per cent of the holdings. A more accurate picture might be achieved by excluding ten holdings (atypical for reasons explained below), each shared between five men or more. In this case, nearly half of the remaining 81 men held substantial farms of more than 60 acres. Twenty-five men held between 31 and 60 acres, while only eighteen held fewer than 30 acres. These men were characterised by a wide range of economic and, presumably, social status, and the position of men holding 60 acres or more might approach that of 'Ceorls [who] with a hide of land are surely nearer to yeomen, even gentlemen, than to crofters'.[19] They may have been small proprietors by the standards of men holding estates of 3 hides or more, but they were no doubt key players within their own communities, holding several times the 10 to 15 acres held by most villeins in the valley in 1279.[20] Many may well have had tenants of their own, whether bordarii, slaves or tenants more like the villani of DB.

The low number of manors in the valley in 1086 implies that freeholding farmers in the Bourn Valley were independent of manorial control, even for payment of the geld (Figure 6.1).[21] There were manors in just four of the twelve parishes, compared with an average of 58 per cent in each Cambridgeshire hundred, illustrating Palmer's comment that 'Eastern Cambridgeshire was as manorialised as most parts of old Wessex ... Not so in Wetherley Hundred'.[22] Two sets of evidence suggest that these four manors had been derived fairly recently from just one, that of the king at Haslingfield (Figure 6.1 and Table 6.2). First, a number of manors appear to have a connection with royal demesne: the king's ancient demesne in 1066 included holdings at Haslingfield, Comberton, Kingston

---

17. Welldon Finn, 'Cambridgeshire Domesday', p. 31.
18. This assumes that, on the twenty-five holdings where there was more than one holder, the land was equitably shared between them. There is no documentary basis for this assumption beyond a statistical interest in establishing mean sizes of holdings. It is not known whether multiple holdings were those of family members who had received partible inheritances, or whether they were small conglomerates of local farmers who agreed together to buy a piece of land or take on a lease.
19. Aston, 'Origins of the Manor', p. 2.
20. Rot. Hund. ii; VCH 5, parish essays.
21. Maitland, Domesday Book and Beyond, p. 129; Welldon Finn, 'Cambridgeshire Domesday', p. 36.
22. Palmer, 'Domesday Manor', p. 149.

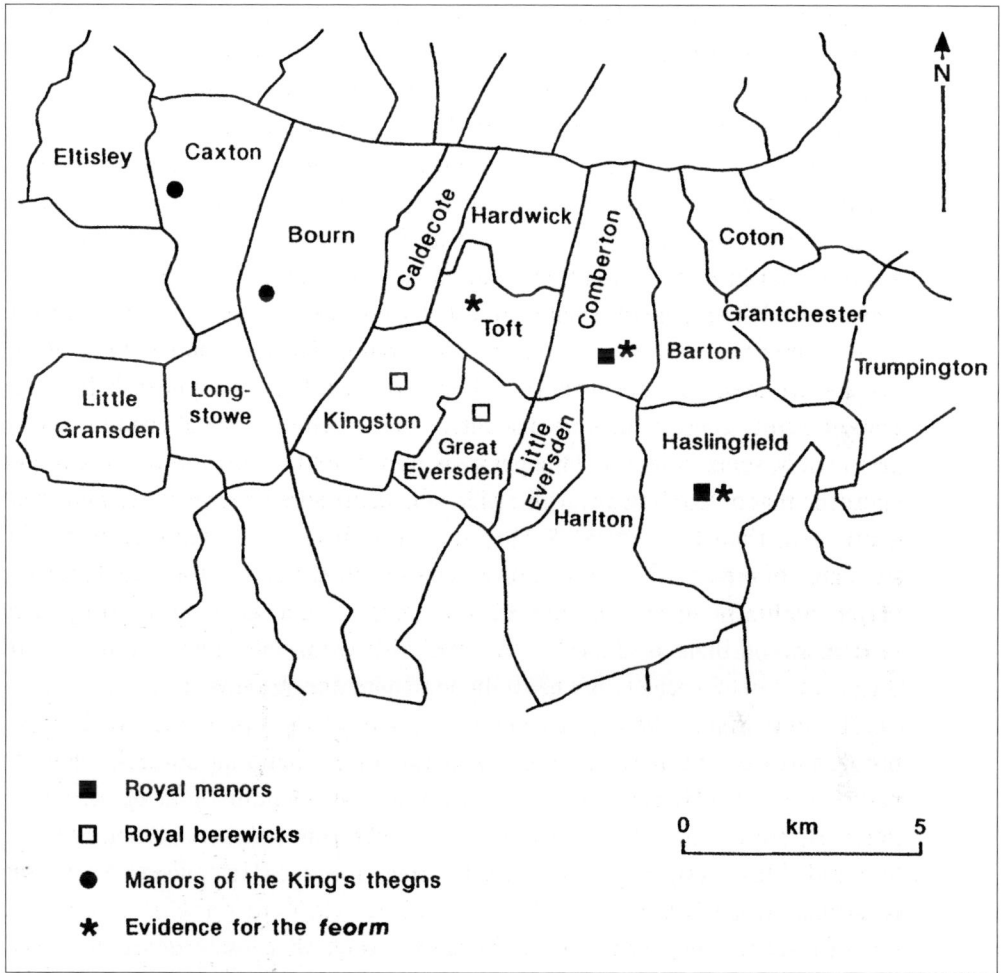

Figure 6.1 Distribution of manors in the Bourn Valley in 1086

and, perhaps, Eversden;[23] Haslingfield was still paying the *feorm* in 1066, an ancient render or tribute that had its origins in the clan territories and *regiones* of the early Anglo-Saxon period. Although the *feorm* had disappeared from the king's manor at Comberton by 1086, the medieval sergeanty attached to the royal manor there is very similar to pre-Conquest forms of *feorm* from manors detached from the *caput*: the care, from Michaelmas to Candlemas, of two of the king's lanner falcons and one retriever trained to catch herons.[24] Since all food farms are believed to have been derived from *feorm* originally rendered to the king, and since

---

23. DB 1:6–7.
24. DB 1:6; Faith, *English Peasantry*, p. 102; VCH 5, p. 177.

Toft also paid one week's food farm to the Abbey of Ely as late as 1035, perhaps Toft too had originally been part of the royal demesne. It is possible that the hide 'missing' in the DB account of Eversden was omitted because it was royal demesne, something that is routine in the ICC.[25] The second indication that the four manors of 1066 were later subdivisions of a single estate is found at Bourn and Caxton whose manors were held by the king's thegns (probably minor officials of the royal household) in 1066. A third thegn held land, though not a manor, at Harlton. The thegnly status of these men may mean that their manors were relatively recent grants from royal demesne – in Yorkshire, for example, the lands of the king's thegns were explicitly assigned to royal demesne in DB.[26] If ancient demesne, *feorm* and the estates of royal thegns are indicators of royal origins, then the implication is that much of the valley had lain within a single royal estate, perhaps not very long before 1066.

At the time of the Norman Conquest, royal demesne lay scattered in relatively small blocks of 1 to 2½ hides in almost every parish: in Harlton, Comberton, Eversden, Kingston, Bourn and Caxton. Only on the estate centre at Haslingfield was the demesne very large at over 7 hides. The scattered nature of the royal demesnes, and their generally small extent, may mean that the royal estate may have been loosely rather than centrally managed and organised. Revenues may have been derived as much from rents and dues from 'rights in meadow, pasture and woodland, [and] the profits of jurisdiction in the hundreds attached' as from the *feorm*.[27] In Oxfordshire, for example, high revenues for royal manors were collected from woods, meadows, pastures and fisheries, and 4 shillings per year were collected in 1086 from 'the men who live in the wood' in Newport Pagnell in Buckinghamshire.[28]

The record of the twelve parishes in DB reveals a landscape of modest holdings of between 30 and 120 hidated acres, generally held by independent, unmanorialised farmers who enjoyed *soca* and *saca* over their holdings, and whose commendation to overlords was the only subordination to which they submitted. They were probably men of some substance in their local communities, with only a loose relationship with the royal centre at Haslingfield. The eleventh-century landscape emerges as a mosaic of small, interlocking holdings, only occasionally – if dramatically – interrupted by large, isolated, lordly demesnes at Haslingfield and Hardwick (Table 6.2). Although they belonged to the generations of men responsible for the extension of common fields across the valley, taking decisions on where new furlongs should lie and what their boundaries should be, the

25. Hart, 'Land Tenure', p. 84; see note 59.
26. Roffe, *Domesday*, p. 40.
27. Harvey, 'Demesne Agriculture', p. 65.
28. Ibid., p. 66.

freeholders of this period seem to have had more in common with English farmers of the seventh and eighth centuries than with the generality of those in the eleventh, and the survival into the medieval landscape of the communally controlled Offals and pastures familiar to middle Anglo-Saxon men in the valley fits well with this conclusion.

The origins of freeman and sokeman tenure in the Bourn Valley

The impression of archaic patterns of landholding in the valley in the eleventh century can be explored through an examination of the three different forms of land tenure that are believed to have evolved by the later Anglo-Saxon period: warland, bookland and leaseland.

Warland

Warland is believed to be the oldest form of landholding in Anglo-Saxon England, and was land in whose products the whole community was entitled to share and over which the whole group, rather than individuals, had rights.[29] It is significant that it was also sometimes known as *folcland*, since its origins lay in the seventh-century *regiones* or clan territories whose land had belonged to the whole community, linked by kinship (the 'folk', analogous to the Germanic *volk*).[30] Archaeologists have seen the relationship between community and landscape reflected in cemeteries, where kinship 'determined personal status, provided genealogical links, and gave access to land'.[31] It is believed that warland formed the basis of 'ancient royal demesne', created as the Anglo-Saxon kingdoms of the seventh and eighth centuries emerged out of or absorbed the clan territories of the sixth and seventh centuries.[32] In the Bourn Valley, for example, the kings of Mercia may have subsumed the clan territory of the *Hæslingas* into a royal estate. Some elements of the view that warland belonged to a community defined by kinship survived into the late Anglo-Saxon period. Individuals were entitled to holdings partly on the basis of their membership of that community and partly on proper trusteeship of their holdings, rules rather like those of modern allotments. Communal ownership of this land meant that only the king, as the representative of the community, had the authority to make grants of land from warland – that is, to transfer it permanently from the community to an individual.[33] Although its

29. Reynolds, 'Bookland, Folkland and Fief', p. 219.
30. Faith, *English Peasantry*, pp. 89–90.
31. Härke, 'Early Anglo-Saxon Social Structure', p. 137.
32. Bassett, *Anglo-Saxon Kingdoms*, pp. 8–17.
33. Reynolds, 'Bookland, Folkland and Fief', pp. 218–19.

association with the kin group became eroded over time, particularly by the evolving rights of individuals from the eighth century onwards to inherit and to hold land individually, there was a close association between warland origins and freeman status throughout the Anglo-Saxon period, since only those men whose holdings had originated as warland paid the *geld* and were required to attend the public courts – precious indicators of their freeholding status.[34]

It might be possible to identify warland holdings in the Bourn Valley in the eleventh century using the record in DB of the ancient and distinctive services they rendered to the king:[35] riding duties (also called escort or *inward*, for example, escorting the king or his representative when called upon), and duties of carriage or cartage, called *averian*.[36] In Cambridgeshire, the DB and ICC accounts of warland duties of carriage and escort appear to have been compiled from a contemporary list supplied by the sheriff on the king's behalf.[37] In Barton, for example, twenty-three men 'provided 6 carrying services and 17 watchmen *for the King's sheriff* by custom'.[38] Twenty-one per cent of the hidated land in the twelve parishes provided riding duties or carriage for the king or the sheriff, while 62 per cent of the 175 holders of land were rendering warland services of some kind to the king in 1066.[39] This is a greater proportion than almost anywhere else in Cambridgeshire. Only Wetherley Hundred, with which the Bourn Valley overlaps, has more.[40] Three factors suggest that the proportion of warland in the valley may have been higher in or shortly before 1066 than DB indicates. First, as has already been noted, only those duties rendered to the sheriff seem to have been included in the compilation of the Cambridgeshire folios of DB, and it is likely that other lists existed. Second, Toft and Hardwick were exempt from warland duties because they belonged to an ecclesiastical estate (the Abbey of Ely), although this may not have been the case

---

34. Faith, *English Peasantry*, p. 117.
35. The service was attached to the land rather than to the landholder. At Caxton, for example, '½ virgate found 3 escorts', and '*wara* acres' could also be identified in eleventh-century Suffolk: DB 26:42; Faith, *English Peasantry*, p. 115.
36. Ibid., pp. 108–9; Aston, 'Origins of the Manor', p. 81.
37. S. Baxter, personal communication.
38. ICC, p. 420, my emphasis; it is worth noting, though, that DB may not be a complete catalogue of warland services in the county, since it may have omitted lists of warland duties rendered through other officers of the king. If this is the case, then land in Cambridgeshire that did not render escort and carriage services in 1066 cannot certainly be excluded from calculations of warland (S. Baxter, personal communication).
39. This figure includes eighteen men commended to Earl Algar who held 6 hides less ½ virgate at Caxton: DB 26:42. DB does not list warland duties for these men, but their pattern of landholding is so similar to the distinctive pattern of men holding warlands in the valley, and so unlike those holdings not held as warland, that they have been included here.
40. The parishes of Wetherley Hundred are Arrington, Barrington, Barton (including Whitwell), Comberton, Coton, Grantchester, Harlton, Haslingfield Orwell, Shepreth and Wimpole.

when they were owned by Wulfwin. And third, there were so many freemen in the Bourn Valley at the time of the Norman Conquest – nearly twice as many as the mean for the county as a whole – that it seems likely that many of their holdings had also originated as warland, even if their services had atrophied by 1066.

Warland was characterised by a great diversity in the status of its inhabitants. Those providing riding services, for example, must have owned horses and may have been men of some economic substance, compared with those providing duties of carriage. While the warhorse was 'always more costly than any other horse' particularly because of the expense of its accoutrements, any 'old nag' sufficient to provide escorts or riding duties would still have been relatively expensive to maintain, even if it did not signify particularly high social status or wealth.[41] By the eleventh century, Edward the Confessor regarded the maintenance of a cavalry unit as so important that he created the post of the staller to take charge of it, and Sigar, the reeve of Asgar, Edward's staller, held 5 hides on the royal estate at Haslingfield in 1066, perhaps to co-ordinate the services of the fifty-one local men from the Bourn Valley who provided riding services to the sheriff at that date.[42]

Had a member of the Hæslingas been able to visit the valley in the eleventh century, he would probably still have been able to recognise elements of his own world in the local landscape. The large pastures and Offals that he had called *feld* were still there, still interspersed on the clay-topped plateaux by ancient woodland and wood pasture. The introduction of the proto-common field and the steady encroachment on the grasslands by common-field agriculture might have been less familiar, nor might he have recognised the new seigneurial complexes at Hardwick, Bourn or Harlton. Although the valley was almost certainly more populated in 1066 than in 650, he could have recognised the locations of some at least of the farmsteads of eleventh-century freemen, some of whom might have been his own descendants, still pasturing their horses on the commons and paddocks around their farms.[43]

---

41. Graham-Campbell, 'Equestrian Equipment', p. 77; J. Campbell, personal communication.
42. Graham-Campbell, 'Equestrian Equipment', p. 88; DB 22:8.
43. Some perspective on these figures can be gained from Härke's view that between the fifth and seventh centuries local communities generally included no more than fifteen to fifty people, and seldom as many as 100: 'Early Anglo-Saxon Social Structure', p. 140. If these 'local communities' were comparable with the population of each vill in 1086, then the number of people in each vill in 1086 calculated by Darby in 1936 – likely to have been just over 150 – might perhaps have been three times their seventh-century populations: Darby, 'Domesday Geography of Cambridgeshire', Figure 3.

Booklands

Booklands were estates that had been granted from warland by charter (*boc*), a process that began with royal endowments of monasteries and minsters in the seventh century. After a time, charters began to be used to grant estates to the Anglo-Saxon aristocracy and eventually to lesser thegns. By the mid-tenth century 'bookland was ... by and large, what belonged to thegns', a signal of social status.[44] Bookland could only be created from warland, and only by the king.[45] It inherited from its warland ancestry the rights of *saca* and *soca*, but – unlike warland, which could be subject to partible inheritance – it was free from the demands of co-heirs.[46]

David Roffe has suggested that bookland can be identified in DB where that record states that a named pre-Conquest tenant simply held (*tenuit*) his land without any overlord, with the right to grant and sell, since these characteristics may be an indication that the holder was a king's thegn.[47] This proposition appears to hold true in the Bourn Valley, in the case of Aelmer of Bourn, for example, who in 1066 held lands amounting to over 15 hides, principally in Bourn (Table 6.1).[48] The formula used by DB in relation to his holdings is uniformly 'In x tenuit Almar ... '. He had rights of grant and sale over all his holdings, like other men we have already considered. His estate was made up of two sets of holdings. First, those lands in which he was named as a thegn, in which he was commended to the king and which appear to be booklands because he was termed a thegn in DB in relation to them, and which were classified as 'manors' before 1066. Only this part of his estate was used to form the *caput* of the post-Conquest barony created by Picot, the Norman sheriff of Cambridgeshire.[49] In this they conform to the pattern that baronies 'represent pre-Conquest [bookland] estates in both form and composition'.[50] Aelmer's booklands seem likely to have been granted by the king not very long before 1066, either from warland or from royal demesne, and his commendation to the king in respect of these holdings may be related to these estates. Aelmer's other lands were those which he probably held as a *liber homo*, as he had the rights of grant and sale, like the other freemen we have already considered. They appear in DB as those in which he was commended to Edeva

---

44. Reynolds, 'Bookland, Folkland and Fief', p. 219.
45. Faith, *English Peasantry*, p. 160.
46. Reynolds, 'Bookland, Folkland and Fief', p. 217; Abels, 'Bookland and Fyrd Service', pp. 4–5; Hadley, 'Multiple Estates', p. 6.
47. Roffe, *Domesday*, p. 34.
48. DB 31:1.
49. VCH 5, p. 6.
50. Roffe, *Domesday*, p. 45.

Table 6.1 The estates of Aelmer of Bourn in 1066 and 1086

Parish	Size of holding	Commended lord in 1066	Overlord TRW	Holder in 1066	Holder TRW
Bourn	4 hides[1]	King	King	'a thegn of the king'	Picot
Bourn	1 hide 3 virgates	King	Sheriff of Essex	Aelmer, King Edward's thegn	Picot
Bourn	4 hides 1 virgate	Edeva	Count Alan	Aelmer	Aelmer
Caldecote	½ hide	Edeva	Count Alan	Aelmer	Aelmer
Croydon	2½ virgates	Edeva	Count Alan	Godiva	Aelmer
East Hatley	1 hide 3 virgates	Edeva	Count Alan	Aelmer	Aelmer
Hatley St George	1 virgate	Edeva	Count Alan	Aelmer	Aelmer
Kingston	1 virgate	Earl Algar	Count Alan	Alfgeat	Aelmer
Longstowe	1½ virgates	Edeva	Count Alan	Aelmer	Aelmer

Source: DB 32:23, 33:1, Index of Persons.
Notes: 1. These 4 hides at Bourn almost certainly include the hide held by two priests, 'this thegn's men', which could not be separated from the church. St Helen's church lies on the periphery of the present Hall complex: DB, 32:23.

before 1066, which he held from the Honor of Richmond, Edeva's successor, after 1066 and were those which he tended to retain after the Norman Conquest.[51]

The bare outlines of Aelmer's seigneurial complex can still be discerned at Bourn (Figure 6.2). A motte-and-bailey castle was constructed here immediately after the Norman Conquest on the crest of a pronounced scarp at the interface between woodland and cleared land. It may have been erected on the site of Aelmer's hall, since 'the building of a [Norman] castle over an existing [Anglo-Saxon] manor house was a deeply symbolic act that affirmed the legitimacy of the new lord'.[52] The parish church of St Helen is an integral part of this landscape, lying immediately north of the bailey, and recorded as Aelmer's estate minster in DB.[53] Castle/hall and church were set in a roughly rectangular block of extensive demesne land, defined by two sinuous roads that enclose an area reaching from Bourn Hall and the parish church in the north-east to Ermine Street in the south-west.[54] The south-eastern boundary of this estate is followed in part by a very substantial bank (Figure 6.3). This block of land is very similar in layout to other small late Anglo-Saxon estates, like that, for example, at Aston Magna in Gloucestershire.[55] The area includes wood and wood pasture (whose core was in

51. DB 32:23, 14:47–52.
52. Liddiard, 'Population Density and Castle Building', p. 44.
53. DB 32:23.
54. An estate of 4 hides at Bourn includes a hide held by two priests, 'this thegn's men', which could not be separated from the church: DB 32:23.
55. Faith, English Peasantry, p. 173.

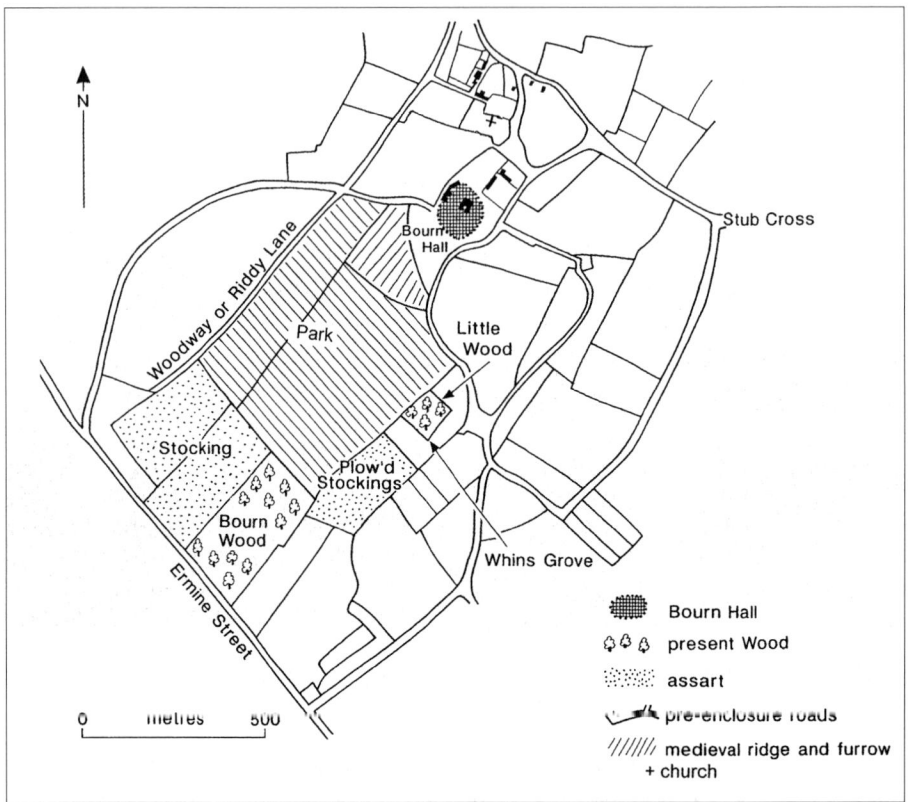

Figure 6.2 The landscape around Bourn Hall in the early nineteenth century, before parliamentary enclosure (after ChC, early nineteenth-century map and Ordnance Survey 1886). The sinuous roads which lead into Bourn from Ermine Street meet at Bourn Hall, enclosing wood, parkland and areas of possible assart, perhaps a late Anglo-Saxon enclosure for hunting

Stocking and Bourn Wood), arable furlongs covered by medieval ridge and furrow, and post-medieval fields called Great, Little and Middle Park Fields.[56] Woodland and arable might be expected in the inland of any late Anglo-Saxon estate; parkland may also have been part of this landscape. Parks for hunting 'seem to have been widespread ... in Britain by the twelfth century, perhaps even by the eleventh'.[57] An earlier date for parkland is suggested, for example, by the tenth-century hunter of Aelfric's *Colloquy* and the place names derived from *haga* discussed in Chapter 2.[58]

56. These names probably mean 'pale', the park fence: Field, *English Field-Names*, p. 28. Two mid-sixteenth century field names also refer to a park: *pales hoke* and *palys hyl*: ChC Bourn M and ChC early 19thC map.
57. Taylor, 'Medieval Ornamental Landscapes', pp. 46 and 48.
58. Swanton, *Anglo-Saxon Prose*, p. 170; see Faith, *English Peasantry*, p. 168 for other examples.

Figure 6.3 The high bank towards the south-east of Bourn Hall may preserve part of the boundary of the earlier manorial complex

In all, only 22 per cent of the hidated land of the valley was held in demesne on bookland estates in 1066, while a further 9 per cent of bookland was leased out (Tables 6.2 and 6.3; and below). Once the royal demesnes are added, it appears that just over a third of the hidated land lay in royal and bookland estates in 1066.[59] This is a relatively low proportion, leaving nearly two-thirds lying in other forms of tenure, and suggesting that the process of fission from a single extensive estate into bookland holdings was a fairly recent innovation here. The conclusion that bookland estates in the valley were not very ancient is supported by the restricted group of owners of these estates in 1066 and their close connection with the royal household. They were all the king's thegns, members of his household, religious houses or senior members of the royal court. There were no local gentry holding bookland estates here in the eleventh century, independent of royal patronage.

It is possible that the holdings of the freemen who could grant and sell their holdings, but who did not provide carriage and escort, may also have originated as

---

59. Hart, 'Land Tenure', p. 84; this calculation of the royal demesne includes a hide at Eversden which appears in the total for the parish, but for which no antecessor is mentioned. Hart believes that it may have been part of the royal demesne in 1066, and this seems likely, since royal demesnes were omitted from ICC, but included in DB: Ibid.

Table 6.2 Royal 'inland' and other bookland demesne in the Bourn Valley in 1066

Owner in 1066	Type of land	Parish	Extent measured in hides
Abbey of Ely	Bookland demesne	Hardwick	3 hides 1 virgate 12 acres
Abbey of Ramsey	Bookland demesne	Bourn[1]	1 hide
Aelmer of Bourn, thegn	Bookland demesne	M Bourn	4 hides 3 virgates
Aki of Harlton, thegn	Bookland demesne	Harlton	3½ hides
Edeva	Bookland demesne	Haslingfield[2]	½ hide
Edeva	Bookland demesne	Toft[3]	2 hides 1 virgate 8 acres
Judicael, the king's huntsman	Bookland demesne	Barton	2½ hides
Judicael, the king's huntsman	Bookland demesne	Grantchester	1 virgate
Thorgar, thegn	Bookland demesne	M Caxton	3 hides
King Edward	Royal demesne	M Haslingfield	7 hides 1 virgate
King Edward	Royal demesne	M Comberton	2½ hides
King Edward	Royal demesne	Kingston	1 hide 3 virgates
King Edward?	Royal demesne	Eversden	1 hide
Total bookland			22½ hides 20 acres
Total royal demesne			12½ hides
Total demesne: bookland and royal			35 hides 20 acres

Source: DB; ICC.
Notes: (M = manor in DB)
1. Berewick of the Abbey of Ramsey's manor at Longstowe (DB 7:1).
2. Berewick of Edeva's manor at Swavesey (DB 14:37, 14:48).
3. Berewick of Edeva's manor at Swavesey (DB 14:37, 14:48).

bookland. While they conform in many ways to criteria used to identify bookland estates (many who are named held – *tenuit* – their land without any overlord, and had the right to grant and sell), none was named as a king's thegn, and their estates were generally too small to have been granted by charter – most were between 30 and 60 acres. Bookland estates were usually bigger, even in the Bourn Valley where their mean extent was 3 hides 25 acres, about five times the size of the average holdings held by freemen. In Wessex bookland estates amounted on average to 13 hides.[60] It is possible that freeman holdings were small because they were booklands that had become fragmented over time, but there is no evidence for or against this proposition, and the holdings of these men are more likely to have originated as warland than as bookland.

Recent archaeological excavation in Cambridgeshire has revealed what a minor manorial centre of the late ninth to mid-tenth centuries might have looked like, perhaps something that might have not have been out of place in Harlton or Hardwick.[61] The site at Cherry Hinton was defined by a substantial D-shaped ditch

60. Costen, 'Settlement in Wessex', pp. 97–8.
61. This and the following information are taken from Cessford and Dickens, 'Manor of Hintona', pp. 51–72.

which enclosed an area about 492 yards long by 186 yards wide (450 metres by 170 metres). Within the ditch, the complex was subdivided by further ditches, perhaps for control and penning of livestock, and by a large trackway about 11 to 13 yards (10 to 12 metres) wide which may have been used to lead animals to areas of grazing beyond. Animal bones indicate that cattle were kept predominantly for ploughing and survived to a good age; sheep were kept until they were two years old and then butchered for meat. The dominant arable product was wheat, although significant quantities of barley and oats were also grown. Other parts of the site were used for small-scale smithing and leatherworking. Although the main dwelling was not located, the site included a small timber chapel and a cemetery with nearly 700 burials. It is tempting to see the large green at Harlton as a similar site, with manor and church located in close proximity to the green, with arable fields lying beyond.

Leaseland

Leaseland was the third form of land tenure in the later Anglo-Saxon period and might be identified in DB in, for example, the record of a man who 'could not withdraw' from a holding or a holding which 'could not be withdrawn' from a lord's jurisdiction. Leased holdings were not alienable – they could not usually be sold or granted away by the lessee, unless the new holder was also a sokeman of the landowner.[62] Lessees were personally subject to the jurisdiction (*soca*) of the landowner, who had full rights (*saca*) over the land itself – they were therefore 'sokemen'.[63] This is consistent with the view that 'a notice of freedom to go with land and the like is in effect a record of subordination to a booklord' although 'during the term of a lease, its results were not distinguishable from those of a permanent grant'.[64] In all, 11 per cent of the hidated land of the valley seems to have been leaseland in 1066. Thirty-two per cent of the fifty-eight holdings were constrained by the right to withdraw, and 26 per cent of the 146 men whose status was known held leaselands. The relatively low proportion of land held as leaseland in the mid-eleventh century suggests that neither the many holdings nor the multiplicity of freemen in the valley at that time had their origins in leaseholds. Miller also concluded that leaseland 'looks rather like a new category of landholding' in this period.[65] In Aston's view, leasehold was one of the 'major factors in the long- no less than short-term fragmentation of manors', but this

---

62. Roffe, *Domesday*, p. 34.
63. VCH I, p. 349.
64. Aston, 'Origins of the Manor', p. 22.
65. Miller, *Bishopric of Ely*, p. 57.

Table 6.3 Percentages of royal demesne, bookland, leaseland and warland in the Bourn Valley in 1066

	Hides (total = 101 hides 3 virgates)	Percentage of total hidage
Royal demesne	12.5 hides	12.2
Royal leaseland	2 hides 1 virgate 15 acres	2.3
Total royal land	14 hides 3 virgates 15 acres	14.6
Bookland (excluding royal demesne)	22 hides 2 virgates 20 acres	22.2
Leaseland (excluding royal land)	9 hides 26 acres	9.1
Total book and lease land	31 hides 3 virgates 16 acres	31.3
Warland (incl. 2½ hides royal leaseland[1])	21 hides 3 virgates 13 acres	21.4
Land held by freemen and not so far accounted for	35½ hides 16 acres	35
Probable total warland	55 hides 12 acres	55.1

Notes: 1. *DB*, 17:4 and 32:2.

process seems only to have been beginning in the twelve parishes in the eleventh century.[66] The owners of land leased in 1066 were the same group of royal officials or senior members of the royal court who held bookland estates here. Leaseland was evidently simply that part of their estates which was not farmed in demesne. In some cases, as for example in Earl Waltheof's lands in Caldecote, these non-demesne areas were leased out to local farmers in their entirety.[67] In other cases the leased holdings were so small – like that of 10 acres leased by Waltheof in Kingston – that they may represent the loss of freedom over a holding by its owner, for reasons we cannot now discern.[68] Nevertheless, the accelerating process of fission of bookland estates by grant or lease from the tenth century onwards is illustrated by the history of the estate of 10 hides at Toft/Hardwick granted to Wulfwin at some date before 975, when they were given to the Abbey of Ely. The Abbey still held the two parishes as a single estate in 1035 when they paid a week's *feorm*.[69] By 1066, however, almost all its holdings in Toft had been sold or granted away: 2 hides, 1 virgate and 8 acres had gone to Edeva, 1 hide and 4 acres was held by a freeman with full rights over it, and a further 1½ hides and 6 acres had been leased to six sokemen. Only Hardwick continued to form part of the Abbey's demesne holdings.[70]

Holdings identified as warland, bookland and leaseland account for about two-thirds of the twelve parishes in 1066. However, the men who held the remaining third also paid the *geld* and had full rights of *soca* and *saca*. There is no

66. Aston, 'Origins of the Manor', p. 22.
67. DB 39:1.
68. DB 25:8.
69. Hart, 'Land Tenure', p. 85; LE, pp. 152–3.
70. DB 14:48, 32:22, 44:2.

evidence that they held their land as bookland, and it was not leaseland. It can therefore only have originated as land once belonging to the community at large, whether or not it was subject to warland duties (Table 6.3). 'Some free holdings', according to Faith, 'represent the unmanorialised peasant economy of the warland farmer.'[71] This last third, together with the warland holdings which rendered duties of carriage and escort, accounts for 54 per cent of land here in 1066, inhabited by men, nearly three-quarters of whom were freemen. The independent, unmanorialised character of these holdings and their free status have more in common with the men who belonged to the clans and kinship groups of the sixth and seventh centuries than the villeins, dependent on their lords in and after 1086.[72]

The social function of escort and carriage duties

The warland holdings in the Bourn Valley to which services were still attached in 1066 share other, less formal but nevertheless distinctive characteristics, which make most of them easily identifiable in the Domesday account: there was at least one holding in almost every parish which rendered these services; at least one of these warland holdings in each parish was held collectively by five or more men; in most cases the number of escort and carriage duties that they owed was exactly the same as the number of men on the holding. There were just ten of these holdings in 1066 and eight of them were larger than 1 hide. Their average hidated acreage was generally low, at between 11 and 30 acres. Yet 62 per cent of the 175 freemen of the valley were associated with them. Furthermore, of the 109 men whose commendations are known, 82 were commended to the king. Perhaps warland holdings performed another function than simply their duties of carriage and escort?

Economic benefit does not seem an obvious motive for taking on a warland holding, since they seem to have been relatively small. Furthermore, the 51 men owing escort duties in the valley will have incurred some disproportionate expenses in supplying a horse – even 'any old nag' – from an arable holding of between 11 and 30 hidated acres, even if some of them did not derive their principal income from arable farming.[73] They may well have had other holdings in the valley, perhaps of greater value and in relation to which they were likely to have

---

71. Faith, *English Peasantry*, p. 207.
72. Ibid., pp. 216–7.
73. DB 1:16 and 29:12; a riding horse found at a late Anglo-Saxon manorial site at Cherry Hinton in Cambridgeshire had survived to twenty years, but showed signs of excessive riding at a young age; Cessford and Dickens, 'Manor of Hintona', p. 61.

been commended to other lords, in order to bear the expense of escort duties. This is not unlikely. In 1279, for example, local farmers commonly held portfolios of property from a number of different lords, some as freehold, some as customary land.74 The clue to the unusual characteristics of warland holdings and perhaps to their local survival into the eleventh century, emerges in a comparison of the commendations of men rendering warland duties with those men who did not. Ninety-eight of the 175 freemen in the valley were commended to the king – three-quarters of those performing warland services – but only four men who did not provide carriage and escort were similarly commended.

The combination of the small size of individual warland holdings, the cost of supplying the service, together with the almost unique access to commendation to the king apparently provided by these warland acres, may mean that local men used these holdings to gain access to status and protection through a personal contact with, at best, the king or, at very least, a member of the royal household. While on the one hand they played an important role in the running of the royal estate and thus undertook duties that took them away from their own farms, on the other hand the contact that these duties allowed with the king or his entourage may have made this burden worthwhile. In Faith's view,

> the riding men's distinct status was more than simply a matter of wealth, it had also to do with personal service of a responsible kind that brought them closely in touch with the great figures they served. A supply of trusted people like this was essential to the running of a large estate.75

The suggestion that commendation to the king was particularly associated with warland duties in the Bourn Valley is especially interesting because personal relationships with the royal household derived from the period of early Anglo-Saxon kingship, when kings surrounded themselves with unmarried fighting men who received warland homesteads when they married.76 The close relationship between freemen, hidated land and military service may indicate a wider significance to the name *fferdmanweye* for the Roman road (the present A603) in Little Eversden, which survived into the sixteenth century (the *fyrd* was the Anglo-Saxon army).77 Since 73 per cent of the 146 men whose status can be inferred from DB had rights of *soca* and *saca* over their land and paid the *geld* upon it, it can be inferred that a similarly high proportion of these men would have had the right and the obligation to join the *fyrd*.

The physical landscape of the Bourn Valley during the later Anglo-Saxon

---

74. Rot. Hund. ii, pp. 510–29.
75. Faith, *English Peasantry*, p. 108.
76. Abels, 'Bookland and Fyrd Service'.
77. CUL QC13/3.

period has become familiar through the earlier chapters of this book – greens and commons, ancient hedges, ditches and rights of way, the introduction of common fields. Through this evidence we can almost glimpse the valley as it was seen by the freemen who managed and cultivated it around the period of the Norman Conquest. They looked to the royal estate centre at Haslingfield for contact with the court, they took their horses to ride alongside the sheriff when he required it, or transported goods to and fro on behalf of the king, and rode out to the *fyrd* along the main road between Wimpole and Cambridge. Each man, every time he rode out from his holding, looked out across his fields, attended the hundred court or tended his horse, would have been aware of the social networks and relationships which underpinned this activity – connections with his commended lord, very probably the king; his relationship with the king's representative in the valley to whom he reported; and the interplay between these associations, his family's holding and its history, and his and his family's relationships and standing with the other freemen of the valley. The roads, settlements, fields and pastures of the physical landscape were mnemonics reminding him of his local, regional and national place.

Conclusion: the landscape

The evidence for freemen's holdings in the Bourn Valley suggests that some elements of the relationships between eighth-century kings, their households and the clans that provided their wider context, still lingered in the valley in 1066, in the quantity of warland that still existed, in the number of freemen who occupied it, and in the ways in which it was manipulated by these men to gain personal access to the king. The evidence for manors and bookland estates discussed above suggests that the longevity of the extensive estate that controlled the valley in the seventh or eighth centuries preserved forms of social relationships initially developed in the *regiones* or clan territories of the sixth and seventh centuries. The estate itself may have remained intact as late as the mid-tenth century, the process of fission accelerating thereafter. It was, however, a form of social organisation which was, like the freemen who inhabited it, becoming increasingly archaic by the mid-eleventh century. It is unlikely that contemporaries were unaware of the growing emphasis on manorial control across England as a whole. They probably noticed how surrounding lords like Aelmer or the Abbey of Ely, 'farmed their inlands using the regular labour of their inland workforce of bordars, slaves and *geburs*' and the contrast between the conditions of tenure of these dependent tenants and their freedoms may have been a sharp one.[78]

78. Faith, *English Peasantry*, p. 176.

The substantial peasant families of the eleventh century cultivated independent freeholdings set in a landscape of communally managed greens and commons which had perhaps originated four or five centuries earlier. Social and tenurial conservatism was expressed in conservatism towards implementing large-scale change in the landscape as the process of extending the selions and furlongs of the proto-common field across the valley gathered momentum. The role of these men in implementing this change may be analogous to that of similar groups of landholders who were responsible for undertaking the process of parliamentary enclosure in the valley and beyond, although the analogy should not be pushed too far. When the Eversdens were enclosed in 1811, for example, the surveyor drew up an enclosure map which showed little relationship between the straight boundaries of the proposed allotments and the boundaries and divisions of the medieval furlongs that they replaced. Lord Hardwicke, for example, received an allotment whose generally geometric boundaries were typical of enclosure and made little reference to the pre-enclosure landscape except where they followed parish boundaries. Yet over seventy years later, the Ordnance Survey's first large-scale edition tells a different story (Figure 6.4).[79] Within the borders of Lord Hardwicke's allotment, many post-enclosure field boundaries preserve the sinuous curve of medieval ploughing. It seems that his tenants reused medieval alignments – hedges, ditches or headlands – wherever they could in setting out the post-enclosure fields. The enclosure map defined radical changes in tenure, but it had less impact on the physical process of land division, which tended to be more conservative. This example highlights the obvious distinction between the surveyor, from outside the parish, who planned the new post-enclosure order and those, part of a long local farming tradition, who implemented his plans on the ground.

A similar process may have resulted in the reuse of pre-medieval field boundaries when the mature common fields were introduced from the later Anglo-Saxon period onwards. Practically, it is difficult to understand how the change from the boundaries of pre-common-field agriculture to the selions, furlongs and fields of early medieval cultivation could have been undertaken unless there was at least some continuity between field boundaries of the earlier system and those of the new, since cultivation could not be halted for the months and, perhaps, years it may have taken before the process was judged to be complete. Cultivation certainly continued throughout the process of parliamentary enclosure, which was timed to cause the least disruption, generally taking place either between December and March when there was little pressing agricultural

---

79. OS 1886, 1903 edn.

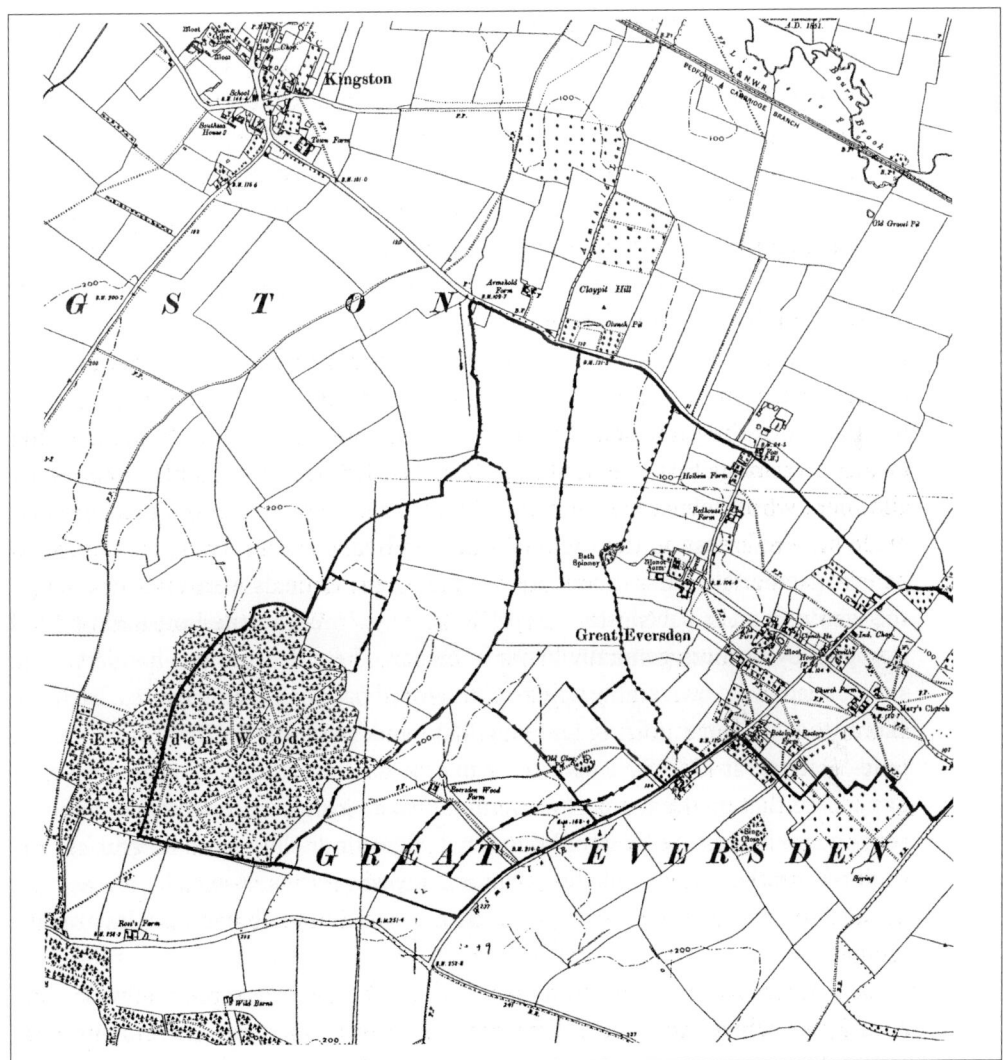

Figure 6.4 Medieval field-divisions conserved in the hedges of the post-enclosure landscape of Great Eversden in 1886 (Ordnance Survey 1886 with additions). The solid lines are those of Lord Hardwicke's allotment at enclosure in 1811; the dotted lines show the boundary between ancient enclosures and arable land at the same date; and the dashed lines highlight medieval furlong boundaries reused in the subdivision of Lord Hardwicke's allotment

work or in the interval before harvest.[80] Even so, there was considerable disturbance to the cultivation of arable and the exploitation of pasture, and it is likely that similar disruption would have accompanied the creation of common-

---

80. Becket et al., 'Farming through Enclosure', p. 149.

field furlongs. New boundary ditches had to be dug; new hedges had to be planted and needed time to come to maturity.[81] Throughout this process, which could take several years (in the case of parliamentary enclosure, ten to fifteen years was not uncommon), the occupiers of selions ploughed and sowed their crops as best they could within the pre-enclosure arrangements until the moment of transition.

There is no evidence for the practical methods adopted by the farmers who implemented the introduction of mature common-field layouts in the Bourn Valley or elsewhere. However, the similarities in crops, in much cultivation technology and in many cultivation methods between late Anglo-Saxon farmers and unmechanised early nineteenth-century farmers may mean that at least some of the forces acting on each group within the same landscape may have been the same. An additional pressure on Anglo-Saxon farmers, presumably not experienced to such an intense degree by those of the nineteenth century, would have been the absolute necessity to ensure each year's harvest in an economy that had restricted access to other sources of grain. With these reservations in mind, let us explore the following model. Before the common fields were extended across the whole of each parish, the rural landscape of most of the Bourn Valley was occupied by farmers generally living in dispersed farmsteads and hamlets, each surrounded by its own arable fields and enclosed paddocks and pastures; each had access to communal grazing and woodland and, perhaps, to the proto-common field. Hedges and ditches divided arable areas from those open to livestock. Supposing that the transition to a common-field layout was undertaken between sowing and harvest, redundant boundary hedges or ditches could be grubbed out or filled in without too much disturbance to growing crops. New field, furlong and selion boundaries could be laid out at the same time, but might involve the destruction of crops already growing and an associated potential loss of food and income, as well as the labour and other costs already invested in cultivating and sowing these pieces of land. The reuse of existing boundaries, where they were useful, would minimise this loss and would have the additional advantage that only the land underlying those old hedges and ditches that had been grubbed up or filled in would be barren of crops, rather than both that land and any land on which new boundaries had been constructed.

This model allows for complexity: for some continuity of existing boundaries, for some reuse of relict boundaries where they survived as hedges, ditches or earthworks in grassland, and for some completely new layouts. It does not depend on medieval fields being created either as a single event or by piecemeal accretion. Such an approach would also be consistent with the survival into the early

---

81. Ibid., pp. 144–5.

medieval period of prehistoric boundaries and early Anglo-Saxon commonable pastures. The model raises, but does not answer, the question as to why this process, which conserved very old land divisions and ancient greens and commons, should have occurred in the Bourn Valley, when it did not occur in other similar parts of the Central Province. It is Faith's view that 'where the warland peasantry had retained more autonomy, perhaps too where pressure on land was lightest, an older regime of shared rights in land persisted, becoming associated with the other "free" characteristics of the warland, and eventually becoming itself a sign of free tenure'.[82] The valley appears to conform to this conclusion in many ways (although it was an area of high, rather than low, population), particularly in its shared rights in non-arable land, and this may have been a key attribute that local men were keen to protect. For example, Chapter 3 has shown that at least some elements in the landscape appear to have been communally managed long before the introduction of the common fields. The common grazing provided by the Offals is one example; the wood pasture and some of the river meadows in Caxton may be another, since they share the common element *swān* 'peasant': Swansley (*lēah* 'wood pasture') Wood in the north of the parish and Swansom (*holmr* 'meadow') Furlong near the Bourn Brook in the south.[83]

One explanation for the preservation of these ancient elements may have been the expression in the landscape of a conservatism born of the apparently unusual structures of landholding and society explored above. It was argued there that a royal extensive estate, derived from one or more earlier clan territories, may have been created in the Bourn Valley in the eighth century. By the mid-eleventh century, the number and condition of the many freemen of the valley suggests that some very old-fashioned social and landholding customs had been preserved in an estate that was itself slow to change. It was this archaism, it was suggested, that explained the fact that 77 per cent of the men of the Bourn Valley enjoyed full rights over their land, that the warland origins of about 55 per cent of the land of the valley were still identifiable, and that at least some of the surviving warland was manipulated by local men to gain personal access to the king and his court.

It is possible that the conservatism of local society in the Bourn Valley – of which the retention of pre-common-field boundaries may have been the physical

---

82. Faith, *English Peasantry*, p. 137.
83. Reaney, *Cambridgeshire*, p. 157; CUL EDR/H1. Reaney suggested that 'swan', the bird, might be a more likely interpretation, although early forms of these names make it impossible to choose between 'peasant' and 'swan': Ibid. His conclusion was based on the combination of *swan* and *holmr* in Swansom Furlong. However, had he known that Swansley Wood and Swansom Furlong were at opposite ends of the parish, he might have favoured 'peasant', particularly since 70 per cent of the hidated land of the parish was controlled by freemen in 1066: DB 26:42.

expression – resulted from the longevity here of a loosely regulated royal estate in a backwater on the periphery of Mercia before 870 and a long way from Wessex in the tenth century. It can be assumed that, as long as the valley provided its expected renders to the royal household, it escaped very much notice. A correlation between high numbers of freemen and the preservation of elements of earlier landscapes in common-field landscapes cannot, however, in itself be regarded as more than one factor in many in finding a solution to this complex problem. In the heart of the Central Province, in Leicestershire for example, high numbers of freemen were documented in DB and yet this is an area in which pre-common-field boundaries and ancient greens do not occur, as far as is known.[84] Nor is this correlation found in Hertfordshire where most surviving 'co-axial' landscapes are in the south and west, while the highest numbers of sokemen in DB were found in the north and east.[85] In south-east Suffolk, large numbers of sokemen lived within a large estate that may have been part of the dowry of the seventh-century East Anglian princess Æthelthryth.[86] But, while Warner has argued that this area 'contains sufficient archaeological and etymological evidence to suggest a degree of continuity with the Roman past', it is an area in which pre-medieval landscapes have not so far been discovered.[87]

In the Bourn Valley, conditions of landholding, of royal ownership and of the original status of land were each old-fashioned by the tenth century and may have combined to encourage the retention of archaic elements in the physical landscape. In other areas, a preponderance of sokemen over freemen, of estates that had largely disintegrated by the tenth century, and of bookland and leaseland rather than warland, may have led to quite different influences on landscape formation even though a high density of 'sokemen' in DB may imply superficial similarities between these areas. Different patterns of land use in the period after the withdrawal of Roman administration in 410 and before the introduction of common-field agriculture may have been another important factor. Roberts and Wrathmell, for example, have suggested that areas in the Central Province that reverted to or continued to be used as woodland or wood pasture in the fifth and sixth centuries may have experienced very different patterns of land use during the middle and later Anglo-Saxon periods compared with those that remained largely ploughed, and this may in turn have impacted on the way in which common fields were introduced.[88] The proportion of land in the Bourn Valley that was apparently

---

84. Dodgshon, 'Early Middle Ages', Figure 4.2 left.
85. Williamson, *Hertfordshire*, pp. 147 and 157–61.
86. M. Hesse, personal communication; Warner, 'Pre-Conquest Territorial and Administrative Organisation', p. 21.
87. Ibid., p. 15; Dymond and Martin, *Historical Atlas of Suffolk*, pp. 41–2.
88. Roberts and Wrathmell, *Atlas*, p. 34.

used for intensively grazed pasture just before the introduction of the mature common fields may provide just such a factor for explaining the survival of these elements here and not elsewhere in the Central Province. The prehistoric linear boundaries in the valley offered a relatively regular physical framework and could be utilised and amended quite easily. In many parts of the valley, new boundaries would only need to have been set out in those restricted areas where land was taken into arable cultivation from areas of wood pasture or woodland for the first time, that is, where the linear boundaries had either never existed or did not survive. This is certainly consistent with the evidence from Chapters 2 and 4 which appears to demonstrate that there is indeed least evidence for linear land divisions in the valley in the vicinity of ancient woodland and the strongest correlation between the survival of these ancient alignments and areas of pasture or early arable.

The medieval landscape of the Bourn Valley demonstrates gradual change within an existing physical framework as well as shorter 'moments' of transition between pre-common-field and common-field arrangements. It captures in its hedges, banks, ditches and rights of way the complexity of its agricultural history, its social and tenurial structure, demography, existing agricultural practices and the physical limitations imposed by geology, relief and drainage, in regions at a distance from centres of direct royal authority.

7

Conclusions

The origins of common fields and their furlongs in the Bourn Valley, their relationship with the landscapes that preceded them and the role played by administrative and tenurial structures in their survival raise a number of more general questions for the origins of the medieval landscape in the Central Province: the reuse in boundaries and subdivisions of the common fields of earlier hedges, ditches and other barriers; the processes through which common fields were introduced; the implications for settlement – particularly the shift from dispersed farms and hamlets to nucleated settlement; and whether it was communities or lords who took the lead in initiating common-field cultivation.

Reuse of earlier landscape features

The survival of prehistoric or Roman field boundaries through the early and middle Anglo-Saxon periods was, of course, an essential prerequisite for their reuse in common-field layouts. There is, indeed, no evidence for any major reorganisation of arable fields anywhere in England between the withdrawal of Roman administration in the early fifth century and the introduction of the common fields 300 or 400 years later. Where arable cultivation continued to be practised between the fifth and the ninth centuries, succeeding generations generally worked within the same land divisions until the fully developed common fields were introduced. Where there was abandonment of arable cultivation in favour of pasture in the fifth and sixth centuries, ditches and banks would be likely to be preserved as grassy earthworks.[1] Hedges for controlling the movement of stock were as useful to pastoral farmers as to those whose income was predominantly derived from arable cultivation. Early and middle Anglo-Saxon

---

1. For example, Bell, 'Environmental Archaeology, pp. 275 and 278; Carver, 'Kinship and Material Culture', p. 142; Rackham, 'Trees and Woodland', p. 8; Hamerow, 'Migration Theory', p. 174; Williamson, 'Early Co-Axial Fields'.

farmers cultivated fields first created in the prehistoric or Roman periods, 'taken over as going concerns by Saxon settlers', while 'Britons ... [continued] to farm their "ancient fields" well into the so-called Anglo-Saxon period'.[2]

Once common fields were introduced into the Central Province from the ninth century onwards, the fields created and cultivated by prehistoric or Roman farmers and their descendants are believed to have been almost universally destroyed to make way for selions and furlongs. Prehistoric or Roman fields generally survive in central and southern England only as marks in crops or on plough land, cut across and ignored by later field boundaries.[3] Almost the only examples of prehistoric or Roman fields which survive as earthworks lie outside the Central Province in areas that never experienced classic common-field agriculture.[4] In Somerset, for example, there was 'considerable continuity [of settlement and land units] from the Roman, through the Anglo-Saxon to the medieval periods with little evidence generally for disruption or major upheaval'.[5] Nevertheless, as outlined in Chapter 1, in the Central Province there is a little evidence – generally regarded as atypical – for continuity from prehistoric and Roman landscapes into that of the common fields both from the central areas of classic common-field arrangements like Cambridgeshire, where common fields continued to be cultivated into the nineteenth century, and from areas where most common fields disappeared under late medieval and early modern enclosure, although these examples are believed to be the exceptions that prove the rule.[6]

The earthworks, ditches, lanes and hedges of the Bourn Valley, by contrast, demonstrate considerable reuse of prehistoric or Roman field boundaries in the common fields as boundaries between fields, furlongs or sometimes selions. The whole landscape of the valley appears to have been fully exploited from an early date and is likely to have been divided into fields and pastures long before the common fields were introduced. Romano-British farmsteads, for example, lay just a few hundred yards apart even on the heavy clay along the upper slopes of the valley.[7] The lack of evidence for wildwood here suggests that there was little reversion to woodland in the early and middle Anglo-Saxon periods. The common

2. Taylor and Fowler, 'Roman Fields', pp. 160–1.
3. For example, Addyman, 'Maxey'; Hall, *Medieval Fields*, p. 55; Unwin, 'Vills and Early Fields' and 'Anglo-Scandinavian Rural Settlement'; Rackham, *History of the Countryside*, p. 164; Hooke, 'Regional Variation'; Gelling, *West Midlands*, pp. 172–3.
4. For example, Drury and Rodwell, 'Asheldham'; Fleming, 'Dartmoor: Part 1' and 'Dartmoor: Part 2'; Williamson, 'Co-Axial Fields'; Roberts and Wrathmell, *Region and Place*, p. 144. See also Chapter 1 above.
5. Aston, 'Medieval Settlement', p. 229.
6. Taylor and Fowler, 'Roman Fields'; Bassett, 'Lichfield' and 'Goltho'.
7. Wessex Archaeology, Reference: 33220, Report 45970, Report 45977.1; Oakey, *Highfields, Caldecote*.

fields did not, therefore, colonise virgin tracts of the Bourn Valley, but replaced other fields and enclosures that had continued to be used throughout the Anglo-Saxon period and that had survived in hedges, ditches or earthworks.[8] There were, therefore, many opportunities for reuse of earlier land divisions in the layout of the common fields, and Chapter 4 has illustrated how widely these opportunities were taken up. The most dramatic example is that at Hardwick, where a low, curving bank across a modern field is all that remains of a common-field headland which itself follows the alignment of a Romano-British ditch (see Figure 4.6).[9]

The importance of the Bourn Valley to a debate in which most examples have been drawn from areas outside the Central Province or from areas within the Central Province that suffered late medieval or early modern enclosure, is that the alignment of many prehistoric and Roman boundaries was preserved in common fields which continued to be cultivated into the early to mid-nineteenth century when maps were drawn showing these features. For the first time, the argument for continuity of use of some field boundaries in the Central Province is supported on a large scale by physical as well as map evidence in an area in which medieval and post-medieval common-field cultivation followed the classic two- or three-field system until parliamentary enclosure. These parishes in the Bourn Valley were among the last in England to be enclosed by Act of Parliament.[10] Continuity of patterns of landscape use across millennia in the Bourn Valley may appear atypical at present, but it seems likely that other examples are likely to be found across the Central Province. Here, where the process of transition from one form of arable organisation to another is briefly and incompletely illuminated, it seems that patterns of cultivation and tenure rather than the pattern of fields were substantially changed by the introduction of the common-field system.

Modelling the processes of common-field introduction

Christopher Taylor has characterised the introduction of common fields as 'the second great revolution in the English landscape'.[11] The first revolution was that of the later Bronze Age, when large tracts of land were subdivided by long, parallel ditches, hedges and walls, 'a consciously planned reorganisation on a vast scale'.[12] The second revolution was of a similar magnitude: it covered much of the Central Province, and the fields, furlongs and selions were details within a large-scale, deliberately designed, layout.

8. See Wessex Archaeology, Report 45977.1, p. 11.
9. Chapter 4 above, p. 83.
10. Tate, *Cambridgeshire Field Systems*, p. 61.
11. Hoskins, *Making of the English Landscape*, p. 41.
12. Ibid.

Models for common-field creation in the mid-twentieth century tended to centre on the piecemeal clearance of furlongs from woods or pastures, as uncultivated areas were gradually brought into arable production. The example of Leighton Bromswold has already been cited as an example of a long process in which smaller and then larger furlongs were assarted from woods, waste or pasture to become arable fields, as the population of a vill increased.[13] This explanation depends heavily on the characterisation of the Anglo-Saxon landscape as wooded and relatively empty, a view that was a fair interpretation of known evidence at the time. Hoskins, for example, in his seminal *Making of the English Landscape* described how 'each field covered perhaps a few score acres to begin with, but every decade and generation added to their area by clearing the woodland and other wild ground around their circumference'.[14] Common fields were, it was thought, created from scratch around new settlements, clearings in the forest where isolated groups of Anglo-Saxons hacked at the wildwood. This explanation became increasingly difficult to sustain as archaeologists and landscape historians began to find more evidence during the 1970s and 1980s of survival of Romano-British culture and landscapes into the Anglo-Saxon period, and of a late Roman population which was substantially higher than had previously been conjectured. For the first time, scholars had to confront the possibility that the English landscape was as exploited during the Roman period (and earlier) as it is today. This led to problems in attempts to explain the origins of the common fields. There were undoubtedly some areas – such as Rockingham Forest in Northamptonshire or the wolds of west Huntingdonshire, of which Bromswold is a part – where woodland regeneration had occurred after the end of the Roman period.[15] Here, the common fields were likely to have grown relatively organically, one furlong gradually added after another, while pastoralism continued to play an important part in the local economy.

There are now, however, many examples from Northamptonshire, northern Cambridgeshire, Oxfordshire and Yorkshire of places where common-field cultivation seems to have been introduced across the whole landscape of a vill in a single, brief, impressive event.[16] At Middleton, in North Yorkshire, for example, 'the whole parish seems to have been laid out in two massive blocks with curved strips, preserved in the modern hedge lines, up to 2,000 metres (2,200 yards) long'.[17] These are all parts of England in which there is relatively little evidence for

13. Roberts, *English Village*, pp. 49–51; see Chapter 5 above, p. 91–5.
14. Hoskins, *Making of the English Landscape*, p. 45.
15. Fox, 'Wolds', p. 50; Roberts and Wrathmell, *Region and Place*, p. 77.
16. Hall, 'Late Saxon Topography', p. 64; Harvey, 'Planned Field Systems'; Hall, *Northamptonshire*, pp. 131–5; Hall, 'Distribution and Change', p. 45; Pocock, 'First Fields', 1968.
17. Hall, *Medieval Fields*, pp. 48–9.

Anglo-Saxon woodland, and it seems likely that the landscape in these areas was more or less fully exploited during the early and middle Anglo-Saxon periods.[18] Roberts and Wrathmell have noted that 'the main concentrations [of early Anglo-Saxon cemeteries] coincide broadly with those areas that in late Anglo-Saxon times were characterised by a greater proportion of open land to woodland: in the zone that later developed as the Central Province'.[19] In these areas, the introduction of common-field cultivation may simply have been a different way of organising land already under the plough.

The evidence from the Bourn Valley discussed in Chapters 4 and 5 implies that the processes by which common fields were introduced across the Central Province may have been yet more varied. Here, common fields were introduced in at least two phases: in the first phase, perhaps in the eighth or ninth centuries, a proto-common field was laid out across the southern third of at least four parishes, preserving in subordinate boundaries between furlongs and selions, the prehistoric land divisions which it overlay. In the second phase, the proto-common-field core was extended across almost all the remaining land within each vill. The work was carried out by communities acting independently within their own boundaries – there is no indication of any collaboration between neighbours in co ordinating the alignment of furlong boundaries across the administrative boundaries that divided them (later parish boundaries). This implies that by the time the second phase of common-field creation was being undertaken, each vill had become tenurially, administratively, ecclesiastically and agriculturally independent of its neighbours. The independence of each community indicates that the extension of the common fields was begun after the fragmentation of the middle Anglo-Saxon extensive estate was complete, a process that was certainly underway by the mid-tenth century and concluded by 1086, when each community was recorded in DB. The common fields had reached their greatest extent by about 1300, and the second phase was therefore probably undertaken between the tenth and the thirteenth centuries. Many of the furlong boundaries that formed the dominant framework within each parish were laid out along the banks, hedges and ditches of pre-existing land divisions, some perhaps still in use, others perhaps surviving as earthworks, but nevertheless fossilising prehistoric alignments which had first been constructed at least 1,000 years earlier. The two phases suggested for the development of common-field arrangements in the

---

18. Roberts and Wrathmell, *Atlas*, p. 31 and *Region and Place*, p. 124; Gray's seminal distribution map of medieval two- and three-field systems defined the Central Province nearly a century ago: Gray, *English Field Systems*, frontispiece.
19. Roberts and Wrathmell, *Region and Place*, p. 75.

Bourn Valley offer another model for the origins of common fields, particularly in the proto-common field. This, together with the occurrence of characteristics of ancient *and* champion landscape in west Cambridgeshire, indicates how unlikely it is that common fields had a single origin or were developed by a common process, even within the boundaries of the Central Province. Instead, multiple and multi-factor explanations for the introduction of common fields seem more probable.

Implications for the origins of medieval settlement

It is commonly accepted among archaeologists and landscape historians that early and middle Anglo-Saxon settlement was predominantly dispersed, taking the form of hamlets or farmsteads which shifted periodically within the territories in which they lay.[20] It is also generally agreed that the change from a dispersed to a nucleated pattern of settlement occurred in the Central Province between the mid-eighth and late twelfth centuries.[21] In Leicestershire, for example, 'it is virtually certain that this major change from a dispersed to a nucleated landscape took place between about AD 700 and 900;'[22] middle Anglo-Saxon sites in Northamptonshire were deserted by AD 850;[23] and in Hampshire 'farmsteads, hamlets and possibly cemeteries were commonly abandoned … in the middle Anglo-Saxon period'.[24] The evidence cited above is drawn from excavation as well as from distributions of concentrations of Anglo-Saxon pottery during field-walking. David Hall has suggested that the process resulted from the creation of the common fields, as his extensive field-walking discovered no pottery later than the mid-ninth century under the common fields of Northamptonshire, and this suggestion has been widely confirmed and accepted.[25] Hamerow, in her recent review of the literature, proposes that the process is related to the long process of intensification of agriculture in the seventh and eighth centuries during which arable cultivation moved from the easier soils of the river valleys to the heavier soils of the upper slopes.[26] These are clearly important issues in the context of the Bourn Valley where, for the first time, there is physical evidence in the huge, intensively cultivated, proto-common field for increased specialisation in arable

---

20. For example, Foard, 'Systematic Fieldwalking', p. 367; Bellamy, 'Anglo-Saxon Dispersed Sites'; RCHM(E), *North-East Northamptonshire*, for example, pp. 7, 21, 62, 72, 92.
21. For example, Taylor, *Village and Farmstead*, pp. 130–1; Hamerow, *Early Medieval Settlements*, pp. 120–4.
22. Liddle, 'Medbourne', p. 35; Knox, 'Anglo-Saxons in Leicestershire', p. 103.
23. Brown and Foard, 'Saxon Landscape', p. 76.
24. Klingelhöfer, *Manor, Hundred and Vill*, p. 24.
25. Hall, 'Late Saxon Countryside', pp. 100–3.
26. Hamerow, *Early Medieval Settlements*, pp. 122–3.

cultivation during the late eighth or ninth centuries, raising questions about the relationship between field layout and settlement.

Archaeological evidence for Anglo-Saxon settlement is generally sparse in the Bourn Valley. Excavations have found evidence for early Anglo-Saxon settlements both in the river valley at Grantchester and on the high boulder clays across the northern section of the parish boundary between Caxton and Bourn, suggesting that the clay-topped plateaux were not abandoned by settlement in this period, from which one might infer that the whole valley continued to be occupied.[27] Although there is no evidence to indicate the form of this settlement, it seems very likely to have been dispersed, by analogy with the evidence from other parts of the Central Province. If this is the case, then at least some hamlets and farmsteads lay within the area later covered by the proto-common field, particularly since this large infield overlay the more tractable lands of each parish, and the lower spring line. What happened to these sites when the new furlongs were laid out? The continuity of alignment of each of the long, narrow commons across the proto-common field indicates relatively little disruption from settlement at the time that it was created or later and suggests that any settlement that predated the infield was abandoned at the time the proto-common field was laid out (although there is no reason why dispersed settlements that lay outside the proto-common field should not have continued to be occupied).

None of the medieval settlements of the Bourn Valley demonstrate any evidence of occupation before the eleventh century at the earliest, although investigation is impeded by modern buildings and gardens.[28] The medieval settlement at Hardwick, as we have seen, seems to be a deliberate foundation of the early or mid-eleventh century by the Abbey of Ely; planned settlements at both Eversden and Comberton appear to have been laid out immediately following the Norman Conquest; post-medieval settlement at Toft has simply 'rolled over' onto its common fields; and the location of the eleventh-century churches at Harlton and Haslingfield implies that the clustering of contemporary settlement around the edges of the very large greens in those parishes did not become intensive until after the Norman Conquest. From this, one might infer that the process of development of later Anglo-Saxon settlement in the valley went through several stages: it was dispersed before the proto-common field was laid out across the southern third of the northern valley slope; after the proto-common field was created, settlement underneath it was abandoned and the men and women who had lived in these farmsteads and hamlets moved their farms elsewhere (of which, more below); dispersed settlement continued to be occupied on the pastures and

---

27. Alexander and Trump, 'Grantchester'; Wessex Archaeology, Report 45977.1, p. 11.
28. Oosthuizen, 'Medieval Settlement Relocation', and Chapter 3 above.

moors north of the proto-common field; in the eleventh century planned nucleations began to be laid out and by the end of the twelfth century almost every settlement in the valley showed some signs of formal planning, sometimes in several phases. The period that interests us here is that between the abandonment of settlement under the proto-common field and the creation of planned settlements in the years around and after the Norman Conquest.

Such slight evidence as exists suggests that the planned settlements of the eleventh century were preceded by relatively informal, loose nucleations on areas of pasture or meadow. At Comberton, for example, the properties around the church share a common curvilinear external boundary. This land belonged to nine freemen before 1066 and it seems very likely that this was the site of their settlement – perhaps informally nucleated around a narrow green, a southward extension of Comberton Offal towards the Bourn Brook.[29] At Toft, the church and earthworks of deserted medieval settlement are each located on relatively small areas of meadow. At Great Eversden there is tension between planned settlement lying along Wimpole Road, almost certainly post-Conquest in origin, and that around the parish church, where the location of late medieval farmhouses implies another, less formal, settlement focus around a large area of common pasture.[30] This seems, too, to have been the pattern at Harlton and Haslingfield, already referred to above. In this the pre-Conquest settlements of the Bourn Valley are similar to that at Chalton in Hampshire, where middle Anglo-Saxon settlement 'was in an area of Romano-British pasture surrounded by arable', and to those settlements in Northamptonshire which predated the planning of the eleventh century and which were 'very close to later villages but apparently of a formless nature and unrelated in morphology to the subsequent layout'.[31] Later work, also in Northamptonshire, has resulted in the suggestion that settlement nucleation occurred in two phases: the first phase, in or soon after the mid-ninth century, may or may not have involved planning; the second, in or after the tenth century, certainly did include elements of settlement planning.[32] This seems also to have been the case in the Bourn Valley and, for the first time, the relationship between planned settlement and common field begins to emerge a little more clearly. It is proposed here that the creation of the proto-common field led to the abandonment of dispersed settlement in the area of the new infield, and that those who were displaced relocated themselves in informal clusters around areas of pasture or meadow. Thereafter the development of common fields and planned

29. Oosthuizen, 'Medieval Settlement Relocation'.
30. Ibid.
31. Bell, 'Environmental Archaeology, p. 278; Taylor, *Village and Farmstead*, p. 122.
32. Brown and Foard, 'Saxon Landscape', p. 76.

settlement seem to have occurred relatively independently: the common fields were gradually extended across most of the land of each parish from the eleventh century onwards. Although planned settlements also began to appear in the valley from the eleventh century onwards, these new foundations were laid out across existing common-field furlongs and there is no necessary relationship between settlement planning and common-field creation, existing nucleated settlements forming an obvious focus for the relocation of settlement gradually displaced by the encroachment of common fields. Only in Hardwick is the framework of settlement integrated with the layout of common fields and only here is there any suggestion that the creation of common field and the planting of planned settlement were connected processes. The evidence from the Bourn Valley offers some illumination, then, to the proposition that common fields and nucleated settlement are interlinked processes with a common origin.

Lord or community as the instigator of change

There is a substantial argument between scholars on the relative roles of lords and community in instigating changes in the landscape in the pre-Conquest and medieval periods. Some have argued that only lordly direction could have initiated and carried through the creation of common fields and the development of planned settlement, since the problems of engaging whole communities in such dramatic changes to their lives and livelihoods would have been insuperable otherwise. Hooke, for example, has suggested that the essentially conservative agricultural economy makes it unlikely that common-field cultivation would have been initiated by communities acting collectively, a view that will resonate with many parish councils.[33] Harvey, too, argues that 'lordship tended to be strongest in matters affecting the community as a whole'.[34] On the other hand, in north-west Bedfordshire 'a high proportion of free tenants were living in nucleated villages' in 1086, implying that settlement nucleation there was achieved by communal consent and cooperation.[35] Dyer, too, has argued that, since nucleated settlement and common fields often occurred in vills that were divided between several lords, communities must have been actively involved in laying out fields which united them all in common farming arrangements:

> Village communities, which were capable of taking on the management of manors as collective lessees in the eleventh century, may well have been involved in village

---

33. Hooke, Anglo-Saxon England, pp. 119–20.
34. Harvey, 'Initiative and Authority', p. 36.
35. Lewis et al., Village, Hamlet and Field, p. 209.

reorganisation. In which case the regularly planned village is evidence not of close seigniorial control, but of the limitations on the power of manorial lords, who had to deal with a strong and cohesive village community.[36]

This view is supported by the argument that, in the case of a vill divided between a number of manorial lords, consensus between lords would have been as necessary as consensus among villagers: 'If a committee of lords has to be envisaged, why not bring the tenants into the decision-making as well?'[37] The Bourn Valley offers a chance to explore the extremes of these arguments from the agency of the lord on the one hand to local communities of freemen on the other in instigating major changes in the landscape – first, in the creation of the proto-common field, and second, in the extension of the common fields across the remaining lands of each vill.

The proto-common field, probably created between about 700 and 900, lay across the southern third of four communities from Toft to Grantchester and appears to have been a single, intensively-cultivated infield. The implication follows that the labour it demanded and the crops it produced were shared at least between those four communities and perhaps more widely among all the communities of the valley which lay within the extensive estate controlled from Haslingfield, providing a common arable resource for the whole valley just as the Offals provided pasture. As Klingelhöfer has pointed out, 'a "community-wide" division of land use ... could only flourish in a period before the appearance of a discrete cooperative agricultural unit, the vill'.[38] The period within which the proto-common field was created was one which also saw the emergence of extensive estates, centred on high status 'great halls' such as those at Pennyland in Buckinghamshire or Flixborough in Lincolnshire, and this suggests that the period was one in which lordly intervention was the more likely cause for large-scale landscape change.[39] The extent of the proto-common field does nothing to contradict this, nor does the cohesion of the extensive estate in the Bourn Valley at the time. Earlier chapters have shown that the proto-common field and informal nucleations of the eighth and ninth centuries developed substantially before the disintegration of the middle Anglo-Saxon extensive estate into independent vills, even if local communities were identifiable within the estate. It therefore seems likely that, had each community been left to devise its own response to the increased pressures for greater grain production, a single infield running from

---

36. Dyer, 'Lords, Peasants', pp. 306–7.
37. Lewis et al., *Village, Hamlet and Field*, p. 208.
38. Klingelhöfer, *Manor, Hundred and Vill*, p. 23.
39. Hamerow, *Early Medieval Settlements*, pp. 98–9; Loveluck, 'Flixborough', pp. 146–61.

Grantchester to Toft would not have been created. Each group of local farmers would have been more likely to have laid out their own infield, even if the administrative boundaries that divided communities may not yet have been fully formalised. The unified layout of the proto-common field implies that it was designed by some higher authority that had the power to combine communities in a project in which their own landscapes played just a part at a time before the boundaries between them had become formally established. Some degree of local initiative is demonstrated in the integration of prehistoric cross-valley alignments in furlong or selion boundaries in the new arrangement. There is no evident physical reason why they should have been retained, except for the obvious pragmatic one of not duplicating effort. Their retention may signify their cultural, historical or sentimental value to the men who implemented the construction of the new infield. The retention of local features within a new landscape is unlikely to have been the concern of any central authority and seems more likely to have been the work of those already familiar with these acres, perhaps over many years and with the weight of family tradition behind them.

The later subdivision and extension of the proto-common field into classic two- and three-field cultivation across almost all the land of each parish offers another context within which to explore the degree to which lords or communities undertook significant changes in the landscape. There is no doubt that local freemen were capable of undertaking collective, cooperative ventures. The common fields of Eversden, for example, seem likely to have been created by the twenty-seven freemen of that parish before the Norman Conquest, when there was no manor in the vill. This conclusion is derived from the fact that, by the early nineteenth century, the parishes of Great and Little Eversden could not physically be distinguished from each other by the distribution of manorial land in each parish – the 'occupiers in each vill ... [held] land indifferently in both parishes'.[40] This confused pattern of landholding does not derive from the post-Conquest history of the parish: in 1086 the Eversdens were not distinguished and there was one very large manor consisting of 5 hides and 10 acres (610 hidated acres), two holdings each of 1 hide, and a further holding of 1 virgate.[41] The post-Conquest manorial history is unexceptional; indeed, the extent of the largest manor seems to have changed very little after it was created in 1066. By 1491, when it was sold to

---

40. VCH 5, p. 63.
41. DB 14:46; 26:37; 27:1; 31:7. Great Eversden appears to have been the original nucleated settlement in the parish, and both tenurial and landscape history indicate that Little Eversden was not set out as a separate settlement until the late twelfth or early thirteenth centuries.

Queens' College, Cambridge, it had grown by only 60 acres.[42] Terriers of land held by the College's tenants in the Eversdens show that the number and distribution of selions within each holding remained virtually static between 1491 and 1811. The confused pattern of landholding evident in the early nineteenth century is unlikely to be the result of assarts or transactions in land after the late fifteenth century.[43] If the common fields had been laid out after the Conquest, then it is more likely that the land of each of the Norman manorial lords would have been regularly dispersed and relatively easy to demarcate, as at Leighton Bromswold in Huntingdonshire.[44] The jumbled pattern of landholding in the Eversdens in 1811 only makes sense if the arable land of the two parishes had already been laid out in a single field system by 1066. If this were the case, the redistribution of the land of twenty-seven pre-Conquest freemen, each holding on average 12 to 120 acres, among four new Norman lords *would* have resulted in a confused pattern of landholding. A similar argument can be made for Kingston, where the manor of Picot, the Norman sheriff of Cambridgeshire, was derived from the holdings of fourteen sokemen and became the Kingston Wood estate, with its own field system and settlement focus. The northern third of the parish, centred on the parish church, was cultivated in common fields subdivided into furlongs and selions.[45] The separation of the lands of Kingston into discrete blocks after 1066 makes it likely that the lands that Picot assimilated into his barony were those of a subordinate settlement which might, in other circumstances, have evolved during the Middle Ages into a parish in its own right. Once again, pre-Conquest holdings were preserved in the medieval landscape and once again the common fields were already defined by a group of freemen before 1066. On the other hand, the analysis of Hardwick in Chapter 3 above offers an example in which a lordly hand, that of the Abbey of Ely, appears to have directed the layout of the early medieval landscape. In many cases the freemen of the valley were as intimately involved in

---

42. VCH 5, p. 6. The figure of 5 hides and 10-acre hides is based on the sum in DB of the entries for the antecessors of Guy de Raimbeaucourt (DB 31:7). It is 1 hide short of the total land with which he was credited (6 hides 10 acres), and it may just be possible that the additional hide was made up of royal woodland or pasture which was omitted from the royal account and added to this entry for whatever reason. Although the relationship between actual acres and hidated acres of arable is not known, the record of a land transaction in Chippenham between 970 and 984 shows that 'whatever the original relationship between the hide as a fiscal unit and the actual acres in the field, in tenth-century Chippenham men thought of it as a measurable unit of a hundred and twenty acres', to the extent that they were able to go out into the field to measure it: Spufford, *Chippenham*, p. 9.
43. CUL QC13 and QC15.
44. Roberts, *English Village*, pp. 49–51.
45. DB 1:8, 13:12, 14:47, 25:8, 26:38–9, 32:21.

the second phase of the creation of the common fields as in places where this work was directed by the manorial lord. The second phase of field creation, the extension of common-field furlongs across the slopes and pastures of the Bourn Valley, seems as likely to have been directed by each community as by the manorial lord (or lords) in each parish.

Last words

The fields, paths, boundaries and earthworks of the Bourn Valley preserve a rich history of landscape development stretching back over at least two millennia during which the land of the valley was continuously exploited. Portions of Iron Age land divisions and large tracts of Anglo-Saxon or earlier commons survived into the early nineteenth century in the classic two- and three-field arrangements of the Bourn Valley as earthworks or living boundaries and in grazed pasture. They have survived almost into living memory – 200 years can be spanned in just three generations, as shown by my great-great-uncle Oswin Bull who, as a child in the 1880s, sat on the knee of a man who had fought at the Battle of Waterloo, and on whose own knee I was in turn dandled in the mid-1960s. It is not difficult to imagine a similar oral history for the common fields of the Bourn Valley.

The continued use of prehistoric and Roman land divisions in the layout of the common fields may have been due, at least in part, to the survival of archaic patterns of landholding and social structure in the valley, which linked the freemen of the eleventh century with their ancestors of the seventh and eighth centuries. The preservation of archaic features in the landscape of the valley indicates that the distinction between ancient and champion landscapes may date back to the Roman period or earlier and suggests the development of many distinctive *pays* across southern England. The proto-common field, running along the contours from Grantchester to Toft, offers a new model for the origin of common-field arrangements in the eighth or ninth centuries and, for the first time, provides important physical evidence – some of which still survives – for the workings of the extensive estates thus far evidenced only in documents and place names.

The study of the Bourn Valley in west Cambridgeshire demonstrates how much regional studies of apparently insignificant areas can contribute to our understanding of the origins and development of fields and settlement in the rural medieval landscape. It is an ordinary landscape, cultivated for millennia, and its characteristics are unlikely to be unique. Nevertheless, its ordinariness has extended our understanding of the mechanisms involved in the creation and development of rural landscapes before the Norman Conquest through an examination of the ways in which fields were created and evolved over several hundred years. Its hedges, banks and rights of way do not preserve a relatively narrow period of use like the Dartmoor reaves or the deserted medieval settlements of the midlands, but those of many phases, accreted over a long time. That complexity is a strength. Century after century, local farmers have continued to settle and cultivate their lands within some existing features, abandoning others and creating yet new ones. This landscape is not a palimpsest, but something richer and more dynamic, a kaleidoscope, in whose constantly moving pattern elements of the old are preserved and contribute to the development of the new.

Appendix A: Key to Figure 4.1

Caxton
(a) St Peter Street, its extension towards Gransden and its extension as the boundary between Madledean and Breach Furlongs
(b) Church Way and field boundaries to its east
(c) Part of parish boundary between Caxton and Bourn from Ermine Street as far as the northern end of Long Furlong; the northern part of this parish boundary, near the St Neots ridgeway, may also be on the same alignment

Bourn
(d) Ridhill Dean Common
(e) Stone Haven Common
(f) An unnamed furlong boundary between (e) and (g)
(g) Broadway
(h) Flaxendene or Dundee Road
(i) Furlong boundary along Common Drift Common
(j) Northern part of the parish boundary with Caldecote; the alignment reappears further south between Over and Nether Metwell furlongs
(k) Porter's Way, south-eastern parish boundary between Bourn and Kingston

Caldecote
(l) Strympole Way, the main village street, and the continuation of Crane's Lane in Kingston (Y below)
(m) The eastern parish boundary

Toft and Hardwick
(n) Hatchemer Dean in Hardwick
(o) Furlong boundary along The Joint
(p) Furlong boundary along The Dams
(q) Deadmansway, running from the St Neots ridgeway to (u) below
(r) Continuous furlong boundary from Portway southwards along Mottle Dean and west of Deadmansway
(s) Comberton Mereway: continuous parish boundary from Comberton Offield to the northern ridgeway

(t) Furlong boundaries west of Short Deane aligned with a lane along Puttockdene in Kingston
(u) High Street/Broadway in Toft
(v) Ancient lane forming the eastern boundary of Priory Closes continues as Church Lane and becomes Toftway to Hardwick
(w) Alignment of footpath from Great Eversden continued by the eastern boundary of Lord's Meadow; its line picked up to the north by boundary between Redland and Moor Furlongs, before entering the meadow along Long Deane and continuing into Hardwick
(x) Footpath enters Toft from the south at Scots Bridge (so called before 1637), just a furlong to east of (v) and proceeds north along the western boundary of Horsepit Furlong and thence northwards along field divisions until it becomes part of the boundary between Hardwick and Toft

Comberton
(y) Furlong boundary, part of which forms a section of the parish boundary between Barton and Comberton; runs south from the St Neots ridgeway, continuing southwards through Harborough Field along Longgoodway
(z) Southern section of parish boundary between Comberton and Barton
(A–C) Furlong boundaries in North Field
(D) Long Bellon Way, a furlong boundary in Harborough Field
(E–K) Unnamed furlong boundaries in West Field and Stallow Field

Harlton
(L–P) Unnamed furlong boundaries

Eversdens
(Q) Royston Way, linking the Mare Way with Comberton along Little Eversden High Street; there are suggestions of further balks running on the same alignment between Ermine Street and Little Eversden High Street
(R) Broadfield Way
(S) Stony Green Way
(T) Wimpole Way/Road, continuing as Chapel Lane to the north, and running south into Wimpole
(U) Unnamed furlong boundary in Low Field, Great Eversden
(V) Unnamed furlong boundary, continued alignment of the section of the main street running past the Manor House, Red House Farm and the Fox public house to a bridge across the Bourn Brook shown in a map in 1801; it may link with (w) in Toft
(W) Western parish boundary between Kingston and Eversden along Armshold Lane

Kingston
(X) Footpath along Puttockdene into Toft
(Y) Crane's Lane, continuation of a regional route from Wimpole; forms the village street before continuing northwards
(Z) Southern section of Church Way which may once have formed the eastern boundary of Kingston Wood

Appendix B: Key to Figure 5.1

Comberton
(a) Headland running between furlongs along the brook and Middle Furlong
(b) Headland between Middle Furlong and Broadway Furlong in the west of West Field; the alignment is continued by the southern boundary of Price Meadow Furlong. It was interrupted again by Home Heard Furlong, but its alignment can be traced again in the final section of Stallan Way which leads into Barton. The central western part of this headland is disrupted by the boundaries of a furlong (C on Figure 5.3) lying between Broadway Furlong and Clarkes Hunches. The furlongs in this part of the field have the appearance of the reorganisation of two furlongs into three at some time after these fields were laid out. This is most marked in the north-western corner (D on Figure 5.3) of the middle furlong which projects into Broadway Furlong, creating an unnecessarily complicated junction between the furlongs and cutting across the selions in the central and eastern parts of Broadway Furlong
(c) Broadway Common in the west continued easterly across Fox's Bridge Road as Hensnest Way
(d) Mill Way or Lot Way in the west became Great and Little Hodge Way in the east. Its course seems to have been disrupted by Late Saxon settlement around the church
(e) Meadows of Tid Brook Common in the west and the Slade and Red Ditch in the east formed the northern boundaries of selions in the furlong to the south. While it would have been neater to have laid out this furlong boundary so that it was more truly parallel to (a)–(d), this would have created an area of waste ground between the boundary and the Tid Brook. Instead, the furlongs on either side of Tid Brook simply had to take its rather more winding course into account, which resulted in the rather more 'tortured' appearance of this boundary
(f) Headland between common-field furlongs that was later used to create a back lane when planned settlement was shifted onto the selions to its north after the Norman Conquest. To the east of South Street, it became Swaynes Lane before leading into Gurnalls Meadow. This alignment may be a later subdivision between the headlands (e) and (g)
(g) Present main road from Toft to Barton, called West Street in the west of the modern settlement at Comberton and Barton Road in the east
(h) Back boundary to properties immediately north of the west end of the main street,

Appendix B

whose alignment continued east with just one interruption as far the Barton parish boundary

Toft
(j) Headland shown as (a) in Comberton continued into Toft as the northern boundary of Nether Cresgras Furlong
(k) Headland shown as (b) in Comberton continued into Toft as the northern boundary of Upper Cresgras Furlong
(l) East Way Common, continuation of Broadway Common in Comberton
(m) Lot Way, continuation of Millway Common in Comberton, which led westward across the settlement in Toft – almost certainly a later medieval shift onto former arable land – to a further wide balk, common or headland called Peck's Lane in 1815[1]
(n) Dawes Lane (so called in 1815 – the present main street now called Comberton Road), continuation of Tid Brook Common in Comberton.[2] Although the modern main road turns sharply south at the junction with the present High Street, the alignment of this boundary seems to have continued west as Cambridge Way along the south side of Mill Furlong into Caldecote[3]
(o) Westerly continuation of the present main road from Comberton, in a southwesterly direction into (m) along the northern side of Dovehouse Dole. There is not enough evidence to support or contradict a hint in its alignment that it has been diverted from an earlier, more westerly, course which ran into Copy Lane and, perhaps, further west[4]
(p) Holders Way was the most northerly of these substantial balks in Toft and seems to have been the continuation of (h) in Comberton. It led westerly before coming to an abrupt halt against Stockwell Dean. However, a further substantial balk to the west hints that it too may once have continued further west
(q) Furlong boundary in Toft, continuation of stepped boundary of enclosure south of Comberton Offal, and which is used as part of the parish boundary between Hardwick and Toft

Barton
(r) Headland south of the medieval and modern main road
(s) Wide headland in Barton, continuation of Stallan Way in Comberton. Part of this wide headland underlay a section of the medieval and modern road between Barton and Cambridge
(t) Headland, continuation of Broad/Hensnest Way in Comberton, and continued for a short distance as a common-field division into Barton before being lost in Hensnest Furlong in Barton[5]
(u) Headland which continues alignment of headland in Comberton

1. CCRO Q/RDz 8.
2. CCRO Q/RDz 8.
3. CCRO R60/24/2/11.
4. CCRO Q/RDz 8.
5. CUL EDR/H1.

(v) Wide headland, continuation of Millway or Great Hodge Way in Comberton
(w) Headland, continuation of common which followed Tid Brook for much of its easterly course across Comberton, but which left the brook where the latter turned south, and continued as a headland into Barton where, by 1839, its continuation east had been stopped by the creation of ancient enclosures
(x) Headland and right of way, continuation of alignment of pre-enclosure main road from Comberton into Barton

Grantchester
(y) Section of pre-enclosure road called Stulpe Way, continuation of (r) in Barton
(z) Pre-enclosure road called Mill Way, continuation of (s) in Barton
(A) Wide headland called Mere Way Common, continuation of Mill Way Common (d) in Comberton and Lot Way (m) in Toft
(B) Pre-enclosure road called Deadman Way
(C) Pre-enclosure road called Rivers End Way
(D) Unnamed headland and pre-enclosure road, along northern side of Ridgeway Furlong

Selected primary sources

Manuscript sources

Cambridge University Library (CUL)
EDR/G3/27 Hardwick Ely Coucher Book 1251
EDR/H1 Ely Glebe and Rectory Terriers
Maps.aa.53(1).82.1 Map of the county of Cambridge and Isle of Ely, surveyed by R. G. Baker, 1 inch to the mile, 1816–20
Maps.53(1).01.31 Comberton tithe map 1840
MS Plans r.a.2 Comberton, pre-enclosure map 1839
MS Plans 582 Settlement at Hardwick, 1837
QC13, 15, 16 Eversden Queens' College: terriers of lands
QC 17 Kingston Queens' College: estate papers and terriers
Views.Relhan.3 watercolour paintings

Cambridge County Council County Record Office (CCRO)
124/P39 Caxton, pre-enclosure map, n.d.
124/P51, A-C Hardwick, pre-enclosure map, n.d.
124/P52 Harlton, pre-enclosure map, n.d.
124/P53 Haslingfield, pre-enclosure map, n.d.
124/P80 Toft, pre-enclosure map 1815
152/P2 Barton, pre-enclosure map c. 1839
152/P11 Grantchester, pre-enclosure map c. 1795
152/P12 Hardwick, pre-enclosure map, n.d.
Q/RDc 19 Eversden, enclosure map 1811
Q/RDc 23 Toft, enclosure map 1815
Q/RDc 25 Kingston, enclosure map 1815
Q/RDc 35 Bourn, enclosure map c. 1820
Q/RDc 36 Haslingfield, enclosure map 1810
Q/RDc 49 Caxton, enclosure map and award 1835
Q/RDc 51 Hardwick, enclosure map and award 1837
Q/RDc 57 Comberton, enclosure map and award 1840
Q/RDc 58 Barton, enclosure map and award 1839
Q/RDc 76 Caldecote, enclosure map and award 1854
Q/RDz 7 Eversden, enclosure award 1814
Q/RDz 8 Kingston, enclosure award 1815

Q/RDz 8 Toft, enclosure award 1815
Q/RDz 9 Bourn, enclosure award 1820
Q/RDz 9 Haslingfield, enclosure award 1820
R52/12/5/1 Kingston, Kingston Wood Estate in 1720
R53/16/20 Comberton, Mr Mann's terrier 1806
R60/24/2/11 Caldecote, pre-enclosure map
R86/6 Toft, pre-enclosure map c. 1815
Ordnance Survey Surveyors' draft drawings c. 1810

Cambridgeshire County Council Historic Environment Record (CCC HER)
Records and reports relevant to the study area

Christ's College, Cambridge (ChC)
Caldecote E and L, terriers, 1500s and 1600s

Clare College, Cambridge (CC)
Safe B 38/5, terriers, 1500s–1700s

Gonville and Caius College (G&CC)
XXXII.1 Caxton: grant Henry II
XXXII.2 Caxton: sale 1227
XXXII.18 Caxton: sale of land Elizabeth 1:16
XXXII.28 Caxton: charters
XXXII.29 Caxton: terrier 1661
XXXII.32 Caxton: Broad Close
Caxton: Survey 1762
G04/3/1/15 Caxton: Valuations 1803

Metropolitan Record Office (MRO)
H1/ST/E/107/1 and 2 terrier and maps of Green's Estate, Comberton 1723

Pembroke College, Cambridge (PC)
HI.1–13 papers relating to Pembroke College estate in Hardwick

Royal Air Force (RAF)
Aerial photographs 9 May 1946 (in collection of C. C. Taylor):
106G/UK/1490 nos. 4020–31 and 4228–4236
CPE/UK/2024 nos. 3045–3049 and 4045–4055

Cambridge University Unit for Landscape Modelling, Department of Geography, University of Cambridge (CUULM)
Aerial photographs relevant to the study area

Printed maps

British Geological Survey
1988 *Classical Areas of British Geology, Solid and Drift* 1:25,000, Southampton, Ordnance Survey, Sheets 187 and 204 (CUL maps.c.G.041)

Ordnance Survey of Great Britain
1884 Cambridge surveyed 1810 with later revisions (reprinted 1970, David and Charles), 1 inch to the mile
1886 Sheets XLVI SW, SE, NW, NE, 6 inches to the mile,
1956 TL35 Eversden, 1:25,000 (compiled 1900–37, partial revisions 1938–52 and 1965)

1984 TL25/35 Gamlingay and Comberton 1:25,000
1999 Explorer 209 Cambridge 1:25,000

Published primary sources

Cartulary of St Mary, Clerkenwell, W. O. Hassall, ed. (London, 1949), Camden Third Series, Volume LXXI.
Domesday Book: Cambridgeshire, A. Rumble, ed. (Chichester, 1981).
English Historical Documents c. 500–1042, D. Whitelock, ed. (London, 1979).
English Historical Documents 1042–1189, D. C. Douglas and G. W. Greenaway, eds (London, 1953), Volume II.
Inquisitio Comitatus Cantabrigiensis in Victoria County History of Cambridgeshire and the Isle of Ely, L. F. Salzman, ed. (London, 1938), Volume I.
Inquisitio Eliensis in Inquisitio Comitatus Cantabrigiensis, N. E. S. A. Hamilton, ed. (London, 1876).
Liber Eliensis, E. O. Blake, ed. (London, 1962), Camden Third Series, Volume XCII.
Liber Memorandum Ecclesie de Bernewelle, J. W. Clark, ed. (Cambridge, 1907).
Rotuli Hundredorum 1279 (London, 1818), Volume II.
The 1327 Lay Subsidy for Cambridgeshire, C. Evelyn-White, ed. (Cambridge, n.d.).

Secondary sources

Abels, R. 'Bookland and Fyrd Service in Late Saxon England', *Anglo-Norman St.* 7 (1984), pp. 1–21.
Addyman, P. V. 'A Dark-Age Settlement at Maxey, Northants.', *Med. Arch.* 8 (1964), pp. 20–73.
Alexander, J. and D. Trump, 'Grantchester Excavations' (Cambridge, 1971, unpublished notes held at University of Cambridge Institute of Continuing Education).
Aston, M. 'Medieval Settlement in Somerset', in M. Aston and C. Lewis, eds, *The Medieval Landscape of Wessex* (Oxford, 1994), pp. 219–38.
Aston, T. H. 'The Origins of the Manor in England', in T. H. Aston, P. R. Coss, C. Dyer and J. Thirsk, eds, *Social Relations and Ideas* (Cambridge, 1983), pp. 1–25.
Austin, D., G. A. M. Gerrard and T. A. P. Greeves, 'Tin and Agriculture in the Middle Ages and Beyond: Landscape Archaeology in St Neot Parish, Cornwall', *Cornish Arch.* 28 (1989), pp. 5–251.
Banham, D. (forthcoming) 'Race and Tillage: Scandinavian Influence on Anglo-Saxon Agriculture?' in Kilpiö, M. et al., eds, *Proc. of the International Society of Anglo-Saxonists Congress, Helsinki 2001*.
Barker, P. and J. Lawson, 'A Pre-Norman Field System at Hen Domen', *Med. Arch.* 15 (1971), pp. 58–72.
Bassett, S. 'Medieval Lichfield: A Topographical Review', *Trans. Staffordshire Arch. and Hist. Soc.* 22 (1980–1), pp. 93–121.
Bassett, S. 'Beyond the Edge of Excavation: The Topographical Context of Goltho', in H. Mayr-Harting and R. I. Moore, eds, *Studies in Medieval History* (London, 1985), pp. 21–39.
Bassett, S. ed., *The Origins of the Anglo-Saxon Kingdoms* (Leicester, 1989).
Bassett, S. 'Great Chesterford and Wicken Bonhunt: The Transition from Roman to Anglo-Saxon Control' (unpublished notes, 1993).
Bassett, S. 'Continuity and Fission in the Anglo-Saxon Landscape: The Origins of the Rodings, Essex', *Landscape Hist.* 19 (1997), pp. 25–42.
Becket, J., M. Turner and B. Cowell, 'Farming through Enclosure', *Rural Hist.* 9, 2 (1998), pp. 141–55.
Bell, M. 'Environmental Archaeology as an Index of Continuity and Change in the Medieval Landscape', in M. Aston, D. Austin, and C. Dyer, eds, *The Rural Settlements of Medieval England* (Oxford, 1989), pp. 269–86.

Bellamy, B. 'Anglo-Saxon Dispersed Sites and Woodland at Geddington in the Rockingham Forest, Northamptonshire', *Landscape Hist.* 16 (1994), pp. 31–7.
Beresford, G. *The Medieval Clay-Land Village: Excavations at Goltho and Barton Blount* (London, 1975).
Beresford, M. *The Lost Villages of England* (Gloucester, 1983 edn).
Beresford, M. and J. Hurst, 'Wharram Percy: A Case Study in Microtopography', in P. Sawyer, ed., *English Medieval Settlement* (London, 1979), pp. 52–85.
Beresford, M. and J. K. St Joseph, *Medieval England* (Cambridge, 1979).
Blair, I., E. Barham and L. Blackmore, 'My Lord Essex', *British Arch.* 76, (2004), pp. 11–17.
Blair, J. *Anglo-Saxon Oxfordshire* (Stroud, 1994).
Brown, A. E. and G. Foard, 'The Saxon Landscape: A Regional Perspective', in P. Everson and T. Williamson, eds, *The Archaeology of Landscape* (Manchester, 1998), pp. 67–94.
Browne, D. ed., *Victoria County History of Cambridgeshire and the Isle of Ely* (London, 1977), Volume VII.
Bryant, S., B. Perry and T. A. Williamson, 'A "relict landscape" in South-East Hertfordshire: Archaeological and Topographic Investigations in the Wormley area', *Landscape Hist.* 27 (2005) pp. 5–16.
Bull, E. J. 'The Bi-Axial Landscape of Prehistoric Buckinghamshire', *Records of Buckinghamshire* 35 (1993), pp. 11–27.
Campbell, B. *English Seigniorial Agriculture, 1250–1450* (Cambridge, 2000).
Campbell, J. *Essays in Anglo-Saxon History* (London, 1986).
Carver, M. 'Kinship and Material Culture in Early Anglo-Saxon East Anglia', in S. Bassett, ed., *The Origins of the Anglo-Saxon Kingdoms* (Leicester, 1989), pp. 141–58.
Carver, M. *Sutton Hoo: Burial Ground of Kings?* (London, 1998).
Cessford, C. with A. Dickens, 'The Manor of Hintona: The Origins and Development of Church End, Cherry Hinton', *Proc. Cambridge Antiquarian Soc.* 94 (2005), pp. 51–72.
Costen, M. 'Settlement in Wessex in the Tenth Century: The Charter Evidence', in M. Aston and C. Lewis, eds, *The Medieval Landscape of Wessex* (Oxford, 1994), pp. 97–114.
Crabtree, P. 'Animal Exploitation in East Anglian Villages', in J. Rackham, ed., *Environment and Economy in Anglo-Saxon England* (York, 1994), pp. 40–54.
Current Archaeology, 'Sutton Hoo Before Raedwald', 180 (2002), pp. 498–505.
Darby, H. C. 'The Domesday Geography of Cambridgeshire', *Proc. Cambridge Antiquarian Soc.* 36 (1936), pp. 35–57.
Darby, H. C. ed., *The Domesday Geography of Eastern England* (Cambridge, 1952).
Darby, H. C. *Domesday England* (Cambridge, 1977).
Darvill, T. *Prehistoric Britain from the Air* (Cambridge, 1996).
Dodgshon, R. A. 'The Early Middle Ages, 1066–1350', in R. A. Dodgshon, and R. A. Butlin, eds, *An Historical Geography of England and Wales* (London, 1978), pp. 81–117.
Dodgson, J. McN. 'The Significance of the Distribution of the English Place-Names in -ingas, -inga- in South-East England', *Med. Arch.* 10 (1966), pp. 1–29.
Drury, P. J. and W. J. Rodwell, 'Investigations at Asheldham, Essex', *Antiquaries Jnl.* 58 (1978), pp. 133–51.
Dyer, C. 'Dispersed Settlements in Medieval England: A Case Study of Pendock, Worcestershire', *Med. Arch.* 34 (1990), pp. 97–121.
Dyer, C. *Hanbury: Settlement and Society in a Woodland Landscape* (Leicester, 1991).
Dyer, C. 'Lords, Peasants and the Development of the Manor: England, 900–1280', in A.

Haverkamp and H. Vollrath, eds, *England and Germany in the High Middle Ages* (London, 1996), pp. 301–15.

Dymond, D. and E. Martin, eds, *An Historical Atlas of Suffolk* (Ipswich, 1988).

Elrington, C. R. ed., *Victoria County History of Cambridgeshire and the Isle of Ely*, (London, 1973), Volume V.

English, J. and S. Dyer, 'Surrey Historic Landscape Project: The Polesden Estate', *Soc. Landscape St. Newsletter* (autumn, 1993), pp. 4–6.

Everitt, A. *Landscape and Community in England* (London, 1985).

Evison, N. 'Lo, the Conquering Hero Comes (Or Not)', *British Arch.* 23 (1997), pp. 8–9.

Faith, R. *The English Peasantry and the Growth of Lordship* (Leicester, 1997).

Field, J. *A History of English Field-Names* (London, 1993).

Finberg, H. P. R., ed., *The Agrarian History of England and Wales* (Cambridge, 1972), Volume I.

Fleming, A. 'The Prehistoric Landscape of Dartmoor, Part 1: South Dartmoor', *Proc. Prehistoric Soc.* 44 (1978), pp. 97–123.

Fleming, A. 'The Prehistoric Landscape of Dartmoor, Part 2: North and East Dartmoor', *Proc. Prehistoric Soc.* 49 (1983), pp. 195–241.

Fleming, A. 'The Prehistoric Landscape of Dartmoor: Wider Implications', *Landscape Hist.* 6 (1984), pp. 5–19.

Fleming, A. 'Co-Axial Field Systems: Some Questions of Time and Space', *Antiquity* 61 (1987), pp. 188–202.

Fleming, A. *The Dartmoor Reaves* (London, 1988).

Foard, G. 'Systematic Fieldwalking and the Investigation of Saxon Settlement in Northamptonshire', *World Arch.* 9, 3 (1978), pp. 357–74.

Ford, S. et al. 'The Date of the "Celtic" Field Systems on the Berkshire Downs', *Britannia* 19 (1988), pp. 401–4.

Fowler, P. J. 'Agriculture and Rural Settlement', in D. M. Wilson, ed., *The Archaeology of Anglo-Saxon England* (Cambridge, 1976), pp. 23–48.

Fowler, P. J. *Landscape Plotted and Pieced* (London, 2000).

Fowler, P. J. *Farming in the First Millennium* (Cambridge, 2002).

Fowler, P. J. and A. C. Thomas, 'Arable Fields of the Pre-Norman Period at Gwithian, Cornwall', *Cornish Arch.* 1 (1962), pp. 61–84.

Fox, C. *The Archaeology of the Cambridge Region* (Cambridge, 1923).

Fox, H. S. A. 'Social Relations and Ecological Relationships in Agrarian Change: An Example from Medieval and Early Modern England', *Geografiska Annaler* 70B, 1 (1988), pp. 105–15.

Fox, H. S. A. 'Wolds: The Wolds before 1500', in J. Thirsk, ed., *Rural England* (Oxford, 2000), pp. 50–61.

Frere, S. S. and J. K. St Joseph, *Roman Britain from the Air* (Cambridge, 1983).

Gelling, M. *Place-Names in the Landscape* (London, 1984).

Gelling, M. *The West Midlands in the Early Middle Ages* (Leicester, 1992).

Gelling, M. and A. Cole, *The Landscape of Place-Names* (Stamford, 2000).

Graham-Campbell, J. 'Anglo-Scandinavian Equestrian Equipment in Eleventh-Century England', *Anglo-Norman St.* 14 (1991), pp. 77–90.

Gray, H. L. *English Field Systems* (Cambridge, 1915).

Hadley, D. 'Multiple Estates and the Origins of the Manorial Structure of Northern Danelaw', *Jnl. Hist. Geog.* 22, 1 (1996), pp. 3–15.

Haigh, D., 'A Correlation Between Archaeological Sites and Field Names: A Survey of Parishes Along the Line of the North and West By-Passes of Cambridge: An Interim Report' (Cambridge, 1975, unpublished manuscript held in Cambridgeshire Central Library).

Hall, D. 'The Origins of Common-Field Agriculture: The Archaeological Fieldwork Evidence', in T. Rowley, ed., *The Origins of Open-Field Agriculture* (London, 1981), pp. 22–38.

Hall, D. *Medieval Fields* (Princes Risborough, 1982).

Hall, D. 'Field Work and Field Books: Studies in Early Layout' in B. K. Roberts and R. Glasscock, eds, *Villages, Fields and Frontiers* (London, 1983), pp. 115–131.

Hall, D. 'Late Saxon Topography and Early Medieval Estates', in D. Hooke, ed., *Medieval Villages* (Oxford, 1985), pp. 61–70.

Hall, D. 'The Late Saxon Countryside: Villages and their Fields', in D. Hooke, ed., *Anglo-Saxon Settlements* (Oxford, 1988), pp. 91–122.

Hall, D. *The Open Fields of Northamptonshire* (Northampton, 1995).

Hall, D. 'The Distribution and Change in Arable, Common and Waste, 1066–1550', in T. Kirby and S. Oosthuizen, eds, *An Atlas of Cambridgeshire and Huntingdonshire History* (Cambridge, 2000), p. 45.

Hall, R. *The Viking Dig* (London, 1984).

Hallam, H. E. *Settlement and Society: A Study of the Early Agrarian History of South Lincolnshire* (Cambridge, 1965).

Hamerow, H. 'Settlement Mobility and the "Middle Saxon Shift": Rural Settlements and Settlement Patterns in Anglo-Saxon England', *Anglo-Saxon England* 20 (1991), pp. 1–17.

Hamerow, H. 'Migration Theory and the Migration Period', in B. Vyner, ed., *Building on the Past* (London, 1994), pp. 164–77.

Hamerow, H. *Early Medieval Settlements* (Oxford, 2002).

Härke, H. 'Early Anglo-Saxon Social Structure', in J. Hines, ed., *The Anglo-Saxons from the Migration Period to the Eighth Century An Ethnographic Perspective* (Woodbridge, 1997), pp. 125–60.

Hart, C. R. *Early Charters of Eastern England* (Leicester, 1966).

Hart, C. R. *The Hidation of Cambridgeshire* (Leicester, 1974).

Hart, C. R. 'Land Tenure in Cambridgeshire on the Eve of the Norman Conquest', *Proc. Cambridge Antiquarian Soc.* 84 (1995), pp. 59–90.

Harvey, M. 'Planned Field Systems in Eastern Yorkshire: Some Thoughts on their Origin', *Agric. Hist. Rev.* 31, 2 (1983), pp. 91–103.

Harvey, P. D. A. 'Initiative and Authority in Settlement Change', in M. Aston, D. Austin, and C. Dyer, eds, *The Rural Settlements of Medieval England* (Oxford, 1989), pp. 31–43.

Harvey, S. 'The Extent and Profitability of Demesne Agriculture in England in the Later Eleventh Century', in T. H. Aston, P. R. Coss, C. Dyer and J. Thirsk, eds, *Social Relations and Ideas* (Cambridge, 1983), pp. 45–71.

Haselgrove, C. 'The Moated Site at Hardwick, West Cambridgeshire', *Proc. Cambridge Antiquarian Soc.* 72 (1982-3), pp. 48–54.

Hesse, M. 'Domesday Land Measures in Suffolk', *Landscape Hist.* 22 (2000), pp. 21–36.

Higham, N. J. *A Frontier Landscape* (Macclesfield, 2004).

Hill, D. 'Sulh: the Anglo-Saxon Plough', *Landscape Hist.* 22 (2000), pp. 5–20.

Hinton, D. A. *Archaeology, Economy and Society* (London, 1990).
Hinton, D. A. 'The "Scole-Dickleburgh Field System" Examined', *Landscape Hist.* 19 (1997), pp. 5–13.
Hooke, D. 'Early Cotswold Woodland', *Jnl. Hist. Geog.* 4, 4 (1978), pp. 333–41.
Hooke, D. 'Early Forms of Open-Field Agriculture in England', *Geografiska Annaler* 70B, 1 (1988), pp. 123–31.
Hooke, D. 'Regional Variation in Southern and Central England in the Anglo-Saxon Period and its Relationship to Land Units and Settlement', in D. Hooke, ed., *Anglo-Saxon Settlements* (Oxford, 1988), pp. 123–52.
Hooke, D. 'Pre-Conquest Woodland: Its Distribution and Usage', *Agric. Hist. Rev.* 37, 2 (1989), pp. 113–29.
Hooke, D. *The Landscape of Anglo-Saxon England* (Leicester, 1998).
Hoskins, W. G. *The Making of the English Landscape* (London, 1988 edn).
Jones, J. *A Human Geography of Cambridgeshire* (London, 1924).
Klingelhöfer, E. *Manor, Hundred and Vill* (Toronto, 1992).
Knox, R. 'The Anglo-Saxons in Leicestershire', in P. Bowman and P. Liddle, eds, *Leicestershire Landscapes* (Leicester, 2004), pp. 95–104.
Lamb, H. H. 'Climate and Landscape in the British Isles', in S. R. J. Woodell, ed., *The English Landscape Past Present and Future* (Oxford, 1985), pp. 148–67.
Langdon, J. 'Agricultural Equipment', in G. Astill and A. Grant, eds, *The Countryside of Medieval England* (Oxford, 1988), pp. 86–107.
Langouet, L. 'Recherches de Trames Anciennes dans des Parcellaires de Haute-Bretagne', *Les Dossiers du Ce.R.A.A.* 26 (1998), pp. 5–13.
Leith, S. *Late Iron Age, Roman, and Medieval Enclosures and Settlement Features at Highfields, Caldecote: An Archaeological Excavation* (Cambridge, 1997).
Lewis, C., P. Mitchell-Fox and C. Dyer, *Village, Hamlet and Field* (Manchester, 1997).
Lewis, J. 'Heathrow Fields' (presentation to English Heritage seminar on 'Ancient Fields', National Monuments Record, Swindon, 12 June 2002).
Liddle, P. 'The Medbourne Area Survey', in M. Parker-Pearson and R. T. Schadla-Hall, eds, *Looking at the Land* (Leicester, 1994), pp. 34–6.
Liddiard, R. 'Population Density and Castle Building: Some Evidence from East Anglia', *Landscape Hist.* 22 (2000), pp. 37–46.
Loveluck, C. P. 'A High-Status Anglo-Saxon Settlement at Flixborough, Lincolnshire', *Antiquity* 72 (1998), pp. 146–61.
Maitland, F. W. *Domesday Book and Beyond* (Cambridge, 1897, 1987 edn).
McOmish, D., D. Field and G. Brown, *The Field Archaeology of the Salisbury Plain Training Area* (Swindon, 2002).
Meaney, A. 'Gazetteer of Hundred and Wapentake Meeting-Places in the Cambridge Region', *Proc. Cambridge Antiquarian Soc.* 82 (1993), pp. 66–92.
Miller, E. *The Abbey and Bishopric of Ely* (Cambridge, 1969).
Millett, M. *The Romanization of Britain* (Cambridge, 1990).
Mills, D. *A Dictionary of English Place-Names* (Oxford, 1991).
Moreland, J. 'The Significance of Production in Eighth-Century England', in I. L. Hansen and C. Wickham, eds, *The Long Eighth Century* (Leiden, 2000) pp. 69–104.
Morris, D. *The Washing of the Spears* (London, 1965).
Murphy, P. 'Iron Age to Late Saxon Land Use in the Breckland', in M. Jones, ed., *Integrating the Subsistence Economy* (Oxford, 1983), pp. 177–210.

Murphy, P. 'The Anglo-Saxon Landscape and Rural Economy: Some Results from Sites in East Anglia and Essex', in J. Rackham, ed., *Environment and Economy in Anglo-Saxon England* (York, 1994), pp. 23–9.
Oakey, N. *Iron Age and Romano-British Field Systems at Highfields, Caldecote: An Archaeological Evaluation* (Cambridge, 1996).
Onions, C. T. ed., *Shorter Oxford English Dictionary* (Oxford, 1972, 3rd edn).
Oosthuizen, S. *Cambridgeshire from the Air* (Stroud, 1996).
Oosthuizen, S. 'Medieval Settlement Relocation in West Cambridgeshire : Three Case Studies', *Landscape Hist.* 19 (1997), pp. 43–55.
Oosthuizen, S. 'Prehistoric Fields into Medieval Furlongs? Evidence from Caxton, South Cambridgeshire', *Proc. Cambridge Antiquarian Soc.* 86 (1998), pp. 145–52.
Oosthuizen, S. 'Anglo-Saxon Minsters in South Cambridgeshire', *Proc. Cambridge Antiquarian Soc.* 90 (2001), pp. 49–68.
Oosthuizen, S. 'Ancient Greens in "Midland" Landscapes: Barrington, Cambridgeshire', *Med. Arch.* 46 (2002), pp. 110–15.
Oosthuizen, S. 'Medieval Greens and Commons in the Central Province: Evidence from the Bourn Valley, Cambridgeshire', *Landscape Hist.* 24 (2002), pp. 73–89.
Page, R. *Decline of an English Village* (Southampton, 1974).
Palmer, B. 'The Hinterlands of Three Southern English Emporia: Some Common Themes', in T. Pestell and K. Ulmschneider, eds, *Markets in Early Medieval Europe* (Macclesfield, 2003), pp. 48–61.
Palmer, J. J. N. 'The Domesday Manor', in J. Holt, ed., *Domesday Studies* (Woodbridge, 1987), pp. 139–54.
Palmer, W. M. *John Layer (1586–1640) of Shepreth, Cambs* (Cambridge, 1935), Cambridge Antiquarian Society Octavo Series 53.
Petrie, F. 'Proceedings of Meetings of the Royal Archaeological Institute', *Arch. Jnl.* 35 (1878), pp. 169–75.
Phythian-Adams, C. *Continuity, Fields and Fission: The Making of a Midland Parish* (Leicester, 1978).
Pocock, E. A. 'The First Fields in an Oxfordshire Parish', *Agric. Hist. Rev.* 16 (1968), pp. 85–100.
Postgate, M. R. 'The Open Fields of Cambridgeshire' (unpublished Ph.D. thesis, Cambridge, 1964).
Pounds, N. J. G. *A History of the English Parish* (Cambridge, 2000).
Rackham, J. ed., *Environment and Economy in Anglo-Saxon England* (York, 1994).
Rackham, O. *The History of the Countryside* (London, 1986).
Rackham, O. 'Trees and Woodland in Anglo-Saxon England: The Documentary Evidence', in J. Rackham, ed., *Environment and Economy in Anglo-Saxon England* (York 1994), pp. 7–11.
Rackham, O. 'Woodland in the Ely Coucher Book', *Nature in Cambridgeshire* 42 (2000), pp. 37–67.
Ravensdale, J. *The Domesday Inheritance* (London, 1986).
RCHM(E) *West Cambridgeshire* (London, 1968).
RCHM(E) *Central Dorset* (London, 1970).
RCHM(E) *North-East Northamptonshire* (London, 1975).
RCHM(E) *Central Northamptonshire* (London, 1979).
RCHM(E) *North-West Northamptonshire* (London, 1981).

Reaney, P. H. *Place-Names of Cambridgeshire and the Isle of Ely* (Cambridge, 1943).
Reynolds, S. 'Bookland, Folkland and Fiefs', *Anglo-Norman St.* 14 (1991), pp. 211–28.
Riley, H. and R. Wilson-North, *The Field Archaeology of Exmoor* (Swindon, 2001).
Rippon, S. 'Early Planned Landscapes in South-East Essex', *Essex Arch. and Hist.* 22 (1991), pp. 46–60.
Rippon, S. 'Landscapes in Transition: The Later Roman and Early Medieval Periods', in D. Hooke, ed., *Landscape: The Richest Historical Record* (Society for Landscape Studies, 2000), pp. 47–62.
Rippon, S. 'Infield and Outfield: The Early Stages of Marshland Colonisation and the Evolution of Medieval Field Systems', in T. Lane and J. Coles, eds, *Through Wet and Dry* (Sleaford, 2002), pp. 54–70.
Roberts, B. K. *Rural Settlement in Britain* (Folkestone, 1977).
Roberts, B. K. *The Making of the English Village* (London, 1989).
Roberts B. K. and S. Wrathmell, *An Atlas of Rural Settlement in England* (Swindon, 2000).
Roberts B. K. and S. Wrathmell, *Region and Place: A Study of English Rural Settlement* (Swindon, 2002).
Robinson, M. 'The Problem of Hedges Enclosing Roman and Earlier Fields', in H. C. Bowen and P. J. Fowler, eds, *Early Land Allotment in the British Isles* (Oxford, 1978), pp. 155–8.
Rodwell, W. 'Relict Landscapes in Essex', in H. C. Bowen and P. J. Fowler, eds, *Early Land Allotment in the British Isles* (Oxford, 1978), pp. 89–98.
Roffe, D. *Domesday: The Inquest and the Book* (Oxford, 2000).
Salzman, L. F. ed., *Victoria County History of Cambridgeshire and the Isle of Ely* (London, 1938), Volume I.
Schumer, B. *The Evolution of Wychwood to 1400: Pioneers, Frontiers and Forests* (Leicester, 1984).
Scull, C. 'Approaches to Material Culture and Social Dynamics of the Migration Period in Eastern England', in J. Bintliff and H. Hamerow, eds, *Europe Between Late Antiquity and the Middle Ages* (Oxford, 1995), pp. 71–83.
Smith, C. 'The Historical Development of the Landscape in the Parishes of Alrewas, Fisherwick and Whittington; A Retrogressive Analysis', *Trans. South Staffs. Arch. and Hist. Soc.* 20 (1978–9), pp. 1–14.
Spufford, M. *A Cambridgeshire Community: Chippenham from Settlement to Enclosure* (Leicester, 1968).
Stafford, P. 'The "Farm of One Night" and the Organisation of King Edward's Estates in Domesday', *Econ. Hist. Rev.* 2nd series 33, 4 (1980), pp. 491–502.
Stafford, P. *The East Midlands in the Early Middle Ages* (Leicester, 1985).
Swanton, M., ed., *Anglo-Saxon Prose* (London, 1993).
Tate, W. E. 'Cambridgeshire Field Systems', *Proc. Cambridge Antiquarian Soc.* 40 (1944), pp. 56–88.
Taylor, C. C. 'Polyfocal Settlement and the English Village', *Med. Arch.* 21 (1977), pp. 189–93.
Taylor, C. C. 'Archaeology and the Origins of Open Field Agriculture', in T. Rowley, ed., *The Origins of Open Field Agriculture* (London, 1981)
Taylor, C. C. 'Medieval Market Grants and Village Morphology', *Landscape Hist.* 4 (1982), pp. 21–8.
Taylor, C. C. *Village and Farmstead* (London, 1983).
Taylor, C. C. *Fields in the English Landscape* (Stroud, 2000).

Taylor, C. C. 'Medieval Ornamental Landscapes', *Landscapes* 1, 1 (2000), pp. 38–55.
Taylor, C. C. and P. J. Fowler, 'Roman Fields into Medieval Furlongs?', in H. C. Bowen and P. J. Fowler, eds, *Early Land Allotment in the British Isles* (Oxford, 1978), pp. 159–62.
Tolan-Smith, M. 'The Romano-British and Late Prehistoric Landscape: The Deconstruction of a Medieval Landscape', in C. Tolan-Smith, ed., *Landscape Archaeology in Tynedale* (Newcastle, 1997), pp. 67–78.
Unwin, P. T. H. 'Vills and Early Fields in North Nottinghamshire', *Jnl. Hist. Geog.* 9, 4 (1983), pp. 341–6.
Unwin, P. T. H. 'Towards a Model of Anglo-Scandinavian Rural Settlement in England', in D. Hooke, ed., *Anglo-Saxon Settlements* (Oxford, 1988), pp. 77–98.
Upex, S. 'Landscape Continuity and the Fossilisation of Roman Fields', *Arch. Jnl.* 159 (2002), pp. 77–108.
Wager, S. *Woods, Wolds and Groves* (Oxford, 1998).
Warner, P. *Greens, Commons and Clayland Colonisation* (Leicester, 1987).
Warner, P. 'Pre-Conquest Territorial and Administrative Organisation in East Suffolk', in D. Hooke, ed., *Anglo-Saxon Settlements* (Oxford, 1988), pp. 9–34.
Warner, P. *The Origins of Suffolk* (Manchester, 1996).
Welldon Finn, R. 'Some Reflections on the Cambridgeshire Domesday', *Proc. Cambridge Antiquarian Soc.* 53 (1960), pp. 29–38.
Wessex Archaeology, 'Cambourne New Settlement, Cambridgeshire. Archaeological Evaluation Site 13: Phase 1 Landscaping Western Boundary' (Salisbury, October 1998, Reference 33220).
Wessex Archaeology, 'Cambourne New Settlement, Cambridgeshire. Archaeological Evaluation' (Salisbury, March 1999, Report 45970).
Wessex Archaeology, 'Cambourne New Settlement, Cambridgeshire. Archaeological Evaluation School Lane, Lower Cambourne' (Salisbury, July 2000, Report 45977.1).
Williamson, T. 'The Development of Settlement in North West Essex: The Results of a Recent Field Survey', *Essex Arch. and Hist.* 17 (1986), pp. 120–32.
Williamson, T. 'Early Co-Axial Fields Systems on the East Anglian Boulder Clays', *Proc. Prehistoric Soc.* 53 (1987), pp. 419–31.
Williamson, T. 'Settlement Chronology and Regional Landscapes: The Evidence from the Claylands of East Anglia and Essex', in D. Hooke, ed., *Anglo-Saxon Settlements* (Oxford, 1988), pp. 153–75.
Williamson, T. *The Origins of Norfolk* (Manchester, 1993).
Williamson, T. 'Questions of Preservation and Destruction', in P. Everson and T. Williamson, eds, *Archaeology and Landscape* (Manchester, 1998), pp. 1–24.
Williamson, T. 'The "Scole-Dickleburgh Field System" Revisited', *Landscape Hist.* 20 (1998), pp. 19–28.
Williamson, T. *The Origins of Hertfordshire* (Manchester, 2000).
Williamson, T. *Shaping Medieval Landscapes* (Macclesfield, 2002).

Index of place names

Bedfordshire 148
Berkshire 18, 69, 89
Berks., Lambourn (Down) 18, 69
Berks., Letcombe Bassett 18
Berks., Old Windsor 113
Buckinghamshire 17, 120, 149
Bucks., Newport Pagnell 120
Bucks., Pennyland 149
Cambridgeshire 137, 141, 143, 145, 152; Anglo-Saxon 6, 30, 105, 106; 100, 111; in Domesday Book 114, 115, 116, 117; field systems 89, 94, 96; greens 51, 52, 54, 58, 59; manors 118, 122, 124, 128, 131, 151; medieval 36, 39, 43, 44, 47, 48, 49; moats 66; post-medieval 29, 75, 86; prehistoric and Roman 5, 15, 16, 17, 18, 19, 85
Cambs., Barton: Anglo-Saxon 95, 110; appendices 155, 156, 157, 158; field systems 44, 46, 47, 49; greens 56; medieval, 66, 81, 103, 104, 116, 122, 128; post-medieval 49, 96, 98; prehistoric 83; Roman 28, 82, 84, 101, 102
Cambs., Bourn 73; Aelmer of 117, 124, 125, 128; Anglo-Saxon 105, 146; appendices 154, 155; arable landscape 42, 43, 44, 46, 47, 48; at Domesday 116, 120, 123; moats 66; post-medieval 6; wood and pasture 23, 35, 36, 38, 40
Cambs., Caldecote: appendix 154; arable 42, 44, 46, 74; at Domesday 116, 125, 130; post-medieval 25; prehistoric and Roman 81; roads and holloways 72, 87, 89; settlement 27, 64; wood and pasture 38, 39, 40
Cambs., Cambridge 28, 74, 133, 151, 157
Cambs., Caxton 21; Anglo-Saxon 105, 146; appendix 154; arable landscape 43, 44, 49, 88; at Domesday 116, 120, 122, 128; moats 66; post-medieval 6; prehistoric and Roman 82, 83, 84, 85; wood and pasture 35, 40, 137
Cambs., Cherry Hinton 128, 131
Cambs., Comberton: appendices 154, 155, 156, 157, 158; arable landscape 42, 43, 44, 46, 47, 49; at Domesday 116, 118, 119, 120, 122, 128; greens 52, 56, 58; moats 66; post-medieval 79; prehistoric and Roman 29, 81, 82; proto-common field date 100, 101, 103, 104, 107, 109; proto-common field layout 95, 96, 97, 98; settlement 64, 74, 146, 147; wood and pasture 36, 40, 41
Cambs., Duxford 18
Cambs., Eversden 5, 21, 25; appendix 155; arable 43, 44, 46, 47, 48, 49; at Domesday 116, 119, 120, 127, 128; greens 41, 52, 56, 57, 58; moats 66; post-medieval 135; prehistoric and Roman 87, 132; settlement 146, 147, 150; wood and pasture 26, 29, 35, 36, 38, 39, 40
Cambs., Grantchester 21; Anglo-Saxon 30, 106, 110, 146; appendices 158; arable 44; at Domesday 116, 122, 128; prehistoric and Roman 29; proto-common field 91, 95, 96, 98, 149, 150, 152
Cambs., Hardwick 34; Anglo-Saxon 100; appendices 154, 155, 157, 159; arable 43; at Domesday 116, 120, 122, 123, 128, 130, 142; greens 56; lordly intervention 151; moats 66; post-medieval 25; prehistoric and Roman 81, 83; settlement 44, 46, 47, 48, 60, 62, 63, 64, 146, 148; wood and pasture 35, 36, 38, 39, 40
Cambs., Harlton: Anglo-Saxon 110; appendix 155; arable 44, 50; at Domesday 116, 120, 122, 123; greens 52, 53, 55, 56, 57, 58, 66; moats 66; prehistoric and Roman 29, 84, 86; settlement 64, 128, 129, 146, 147; wood and pasture 39, 41
Cambs., Haslingfield: Anglo-Saxon 30, 36, 110; arable 44; at Domesday 116, 118, 119, 122, 123, 128; estate centre at 100, 107, 120, 133, 149; greens 52, 53, 54, 55, 56, 57, 58; prehistoric and Roman 29; settlement 64, 66, 146, 147; wood and pasture 41
Cambs., Kingston 21, 34, 73, 75; appendices 154, 155; arable 44, 46, 49, 51; at Domesday 116, 117, 118, 120, 125, 128, 130; lordly or communal planning 151; moats 65, 66; prehistoric and Roman 29; wood and pasture 35, 36, 37, 38

Cambs., Little Wilbraham 111, 112
Cambs., Longstowe 48, 100, 125, 128
Cambs., Swavesey 36
Cambs., Tadlow 18
Cambs., Teversham 18
Cambs., Toft 5, 21; Anglo-Saxon estate at 120, 130; appendices 154, 155, 156, 157, 158; arable 43, 44, 46, 47; at Domesday 116, 122; post-medieval 81; proto-common field 91, 95, 98, 109, 149, 150, 152; proto-common field date 100, 107; settlement 60, 61, 62, 64, 146, 147; wood and pasture 40, 42
Cambs., Westley Waterless 16
Cornwall 10, 17
Cornwall, Gwithian 15
Derbyshire 18
Devon, Badgworthy 108
Devon, Dartmoor 1, 11, 87, 141, 153
Devon, Exmoor 108
Dorset 11, 43
Essex 6, 69, 77, 111, 125
Essex, Asheldham 69, 141
Essex, Prittlewell 111
Essex, Wicken Bonhunt 111
Glos., Aston Magna 125
Hampshire 21, 145
Hants., Chalton 147
Hertfordshire 69, 88, 89, 138
Huntingdonshire 94, 143, 151
Hunts., Leighton Bromswold 94, 143, 151
Hunts., St Neots: route towards 16, 66, 81, 87, 154, 155
Hunts., Yaxley 69, 86
Kent, Weald 6
Lincolnshire 16, 18, 59, 69, 89, 94, 98, 149
Lincs., Flixborough 16, 149
Lincs., Goltho 18, 25, 69, 77, 141
Middx., Heathrow 11
Montgomeryshire, Hen Domen 109, 110
Norfolk 16, 17, 43, 69, 89, 114
Norfolk, Dickleburgh 10, 86
Norfolk, Hockham Mere 6, 106
Norfolk, Scole 10, 69
Norfolk, Thetford 16
Northamptonshire: Anglo-Saxon 5, 6, 17, 143; work of David Hall in 18, 44, 94, 95, 98; Romano-British 69; settlement 145, 147
Northants., Brixworth 69
Northants., Faxton 17
Northants., Great Doddington 69
Northants., Haddon 69
Northants., Maxey 5, 17, 141
Northants., Rockingham Forest 6, 143
Northumberland, Hadrian's Wall 69
Northumberland, Harlow Hill 69
Northumberland, Horsley 69
Northumberland, Newcastle upon Tyne 69
Nottinghamshire 18
Oxfordshire 6, 9, 11, 120, 143
Oxon., Barton Court 6
Oxon., Cowdery's Down 6
Oxon., Farmoor 11
Somerset 141
Staffordshire 18, 69
Staffs., Lichfield 18, 69, 77, 78, 141
Suffolk: Anglo-Saxon landscape 6, 12, 69, 106, 111, 115; at Domesday 122, 138; open fields in 110; ploughs and ploughlands 16, 43, 44; prehistoric 86, 87
Suffolk, Brandon 110
Suffolk, Icklingham 111
Suffolk, Livermere 110
Suffolk, Nazeing 16
Suffolk, South Elmham 12
Suffolk, Sutton Hoo 111
Suffolk, Thetford 16
Suffolk, Yaxley 69, 86
Surrey, Polesden 98, 99
Wales 10
Warwickshire 35
Wessex 68, 118, 128, 138
Wilts., Overton Down 69
Wilts., Salisbury Plain 11, 21, 34, 87, 88
Wilts., Wylye 18
Yorkshire 11, 18, 94, 98, 110, 143
Yorks., Middleton 143
Yorks., Wharram Percy 69

Index of subjects and people

Aelmer of Bourn 47, 124, 125, 128
Alan, Count of Brittany 125
Algar 122, 125
'Ancient countryside' 11, 19–20, 59, 68
Anglo-Saxon: administration 26, 30; arable 42–5; cattle as status symbols 110–11; common fields 109, 111, 140–5; estates 10, 105, 110, 119–20; 124–30; field systems 12, 18, 87, 90, 106, 114, 136, 140, 152; greens 51–9; kingdoms 9, 30, 106; landholding 121–31; early landscapes 5–8, 10, 12, 79, 87; general land-use 32–4; lordly or communal direction 148–52; migration 10; period 1; heavy plough 14–16; roads 28; transition from Romano-British to 7–8, 30, 88, 90, 138; settlement 59–64, 66, 74, 105, 106, 110, 145–8; social structure 114–18, 131–3, 137–40; wood and pasture 35–42, 88, 94, 108, 137–8
Arable: Anglo-Saxon 6, 8, 42–5, 67; appendix 157; and common fields 90, Ch. 5, 136, 140, 142–5, 149; at Domesday 117, 131, 137; estate 9–10; and *feld*, 58–9; impact of geology 25, 56; land-use origins 1, 14, 17, 19, 20, 61, 91ff., 140, 143, 145, 152; lordly or communal direction 151; medieval 41, 46–51, 64, 75, 76; post-medieval 74, 81, 135; post-Roman 36, 79; reuse of prehistoric boundaries in 34–5, 68, 87–8, 140–2, and settlement 60–1, 126, 129, 145–8
Ard, *see* 'Plough'
Assart 36, 37, 38, 39, 45, 56, 65, 79, 86, 91, 113, 126, 143, 151
Bookland 9, 121, 124–9, 130, 131, 133, 138
Bordarii 116, 118
Boundaries, *see also* 'Field boundaries': appendices 154, 155, 157; boundary between Wetherley and Longstowe Hundreds 26, 27, 81, 98, 100, 104, 107, 109; in Bourn Valley, 26, 27, 87; hundred boundaries 25; parish 18, 43, 56; in relation to prehistoric alignments in Bourn Valley 42, 70, 79–82; and proto-common field 98–110, 134, 146
Burials 7, 8, 16, 129

Cam, River 1, 9, 18, 21, 25, 26, 30, 89, 106, 110
Caput, *see* 'Estate, centre'
Cattle: herding 4, 30, 39, 41, 67, 89, 108, 111–13, 129; relating to status 111–13
Central Province 13; ancient and champion landscapes 17–20; anomalies in relation to 68, 69, 72, 105, 109, 139–41; and common fields 49, 91, 141, 142, 144, 145; and freemen 138; and greens 59, 137; and settlement 59, 64, 65, 66, 146
Ceorl 118
'Champion landscapes' 10, 13, 19–20, 59, 66, 68, 134
Chertsey, Abbey of 110
Church dedications 10, 41
Clan territories 9, 26, 59, 107, 119, 121, 133, 137
Climate 6, 8, 10, 41, 46
Commendation 115, 116, 120, 122; of Aelmer of Bourn 124, 125; to king 131, 132, 133
Common fields, *see* 'Fields, common'
Commons, *see* 'Greens, including commons'
Consumption, conspicuous 111–13
Cottarii 116
Crops 49, 50, 109, 136, 141, 149; cropping 14, 49, 88, 99, 108, 109; crop rotation 91, 109
Danelaw 100, 105, 110, 114, 115
Dean (or 'dene') 23, 36, 39, 40, 56, 60, 154, 157
Deconstructive analysis 77–9
Demesne: arable on 43, 49; bookland 124, 125, 127, 128–30; ecclesiastical organisation of 110, 128, 133; manors in relation to 60, 66, 67; Romano-British 102; royal 30, 117, 118, 120, 128–30; stock raising on 36, 39, 44; tenants and workers on 48, 115; from warland 121
Domesday Book 35, Ch. 6
Drainage 14, 22, 25, 26, 41, 42, 55, 96, 139
Earningas 30, 67, 114
East Anglia 18, 30, 64, 87, 88; kingdom of 9
Economy: agricultural 30, 34, 39, 143, 148; Anglo-Saxon 8, 16; arable in 131, 136; cattle in 111–13;

Index of subjects and people

Romano-British 4, 41
Edeva the Fair 124, 125, 128, 130
Edward the Elder 100, 115, 123
Ely, Abbey of 36, 100, 110, 120, 122, 128, 129, 130, 133, 146, 151
Enclosure: Anglo-Saxon for hunting 126; deconstruction of landscape of 77–81; medieval and early modern 18, 19, 69, 75, 76, 89, 141, 142; Parliamentary enclosure 19, 40, 43, 68, 72–5, 76, 82, 126, 134–6, 142; Parliamentary enclosure, landscape before 84, 91, 95, 96–8, 158; Parliamentary enclosure, maps relating to 72–6, 95–8
Estate 73, 75, 131; of Aelmer of Bourn 124–7; in the Bourn Valley 30, 36, 49, 60, 81, 100, 107, 120, 121–6, 130, 132, 133, 144, 149, 151; centre (*caput*) 9, 36, 100, 119, 120, 124, 133; extensive 9, 99, 110, 124, 131, 132, 144; royal in the Bourn Valley 30, 107, 120–1, 123, 132–3, 137–8, 144
Fallow 4, 13, 14, 43, 59, 91, 108
Feld 41, 52–8, 123
Feorm 60, 107, 119, 120, 130
Field boundaries 34, 77–81, 89, 114, 142, 138; in ancient landscapes 10, 11, 12, 17–19, 69; in relation to greens 55; medieval 76, 95, 134; in pasture 1; prehistoric and Roman 83, 85, 87, 140, 141; in woods and pasture 35, 36, 45, 88
Field names 32–3, 34–45, 46, 47, 77, 79, 88; arable 42–5; assart 38, 56; hunting and parks 38, 126; pasture and meadows 25, 39–42, 48, 56, 107; Scandinavian 105; woodland 35–9
Fields: Anglo-Saxon 10, 13–16, 34, Ch. 5, 135–6, Ch. 7; infield 45, 108, 109, 113, 146, 147, 149, 150; introduction of common fields 12–19, Ch. 7, especially 142–52; medieval 13–16, 34–5, 36, 68, Ch. 4, Ch. 5, 135–6, Ch. 7; outfield 108, 109; persistence of prehistoric into medieval fields 68–72, Ch. 4, Ch. 7; prehistoric 1, 11, 17, 19, 68, 89; prehistoric and Roman 1, 4, 10–12, 14, 19, 34–5, 39, Ch. 4, Ch. 5; proto-common field 62, Ch. 5, 115, 123, 134, 136, 144–9, 150, 152; relationship with settlement Ch. 1, 146–8
Fieldwalking 5, 6, 81, 102, 145
Fyrd 28, 132, 133
Geld 100, 111, 117, 118, 122, 130, 132
Geology 21, 24, 25, 139
Grantasǣte 30, 67, 106, 114
Greens 47, 67, 123, 133, 138, 152; in ancient landscapes 12; Anglo-Saxon 39–42; including commons, and settlement 10, 51–9, 62, 63, 129, 146; long narrow commons in proto-common field Ch. 5; Offals 52–9, 86, 147, 157; survival of 66, 134, 137
Guy de Reimbeaucourt 151
Hǣslingas 30, 52, 53, 58, 67, 106, 114, 121, 123
Headlands: appendices 156–8; long, narrow in Bourn Valley Ch. 5, 156; as represented on maps 107–8; medieval 74, 75, 76, 91, 96, 98, 107; post-medieval reuse 134; prehistoric or Roman underlying medieval 17, 69, 81, 83, 84, 86, 142
Hedges 139, 144; in ancient landscapes 11, 12, 19; and deconstructive analysis 77; medieval 95, 143; post-enclosure 135–6; prehistoric or Romano-British 101, 142; preserve ancient alignments 34, 76, 79, 90, 140, 141, 153; process of enclosure 133–6
Herds and herding 30, 40, 41, 56, 88, 89, 108, 112
Hide 100, Ch. 6
Hummocky ground 54, 55, 64
Hundreds 117, 133; arable in at Domesday 81, 98, 104; and hides 107, 109; Longstowe and Wetherley 25, 26, 100; Wetherley 118, 122
Hunting, *see also* 'Parks' 38, 39, 41, 126; game 38, 41
ICC (*Inquisitio Comitatus Cantabrigiensis*) 35, 44, 115, 120, 122, 127, 128
Infield, *see* 'Fields, infield'
Inland 117, 126, 128, 133
King 115; bookland grants 121, 124–30; commendation to 131–3; and *feorm* 9, 107, 119; royal demesne and manors 107, 117–21; royal estates 137, 138, 139, 151; royal hunting 38; status 112; warland duties owed to 122, 123
Laws: Anglo-Saxon 111, 112
Leaseland 121, 129–31, 138
Liberi homines, *see* 'Sokemen'
Linear boundaries 11–12, 69, 87, 139
Lordship 20, 148
Manors: after 1066 151; of Abbey of Ely 60, 63; appendix 155; and bookland 124, 133; and *feorm* 107; landscape of 64, 65, 125, 128, 151; and leaseland 129; medieval 48; population on 118–20, 150
Meadow 5, 27, 39–42, 67, 88–9, 117, 120, 137; appendices 155, 156; distribution in Bourn Valley 32–3; medieval 12, 46, 48, 49, 56, 57; influence of physical geography 21, 25; previously ploughed 75; Romano-British 4, 101–3; and settlement 60, 106, 110, 147
Mercia, kingdom of 9, 30, 121, 138
Migration: Anglo-Saxon 7; Scandinavian 105
Minsters 105, 124, 125
Moats 19, 27, 63, 64–6
Norman Conquest 133, 152; appendix 156; and break-up of large estates 100; and demesne 120; and field systems 150; and settlement 146, 147; and tenure 115, 123, 125; and villein status 116
Offal, *see* 'Greens, including commons'
Outfield, *see* 'Fields, outfield'
Oxen 16, 111
Parish boundaries, *see* 'Boundaries, parish'
Parks 38, 126
Pasture, *see also* 'Greens, including commons' and

'Meadow' 25, 30, 32–4, 39–42, 67, 76, 94, 111, 117, 123–5, 137–9; alignments and 140, 149, 151, 152; arable, relationship with 43–5; and common fields 75, 89, 91, 94, 95, 107, 143; and enclosure 135, 137–9; and greens 51–65; medieval 26, 51; post-Roman 6, 8; prehistoric and Roman 4, 10, 12; and settlement 147; survival of 79, 87, 88, 99, 120; wood pasture 10, 26, 35–9, 40, 123, 125
Peasants 27, 30, 48, 67, 105, Ch. 6
Picot, Sheriff of Cambridgeshire 124, 125, 151
Pigs 35, 36, 111
Place names 40, 110, 152; Anglo-Saxon 30, 53, 58, 60, 126; Romano-British 29; Scandinavian 105
Plough 67, 96, 144; aerial photography and 74; and DB 43; heavy 14–16; medieval 46, 48, 51; and pasture 40, 75; physical geography and 51; prehistoric and Roman 14–16, 83, 141
Ploughlands 34, 43, 44
Population: Anglo-Saxon 6–8, 10, 58, 95; and climate 16; and common fields 20, 143; in DB 116, 117, 123, 125, 137; medieval 43, 44, 59, 64; Romano-British 4
Pottery: Anglo-Saxon 6, 16, 57, 110, 145; Romano-British 102
Ridge and furrow, *see also* 'Selion' 14, 109; drainage and 5, 25, 50; extent of 41, 49, 51, 53, 58, 69, 75, 79; medieval 46, 47, 74, 76, 126; relationship with prehistoric fields 17, 68, 81, 83
Roads: in ancient and champion landscapes 17, 19, 77, 78, 133; Anglo-Saxon 28, 38, 94, 106, 125–6, 132–3; appendices 154–8; and greens 55, 63;
modern 27–9, 41, 51; and proto-common field 95; Roman 22, 77, 81–7; Roman road A603 28–9, 79, 101–2; Roman roads and landscape 41; Roman roads and prehistoric features 69; and settlement 147
Selion, *see also* 'Ridge and furrow' 14, 47, 74, 75, 96, 97, 105, 109, 136, 150
Serfs 63
Settlement, *see also* 'Moats' 6, 19, 77, 146, 152, 156; Anglo-Saxon 6, 7, 10, 18, 23, 62–3, 105–6, 110, 145–8, 156; dispersed 20, 45, 59, 89; and greens 51–9, 62–3; medieval 52, 53, 54, 56, 59, 60–6, 73, 145–8, 150, 157; nucleation 10, 19, 20, 26, 59–66, 117, 140, 145–8, 150; open field layouts, relationship with 63–4, 69, 145–8; phases of development 60–9, 145–8; planned 62–3, 145–8, 156; prehistoric and Romano-British 4, 7, 10, 15, 86, 88, 101–4, 141; secondary 27, 64–9, 150–1
Sheep 4, 8, 9, 30, 40, 44, 67, 88, 108, 111, 112, 129
Smallholders, *see* 'Sokemen'
Sokemen Ch. 6, 151
St Mary's Nunnery, Clerkenwell 66
St Neots Priory 66
Strip, *see* 'Selion'
Subinfeudation 66
Thegns 38, 117, 120, 124, 125, 127, 128
Tracks, *see* 'Roads'
Villeins / *villani* 62, 63, 116, 118, 131
Virgate 48, 59, 117, 122, 125, 128, 130, 150
Warland 121–3, 124, 128, 137, 138; warland duties 130, 131–3
Wood pasture, *see* 'Pasture, wood pasture'

LIST OF OCCASIONAL PAPERS
DEPARTMENT OF ENGLISH LOCAL HISTORY, UNIVERSITY OF LEICESTER

First Series
1. H. P. R. Finberg, *The Local Historian and his Theme* (1952)
2. H. P. R. Finberg, *The Early Charters of Devon and Cornwall* (1953)
3. Joan Thirsk, *Fenland Farming in the Sixteenth Century* with an introduction by R. H. Tawney (1953)
4. M. Claire Cross, *The Free Grammar School of Leicester* (1953)
5. G. H. Martin, *The Early Court Rolls of the Borough of Ipswich* (1954)
6. H. E. Hallam, *The New Lands of Elloe: a Study of Early Reclamation in Lincolnshire* (1954)
7. C. F. Slade, *The Leicestershire Survey c. A.D. 1130* with a preface by Sir Frank Stenton (1956)
8. H. P. R. Finberg, *Roman and Saxon Withington: a Study in Continuity* (1955)
9. A. M. Everitt, *The County Committee of Kent in the Civil War* (1955)
10 and 11. Cyril Hart, *The Early Charters of Essex* (1957)
12. Basil E. Cracknell, *Canvey Island: the History of a Marshland Community* (1959)
13. W. G. Hoskins, *The Westward Expansion of Wessex* with a supplement to No. 2 in this series by H. P. R. Finberg (1960)
14. Thomas Garden Barnes, *The Clerk of the Peace in Caroline Somerset* (1961)
15. R. B. Smith, *Blackburnshire: a Study in Early Lancashire History* (1961)
16. L. A. Burgess, *The Origins of Southampton* (1964)
17. K. J. Allison, M. W. Beresford, J. G. Hurst et al., *The Deserted Villages of Oxfordshire* (1966)
18. K. J. Allison, M. W. Beresford, J. G. Hurst et al., *The Deserted Villages of Northamptonshire* (1966)
19. John S. Moore, *Laughton: a Study in the Evolution of the Wealden Landscape* (1965)
20. Margaret Spufford, *A Cambridgeshire Community: Chippenham from Settlement to Enclosure* (1965)

Second Series
1. Alan Everitt, *Change in the Provinces: the Seventeenth Century* (1969)
2. R. A. McKinley, *Norfolk Surnames in the Sixteenth Century* (1969)
3. Cyril Hart, *The Hidation of Northamptonshire* (1970)

4. Alan Everitt, *The Pattern of Rural Dissent: the Nineteenth Century* (1972)
5. David Hey, *The Rural Metalworkers of the Sheffield Region* (1972)
6. Cyril Hart, *The Hidation of Cambridgeshire* (1974)

Third Series
1. J. S. Morrill, *The Cheshire Grand Jury 1625–1659* (1976)
2. Katherine S. Naughton, *The Gentry of Bedfordshire in the Thirteenth and Fourteenth Centuries* (1976)
3. Prudence Ann Moylan, *The Form and Reform of County Government: Kent 1889–1914* (1978)
4. Charles Phythian-Adams, *Continuity, Fields and Fission: the Making of a Midland Parish* (1978)
5. B. J. Davey, *Ashwell, 1830–1914: the Decline of a Village Community* (1980)
6. Beryl Schumer, *The Evolution of Wychwood to 1400: Pioneers, Frontiers and Forests* (1984)

Fourth Series
1. Charles Phythian-Adams, *Re-thinking English Local History* (1987)
2. Peter Warner, *Greens, Commons and Clayland Colonization: the Origins and Development of Green-side Settlement in East Suffolk* (1987)
3. K. D. M. Snell, *Church and Chapel in the North Midlands: Religious Observance in the Nineteenth Century* (1991)
4. Christopher Dyer, *Hanbury: Settlement and Society in a Woodland Landscape* (1991)

Associated Volumes
1. Charles Phythian-Adams (ed.), *Societies, Cultures and Kinship, 1580–1850: Cultural Provinces and English Local History*, with contributions by Mary Carter, Evelyn Lord and Anne Mitson (1993)
2. Harold Fox, *The Evolution of the Fishing Village: Landscape and Society along the South Devon Coast, 1086-1550*, Leicester Explorations in Local History Volume 1 (Leopard's Head Press, Oxford, 2001)

Note

Virtually all of the Occasional Papers listed above are out of print. Third Series number 6, by Beryl Schumer, has been republished by The Wychwood Press (Jon Carpenter Publishing), Charlbury, Oxfordshire. *The Evolution of the Fishing Village* may be obtained by writing to 'Explorations', Centre for English Local History, 5 Salisbury Road, Leicester LE1 7QR.